TOM FINNEY

MY AUTOBIOGRAPHY

TOM FINNEY
MY AUTOBIOGRAPHY

headline

First published in 2003
by HEADLINE BOOK PUBLISHING

10 9 8 7 6 5 4 3 2 1

Cataloguing in Publication Data is available from the British Library

ISBN 0 7553 1105 1

Typeset in Garamond by Avon DataSet Ltd,
Bidford-on-Avon, Warwickshire

Printed and bound in Great Britain by
Mackays of Chatham plc, Chatham, Kent

HEADLINE BOOK PUBLISHING
A division of Hodder Headline
338 Euston Road
London NW1 3BH

www.headline.co.uk
www.hodderheadline.com

To my father, Alf, for all his love and support.

Contents

Acknowledgements

Committing to your autobiography is not a decision taken lightly; it is imperative, therefore, that you embark on the project safe in the knowledge that your collaborator is someone you not only respect as a writer but trust as a friend.

Paul Agnew, whom I have known for some twenty years and worked closely with in the past, was always going to be my choice and I would now like to place on record my sincere thanks to Paul for all his assistance, expertise and painstaking attention to detail during the writing of this book.

But, much more than that, he has helped make the re-living of eight decades of my life – on and off the football pitch – an absolute pleasure.

Hours and days and weeks and months of fact-finding and interviewing have proved anything but arduous – to the contrary, the whole event has been a great deal of fun and I am delighted with the result.

Thanks Paul.

Tom Finney
March 2003

CHAPTER ONE

The price of loyalty

'Loyalty – the millionaire footballers of the twenty-first century don't know the meaning of the word. They only know – or care – about stockpiling mountains of money, image rights and commercial deals, and agents who scour the world to set up their next big payday. Their greed borders on the obscene.' That is a commonly held view among the football stars of my generation but it is not my view. Even though today's players can earn in a couple of hours what I earned annually, I do not hold it against them.

At my peak, in a structure governed by the maximum wage, my income from a playing year with Preston North End struggled to reach £1,200. When I first signed as a professional it was for shillings – ten bob a match to be precise. That's 50p. So when you read of players now being paid up to £100,000 a week for doing the same job, you might think I would be envious but you would be wrong.

I would never criticise players for the amounts they are paid. It is not their fault and I say good luck to them, go out there and grasp the opportunity.

The whole deal was so wrong in the forties and fifties. Then, when Jimmy Hill and co. eventually managed to bring about major changes, they were labelled as money-grabbing mercenaries, but I have yet to meet any working man who would turn up his nose at a huge salary. Who would look their boss squarely in the eyes and say, 'Well, thanks for the offer, but I will have to decline because I really don't think I'm worth it'?

It is easy to huff and puff and shake your head in judgement and condemnation, and I must concede that six-figure weekly wages and £50 million transfer fees do take a bit of understanding, but footballers' pay has proved a contentious subject since the dawn of professionalism. I was unfortunate in that the maximum wage was abolished the year after I finished. I say unfortunate because I would have loved to earn more, but I also believe that football treated Tom Finney well. I was never ungrateful, but there were times when I did feel the system was mightily unfair on players, and good players in particular. You were basically denied your right to earn your worth because a limit existed, and I found that fundamentally wrong. Every worker, from footballer to office clerk, farm labourer to accountant, entertainer to shop assistant, should be paid according to their ability – paid their worth in other words. A uniform wage scale might have made life easier for the administrators back in the prehistoric days of the 1950s, but it did not excuse the basic injustice towards the players.

I think the powerful men on the football committees were frightened by the prospect of opening up the system, fearful that only those clubs with the best resources, the wealthy minority, would be able to attract the top stars. They were, of course, quite right to be concerned. The vast majority of players would most certainly have moved to the clubs paying the biggest wages. Those in authority back then stifled football's progress in my opinion. They didn't want to threaten the status quo by allowing the game to develop and produce a rich versus poor scenario.

I was a supporter of a Premier League long before the Premiership came into being. I always believed that a strong top end would raise the standards within our game and improve our chances on the world stage. In fact, I put my name to several articles in both regional and national newspapers, so my ideas and beliefs were well aired. I was considered media friendly and I was outspoken, particularly on matters of finance, publicly questioning the system and the people who made the rules. I called not only for the abolition of the maximum wage, but for international fees to be doubled.

My personal views were well known and I still stand by them. I wasn't looking for profile or notoriety. I just wanted football to show an even hand and I campaigned hard during my playing days to instigate change.

I had many a private conversation with my colleagues and recall one long debate with the England manager Walter Winterbottom. Walter was open enough to see both sides and accepted my points, but he still argued that a maximum wage system was in the best interests of the game at large. Let's just say that Walter and I agreed to differ on that one.

In a typical season at the latter end of my career, I was earning the full £20 a week (£3 less in the summer months), small bonuses for winning and drawing and £50 every time I played for England. Additionally, I qualified for a benefit of £500 every five years and also had the extra income generated through my commercial dealings. All things considered, I suppose I was among the lucky ones –

a big earner! But while I had a lot of sympathy for those less fortunate, I also felt I was robbed of the chance to do much better financially than I did.

The England fee was always a handy top-up even though it counted as yet another example of how the players were exploited. We knew full well that a top international fixture at Wembley – most of them played to capacity 100,000 crowds – generated gate receipts in excess of £50,000. The 11 England players would share £550, and the rest, all £49,450, went somewhere else.

So where exactly did the money go, not just at international level but at club level, too? Now there lies a question. Perhaps it would not pay – no pun intended – to delve too deeply. Suffice it to say that the big money did not go into the pockets of those responsible for attracting the crowds in the first place.

Anyway, I can hear you ask, isn't football a dream job, the sort people would willingly do for nothing? Well, never would I suggest that football was anything other than a most agreeable way of earning a living, but as a former employer, I must say that I have yet to meet anyone prepared to labour for love alone. Football was never designed as a job for life – someone once calculated that the average career lasted little more than eight years – so if ever there was a case for an unrestricted pay scale, football presented it.

The vast majority of players in the years from the war to the abolition of the maximum wage were far from wealthy. We even had a pool – everyone paid in about a shilling a week – to help support those who got themselves suspended. In those days, suspended players had their pay docked by the clubs.

Money has always been important to me and I make no apologies for that. Be it football or business, I have always sought a fair day's pay for a fair day's work and see nothing wrong in that either. It has also been said that I am careful with my money, not spending a quid when ten bob would cover it. Again, quite true. Even when my plumbing business was at its peak, I would spend many a Saturday lunchtime after the lads had knocked off and gone home, searching the yard for bits of copper piping they had discarded and stacking them away for future jobs. To the charge of being careful I plead guilty, but I could never stand accused of greed.

I was a one-club man, and by no means unique in that. There were many others – Billy Wright at Wolverhampton Wanderers and Nat Lofthouse at Bolton Wanderers to name but two high-profile England internationals of my era. We were forever being praised for our loyalty, but it wasn't necessarily loyalty by choice. I cannot speak for the others, but I will say this. Had my career started in 2000 and not in 1940, I very much doubt that I would have spent it all at Preston. For one thing, I don't think the system would have allowed it. The financial pressure to move, probably abroad, would have taken charge.

The maximum wage took away a financial incentive to move, and contracts made moving very difficult. Preston was a big club then and I was very happy there, married with a young family and settled in the town with a successful plumbing business. So if Arsenal, probably the top club of the time, had made a bid for me (if they ever did, no one mentioned it!) what would have been my reasons for giving it consideration? Prestige? Possibly. Money? Certainly not. The Arsenal top earners were only on the same as me and with the cost of living in London being substantially higher than in Lancashire, I could actually have ended up worse off.

Now had Arsenal or Newcastle United or any of the other leading clubs been able to come in with an offer to double my wages, I would probably have signed even though I always considered Preston

North End to be the greatest club in the world. What is so terribly wrong with a free market place?

I am also a lifelong advocate of star pay for star play. David Beckham, as the star turn with Manchester United, demands a substantially bigger salary than others within the same team. People would expect that and quite right, too. But it didn't apply to us; we got the same as everyone else. There were those who said it helped team spirit and morale and that is as maybe, but it certainly didn't do anything to boost the morale of the star turns.

So in English football of the post-war period, you tended to stay put. However, in May of 1952, I did come very close to being one of the first English footballers to snap up a big-bucks offer from overseas until North End put the mockers on it.

I was 30 and probably at my peak, playing to the top of my form both for North End and for England, when I received what can only be described as an offer of a lifetime. The approach was made by an Italian prince, owner of the Palermo club in Sicily.

Prince Roberto Lanza di Trabia, Palermo's millionaire president, was prepared to pay me £130 a month in wages (plus win bonuses of up to £100), provide me with a Mediterranean villa and a brand new Italian sportscar, and pay for the family to fly over as often as they wished. Oh, and there was the little matter of a £10,000 signing-on fee!

The Prince was desperate to turn Palermo into Italy's top club and, by all accounts, he had drawn up a shopping list of potential signings. I was the top target and he was ready to give me the earth. All I had to do was say yes to a two-year deal. At the end of the contract I would be free to return to England. He knew there would be an outcry at Preston and he told me privately that he was perfectly willing to compensate North End for my absence or pay them a straight transfer fee of around £30,000 if they preferred.

So, how did it all come about and what prevented it from going through? Well, it happened while I was on tour with England in Florence. It was spring and I was winning my 37th cap. The game ended all square at 1–1, mainly because of an inspired display by the Italian goalkeeper Moro of Sampdoria. Some of his saves were top drawer and I was among the England forwards to applaud him.

It was the first game of our summer tour and 93,000 came to watch. My room-mate, Ivor Broadis, that gifted inside-forward then playing for Manchester City who also gave sterling service to Carlisle, Newcastle and Sunderland, was the only visitor to find the net. On another day against another keeper, we would have won quite comfortably.

Moro was beaten after four minutes but he wasn't prepared to do any more fishing out of his net, thwarting us time and time again in a one-sided first half. The Italians, jeered at the break, improved significantly and deservedly equalised through the goal-poaching instincts of Napoli forward Amadei.

After the match, we went along as guests to an official banquet laid on by the Italian Football Association. I was deep in conversation with Nat Lofthouse, who had been kicked from pillar to post by the over-physical Italian defenders, when Billy Wright, our skipper, interrupted to say that a fan was asking to see me. It was Prince Roberto. He was a man in his early forties, a polite and articulate individual with a good grasp of the English language, who obviously cared passionately about his football.

Ivor was there, too, and we chatted with the Prince for a while. He told us he had come over from Sicily for the game and was very keen to speak with me, so Ivor suggested we went back to the room for a little more privacy. It was there that he dropped the bombshell.

'I want to take Palermo to the very top and I would like you to sign. I would be prepared to give you . . .' and he ran through the details of the offer, the money, the villa, the plans.

I looked across at Ivor and he looked even more astounded than I must have done. We were speechless and both wondered if it was some sort of joke, the sort of set-up you get used to as part of a football team. We laughed, mainly because we didn't really know what else to do. In jest, I said I would think about it providing the money was right. It was at that point I realised the Prince was deadly serious because he jumped in with, 'I'll give you £7,000 to sign.'

'How much?' I exclaimed, which he must have taken as 'do me a favour, I'm worth a lot more than that' because he immediately upped it to £10,000.

'Wait a minute,' I said, swallowing hard and trying to take it all in. 'I'm afraid it doesn't quite work like that. In England, we're under contract and you would have to put it through my club, make it official.'

The Prince frowned. He was obviously not used to such procedures. He was accustomed to going out and getting what he wanted or, in my case, buying what he wanted. He was not the only one befuddled by it all. As an English footballer in the early 1950s, it wasn't every day that a Continental club made you a prime target. Offers like this were not two a penny.

But my feelings during our conversation were clear – I wanted to say 'yes' and grab the opportunity there and then.

'We have two more games to play, in Austria and Switzerland,' I said, 'but when we arrive back home, I'll go straight to Preston and tell them about you and do my best to pave the way.'

The Prince got up, shook my hand and went to rejoin the official gathering, confident that I was more than interested in his proposition. Ivor sat in a corner, as white as a sheet, and several minutes went by before we picked up the thread. Eventually, he broke the silence.

'Hell fire, Tom. Did you hear that – the fellow wants to give you £10,000 just for going over there, never mind the wages. You'll never get an opportunity like this again – you have got to take it.'

We ended up talking for the rest of the night and even when we tried to get some rest I just couldn't get the offer out of my mind. I agreed with Ivor, only a fool would pass this over – but would Preston allow it to happen? I had a contract with them and contracts were binding so I would have to discuss the matter with the club directors, after I had first gone through it with my wife, Elsie. I knew Elsie's answer would be to go along with whatever I felt to be right.

Ivor agreed not to mention it to the rest of the squad and I tried hard to forget about the Prince and Palermo for the remainder of the tour, but it wasn't easy.

Elsie realised that I had something to tell her the moment I got back home and her reaction was exactly as anticipated.

'It sounds wonderful,' she said. 'I'll leave the decision to you, Tom, but what about all the upheaval, schooling for the children and how will Preston react?'

There was only one way to find out. I rang Nat Buck, the North End chairman, a retired businessman who had made his money out of house building.

'Sorry to bother you, Mr Buck, but I wonder if I could request a meeting with the board.'

'What's on your mind, Tom?' he inquired, in his broad Lancastrian accent.

'Well, it's something of a personal nature so I really would appreciate the chance to speak face to face.' He didn't push me for details and we fixed up an appointment to meet at Deepdale.

'Right, Tom. What's going on?' he said, when I got there. Nat was not a man to mince his words. Renowned as a straight-talker – I liked him for that – he seemed to relish controversy and the profile that usually went with it.

'Well, as I said the other day, I would really rather put this matter to the board as a whole. I think it's the right and proper thing to do,' I responded.

'No need for that at this stage,' said the chairman. 'Tell me and I'll decide whether it needs to go before anyone else.'

To say that he was unimpressed with my story would be grossly to understate the truth. He just brushed it all to one side and refused point blank to consider it, saying there was nothing to discuss and it was all too silly for words. I told him that the idea appealed to me, I had given it a lot of thought and had promised the Prince I would get back in touch. He remained unmoved. No, more than that, he was angered.

'Tom, I'm sorry, but the whole thing is out of the question, absolutely out of the question. We are not interested in selling you and that's that. Listen to me, if tha' doesn't play for Preston then tha' doesn't play for anybody.'

Deep down, I expected no other reaction, but I was still more than a little put out by the way he just dismissed it. However, I accepted the decision without too much fuss and tried to forget about the whole affair.

That was easier said than done. There was a genuine appeal about the prospect of trying my luck abroad, not to mention the money and the standard of living, and I couldn't help but think I might regret this missed opportunity for the rest of my life.

Prince Roberto didn't make it easy for me, either. He was disgruntled by North End's 'nothing doing' stance and he came back and tried to set up a deal to borrow me for a season. It basically amounted to the first known example of the loan system that now operates within the global game. But the regulations of the day didn't allow for such a move. I was registered to the English FA and under the Federation of International Football Association's rules, I could not move to Palermo in any circumstances without a clearance certificate. As a rider, the official line stated 'temporary transfers will not be approved' and Nat Buck tried to prevent any further inquiry from Palermo – or anywhere else for that matter – by placing a £50,000 valuation on my head. That said everything and in some ways it was very flattering. The world record transfer fee of the day was still some way short of £20,000 so it proved just how much Preston valued me.

I wrote to Prince Roberto, thanked him for his kind and generous offer and explained that I was unable to accept owing to Preston's refusal to negotiate a transfer deal. I would be lying if I said that I was happy with the outcome. What right had North End to deny me? The signing-on fee in itself was reason enough for leaving.

In the opulent world of 2003, £10,000 may not sound like an excessive amount of money. It's still a nice pick-up, especially as a one-off payment, but it would not be enough to consider a dramatic change of lifestyle. Some people spend that much on their daughter's wedding, a new conservatory or a smart car. But, believe me, in 1952 it was enough to set you up for life. Back then, you could buy a house in Preston for a few hundred quid, and a decent one, too. Something akin to a three-bedroomed terraced house in a semi-rural location with a lounge, dining room, kitchen and bathroom would have cost around £1,150.

With the average working man's weekly wage standing at £7 10s (£7.50) the vast majority of people couldn't afford a car. But for those who could, it was possible to pick up a good second-hand family saloon, say a Ford Prefect, for around £400, and for about the same again you could hitch a four-berth caravan on the back. But leisure and luxury were hardly to the fore in Britain where the major cities carried the scars of bomb craters, and rationing remained in operation. For the most part, families were still recovering from the war and were happy to see their income cover their outgoings.

Television was just starting to make an impact although it didn't really find a way into most homes until the latter years of the decade. For those lucky enough to be able to afford a night out at the theatre, you could go to see Harry Secombe and Arthur Askey at the main venues for about 3s 6d (17p). A seat in the stalls at the local picture house to see *Snows of Kilimanjaro* with Gregory Peck and Ava Gardner was 1s (5p). A sports jacket and flannels came in at 39s (£1.95) and 25s (£1.25) respectively, and at 1s 2d (6p) a pint, those who liked a drink could get merry for about five bob (25p).

So, after digesting the financial state of play in those days, it is easy to understand the relative value of ten grand. In today's terms, it would equate to at least £500,000 – yes, half a million pounds!

As far as I knew, the Palermo business had been conducted under a veil of confidentiality. It was summer and media interest in football had cooled. Elsie, who found North End's stance easier to understand than I did, suggested a short break, so we took our two children, Brian and Barbara, to Blackpool for a few days of clear-your-head sea air.

Our peace did not last for long. News of the Palermo interest had leaked out, possibly at the Italian end although we never did find out for definite, and I remember sitting with Brian on my shoulders, watching a Punch and Judy show on the seafront, when we were confronted by a national newspaper reporter. Then another one appeared and another, and suddenly I was fending off questions from a whole group of hacks.

Newspaper intrusion was no big deal back then. Papers covered football for the matches rather than the personalities or any off-the-field goings-on and I enjoyed a good relationship with many of the national newspapermen. So much so that I decided to take a couple of them back to the hotel to put them in the picture with all the detail they were looking for, including the financial angle. That backfired on me in a big way.

I honestly thought it was the best course of action and that by giving the facts, the public could make a proper judgement. But the mood of the people, particularly those flying the colours of Preston North End, was decidedly uncertain. For some, I was the target for abuse, labelled a 'traitor' for even considering leaving my hometown club. However, there were others, and the overwhelming majority at that, who believed I had not been given a fair crack of the whip. They thought that North End's directors had done wrong by denying me a glorious chance to provide my family with long-term financial security. Some even went so far as to say that in view of my service to the club – 12 years as a professional – the decision on going or staying should have been mine alone.

Now there lies an interesting scenario – what would I have done given the final say? Despite all the advantages and everything I've said, would I really have gone? The honest answer is I don't know. The Palermo episode has drifted across my mind many times in the past 50 years or so. On the one hand, there was the astonishing offer. Prince Roberto might as well have been offering me a king's ransom. At Deepdale, it would take me about ten years to pull in what Palermo were prepared to give me just to say 'yes' to the move. And I did fancy going across to Italy to give it a whirl, not just for the money, but for the chance to test myself in the Continental game.

On the other hand, there was my family and business life in Preston and my career at North End. These were my roots. The kids were settled at school and moving abroad would have totally disrupted them, while Elsie, like me, was always a home bird.

And what about my club? North End has been a love affair for me. I could never properly explain my level of affection for the place. All I ever wanted to do was play for Preston. Had the Palermo offer not surfaced, I would never have dreamt of leaving.

Knowing myself as I do, I have to admit, if pushed into a corner, that I would probably have chosen safety first and turned Palermo down. All things considered, perhaps I was fortunate to be given the easy way out in that the biggest single decision of my football career was never mine to make. Consequently, I stayed loyal to Preston North End.

Talking of loyalty, Tommy Docherty tells a funny story about the day he went to see the North End management to discuss his contract for the following season and to ask about the possibility of a pay rise. Tommy, blunt and forceful as ever, explained that he felt he had made good progress, played a major role in the team during the previous campaign, was now considered a key senior man in the squad and had shown great loyalty to the club.

'That's right enough and we're very pleased with you, Tommy,' said the club representative. 'And that's why we are delighted to offer you the following terms – £12 a week in the winter and £10 a week in the summer.' Tommy was not impressed.

'But Tom Finney is on more than that and I want the same as him.'

'Look son,' came the stern reply. 'That's just not possible. Quite frankly, you're not as good a player as Tom Finney.'

Tommy could not contain himself and blurted out, 'But I am in the bloody summer!'

CHAPTER TWO

My debt to Dad
– and Shanks

Reflecting on the past is a hazardous business; the memory can play tricks and distort the picture. Life is a mix of events and experiences, joys and sorrows, people and places, and who is to say you can ever recall them with precise detail and total accuracy? But, looking back through my 81 years, there is one thing about which I am certain – the role played by my father, Alf, in shaping me, not so much as a sportsman or a businessman, more as a person. He was my guard and my guide, the biggest single influence on my life and the one to whom I owe a debt of gratitude far beyond words. That is not just for the interest he showed in my football – when I made it to the England team there was not a prouder man on the planet – but for keeping our family together when hardship and tragedy threatened to break us apart.

We were a poor family but let me quickly qualify that by saying we were poor only in financial terms. In the far more important areas of love and unity we were rich beyond measure and that was all down to my father.

When I popped up on the scene, Preston was throwing a party. The on-going battle against poverty – poverty is the only word to describe what many families faced – was pushed to the background for a while because 1922 was a special year, a Guild year. Once every two decades the Preston Guild organises a unique mix of entertainment, pageantry and spectacle. The tradition started in medieval times and it is still celebrated to this day. People keep open house and it is a time of great community festivity and fellowship.

Preston, in line with most Lancashire towns, was highly dependent upon the prosperity of the cotton industry. Cotton was how men and women earned their living and the biggest mill, Horrockses, was once known as the 'world centre for cotton' no less. But the ravages of the post-war depression had left a stark legacy. The town had suffered badly and, by 1922, Preston endured some of the worst living conditions in the north of England and mills were closing at the rate of one a year. Around 10,000 Prestonians were unemployed, and the football club, despite holding First Division status, was crippled by debt.

Such was the state of play when I was born on 5 April and, boy, it was a tough place to be. I was the second son of Alf and Margaret Finney. My brother Joe and I had four sisters, Madge, Peggy, Doris and Edith. Ironically, well ironically for me at any rate, our first family home in St Michael's Road was little more than a couple of hundred yards from Preston North End's famous Deepdale ground.

Coincidentally, North End played a First Division fixture on the day of my birth, losing at home to Manchester City. And in what was clearly a most eventful month, Preston reached the last pre-Wembley FA Cup final. The team had suffered massive injury problems, so severe in fact that officials announced publicly a policy of concentrating on the Cup (a variation on the usual claim). It worked, too, as Preston accounted for some hefty opposition to book a final clash with Herbert Chapman's mighty Huddersfield Town at Stamford Bridge. Victories over Wolverhampton Wanderers, Newcastle United, Barnsley, Arsenal, and Tottenham Hotspur in the semi-final, set up a War of the Roses encounter in London.

Cup finals have always produced administrative headaches, particularly in the distribution of tickets, and it was much the same story in 1922. High levels of unemployment meant money was very tight in Preston and only 3,000 townsfolk made the long journey, the bulk of them on 25 specially chartered trains.

Huddersfield, later to be league champions in successive seasons, were the firm favourites and in Preston's goal was a chap by the name of Fred Mitchell who played wearing spectacles. Apparently, Mitchell did his best to prevent Huddersfield's controversial winner from the penalty spot; in fact, he acted in such an animated fashion that it prompted the FA to introduce the rule restricting goalkeepers' movements the following season.

Home attendances at Preston hovered around the 18,000 mark and the team eventually finished 16th in the table despite setting the unenviable record of playing 13 away games without scoring a single goal.

My dad was a keen North Ender but not a regular watcher, due to financial constraints. He often found himself unemployed, a common state of affairs in our working-class environment, especially during the years after the General Strike of 1926. Those families who could be sure that there would be a job for the breadwinner from one week to the next were the lucky ones. When the father did land work, he was often toiling for a pittance.

I was little more than a toddler when we moved house. We took a property in Daisy Lane in the Holme Slack area of town – still within earshot of the roar of the crowd at Deepdale. It was a council house, three-bedroomed with a sitting room and kitchen, on a typical north-west estate. Facilities were basic but there was a large back garden in which Dad grew a selection of vegetables.

Then, like a bolt from the blue, came the tragic death of my mother. I was four. I can remember her falling ill and the ambulance arriving to whisk her to Preston Royal Infirmary. We were worried, of course we were worried, but the initial diagnosis was appendicitis and that was rarely life-threatening. But the doctors had it wrong and a few days later we were mourning her death. She was 32. How Dad coped with the upset and the subsequent responsibility is still hard to contemplate.

In those days, many youngsters who lost their mothers were sent into special care or handed on to foster homes. Others, even less fortunate, were taken under the wing of charities who shipped them off to 'better lives' abroad, never to see their relatives again.

To be left with six children under 10 years of age to raise was the cross my dad was given to bear and he carried it with real guts. I can only start to think of the strain he must have endured, but there was never a chance of him giving in to the pressure even though it meant him looking for extra work to supplement his income as a clerk with the Electricity Board. He did nights behind the bar in local pubs and, more often than not, he counted no more than 50 shillings (£2.50) in his joint pay packets each week.

He never made a song and dance about what he did. Dad was a quiet, inoffensive man who was popular with lots of close friends.

He encouraged support and got it, especially from our grandmas, a really nice woman called Mrs Edwards who worked a few hours as a housekeeper, and our neighbours the Fishes and the Mashiters.

And then there was our Madge, my eldest sister, who did her best to take Mum's place. Madge was a true heroine at 11 years of age. Good at organising, Madge would draw up lists of jobs that needed doing around the house and share them out between us. The fact that we had four girls around the place didn't mean Joe and I got away with anything. My main duties involved washing and drying up and running errands.

Life in a Lancashire mill-town during the troubled twenties was a dour struggle for the vast majority of folk. It was not a healthy environment, either, the mills and domestic chimneys spewing out smoke that frequently enveloped the town in a layer of sooty smog. I once read somewhere that up to five tonnes of soot fell on each and every square mile of Preston annually – smokeless zones were very much for the future. Local corporation parks not only provided a centre for amusement and recreation and general escapism, but also somewhere where you could inhale a few deep breaths of fresh air.

The town was very noisy, too, with the clatter of trams on the tracks, clogs on the cobbles, and the intense rhythmic sound of heavy textile machinery carrying well beyond the mill walls. You could tell those who worked in the mills – they shouted when they spoke. It was little wonder so many of them experienced hearing problems in later life. They never had much money, either, but who did?

By the middle of the 1920s, a cotton weaver could expect to earn little over £3 a week, about half what a bricklayer or a baker could earn and just a few shillings more than the poor old farm labourer. The professionals – teachers, police and solicitors – did better at between £500 and £1,000 a year while the average working man would bring home around £4 per week, and that didn't go very far when you consider the cost of living.

Milk, delivered to your doorstep by a milk cart pulled by a horse, came in at 5d (2p) a pint and a sack of coal cost 1s 9d (9p). Then there were the 'luxury' items, beer at 5d a pint, chocolate at 6d (3p) for a half-pound bar, cigarettes at 10d (4p) for eight and petrol, for the select few who owned a car, at 1s 4d (7p) a gallon.

Religion was enjoying a heyday and I well remember my time as a choirboy. It involved three trips to church on a Sunday for morning service, Sunday school in the afternoon and evensong. We were Church of England and both Joe and I did our time in the choir. Lads started at about eight or nine years old and stayed on until they were 13 or 14, or whenever their voices broke.

The heavily varnished choir pews by the pulpit were pitch-pine, very hard and decidedly uncomfortable, especially as the sermons always seemed to last for an eternity. Many a time I would find myself yawning as I daydreamed about a game of football.

Football was our main pastime but the gang of kids played a variety of other street games as well. I say 'gang' advisedly, for sometimes it seemed as though there were hundreds of us. All the lads liked tig and chase and marbles, especially if you had one or two of the big glass alleys in your treasured collection. The girls could perform wonders with skipping ropes and a stone to mark out a dancing area on the flags.

Unless it was raining – and I mean non-stop torrential rain – we played out. If the weather deemed otherwise, we would stay indoors and play board games, cards, read a book or spend time crayoning.

Most of my clothes were hand-me-downs from our Joe – not that you ever thought about things like that. A jumper was a jumper wherever it had come from. We all had clogs and no one was what you might term smartly dressed, but did anybody notice? I don't think they did. Most of the kids were in the same boat. Families scrimped and scraped to make ends meet, and anyway, clothes were not fashion statements. They were functional. They kept you dry and warm.

The neighbourhood shops were the usual mix – a confectioner's, a grocer's, a hardware store, plus a chip shop and a pub or two. Kids were actively discouraged from going anywhere near the pubs although the smell of alcohol often wafted across the streets. We saw the occasional drunken man stumbling his way home but, by and large, we were brought up to steer well clear of the demon drink.

The chippy was a different matter altogether. It was a favourite haunt of mine and I loved Friday night teatime with my Grandma Finney and Auntie Martha because we invariably had fish, chips and peas. It is easy to see why they were so popular back then – for the same reasons they are popular now. Fish and chips are quick and easy, you can vary the portions to suit appetites and wallets, and they are bloomin' tasty into the bargain. People queued in numbers, watching with mouths watering as the fish fryer conjured up his magic. I can still hear the hissing sound as the sliced potatoes were dropped into the sizzling hot fat, the smell of vinegar on newspaper and the banter between customers. You always hoped that you didn't get behind someone ordering for an army – like me, standing there with the huge family order clenched tightly in my hand.

Kids were often given lists to go shopping. I was a regular volunteer for my grandma. All you had to do was hand over the list and your money (unless you were paying on 'tick') to the shopkeeper and wait until the bag was packed and ready to carry home. Grannie paid me tuppence for my efforts. Easy money.

I spent most of it on sweets. There was little else for kids to buy. Dad or Gran always paid for the major treats like a trip to the pictures or, at Christmas, the local pantomime. Don't think for a minute that we were always going out – you were very lucky if you got to the pictures more than a couple of times a year.

Then there was old Mr Gabbutt, the barber, who could give you a tuppenny short back and sides before you realised what was happening. Dad took us along about once every six weeks and his instruction was always the same: 'Plenty off, please – got to make it last.'

The barber's shop was not a place I particularly cared for, all a bit cold and clinical and I didn't like watching the men get shaved with a cut-throat razor. The rough sound of steel against bristle made me cringe. It wasn't half as much fun as the chippy!

So, given the general state of play, our dad was in every sense a hero. For all his troubles and the need to work long hours, he always had his football to help keep him sane. Dad was never too tired to talk football with Joe and me, relaying tales of the great games and great players he had seen. Perhaps he exaggerated at times – who doesn't to make a story stick? – but I loved him all the more for it. He never told us, or anyone else for that matter, that he harboured a desire for one or both of us to make the grade as a professional footballer but I am quite sure that wish was lurking in the back of his mind.

With times tough and money tight, we weren't quite penniless but we were the next best thing. We certainly missed out on some of the niceties of life. As for holidays, well I didn't know what a holiday was until I was 16 and working as an apprentice plumber. A friend and I decided to take a few days at the seaside, but our money couldn't buy us much and we had difficulty spinning it out for the duration. As for going abroad, that was what the wealthy mill owners did and very few others. I had to wait until I was 20 for a taste of life overseas and that was via the *Queen Mary*. She had been converted to a troop ship and was taking us to Egypt.

I do remember the odd day trip to Blackpool, a walk on the promenade and a ride on a donkey on the sands. I also recall being shipped off to Lytham St Anne's for a week to give Dad a break. It was linked up to what was known as the 'Clog Fund', a charitable organisation that arranged for underprivileged children to go off on special holidays. Joe and I were sent to a hostel in Lytham along with some other local kids. I was about seven and Joe would be 12. We lived in as temporary residents and I was quite taken aback by the place to start with, not least by the amount of food on offer. It was all laid out on a huge table and our eyes lit up when we saw it. Our first reaction was to help ourselves and tuck in but we soon got rapped over the knuckles for forgetting our manners and failing to say grace. Things went downhill after that and we were glad to get back home.

Then Dad got married again, to an Irish girl called Mary. She had an uphill task, inheriting a large family when future prospects were far from encouraging and the present wasn't too clever. I don't remember much about the wedding, but I do remember it taking a long time to adjust to having another woman in the house, a new mother. To be candid, I don't think I ever did properly adjust. Mary was a feisty woman, quick-tempered and quite strict, and we all tended to resent her interference. That was probably most unfair but as a child you don't always appreciate just what someone is trying to do for you.

Mary's cause was not helped by the fact that my Grandma Finney didn't like her and made it fairly plain. By contrast, Grandma

Mitchell – who as my mother's mother might have been more likely to object – was smashing with her. When we complained about this, that and the other, most of it trivia, Grandma Mitchell would say, 'Now come on, Mary is doing her best. You must respect her and help her all you can.'

Mary and Dad had two children, Dennis and Roy, and we accepted them as brothers. Later in life, both of them came to work at Tom Finney Ltd, Dennis as a plumber and Roy as an electrician. Dennis eventually went to work for British Aerospace and travelled the world while Roy set up a successful business of his own.

Dad was never slow to offer advice but he had a way of delivering the message. He didn't impose it on you, just left you to think things through. 'Get a trade in your fingers,' he'd say. 'You never know when you may need it. Football is all well and good but it's not a certainty that you'll make it, and what about injury? You have to plan, so plan well.' It has always amazed me how few footballers of my time, and subsequently, took the time to plan ahead. With the financial situation these days, I don't suppose it is important now, but up until the explosion of money in the game, it was almost as though players felt they could go on indefinitely – a fool's philosophy and one that caught out quite a few down the years.

'Don't get involved in borrowing money,' was another piece of advice. 'Save up for the things you want and then buy them, and if you can't afford them, do without.' I have always followed those wise words, never running up any debts either at home or in business, and I have always paid my way.

'Accept the rules of the game,' Dad would say. 'The referee is always right and nothing you can do or say after a decision has been made will alter anything.' Perhaps that is why I managed to go through my entire career without getting booked or sent off. It wasn't that I never thought the referees were wrong; it was just that I never let them know it.

Although football dominated my early life – that should probably read my entire life come to think of it – opportunities for watching the game were restricted. Apart from anything else, I was always too busy playing. But as a proud Prestonian, I was acutely aware of Preston North End Football Club and, in common with the other lads who kicked a rubber ball around the back fields of Holme Slack, my dream was to be the next Alex James.

James was the top star of the day, a genius. There wasn't much about him physically, but he had sublime skills and the knack of letting the ball do the work. He wore the baggiest of baggy shorts and his heavily gelled hair was parted down the centre. On the odd occasion when I was able to watch a game at Deepdale, sometimes sneaking under the turnstiles when the chap on duty was distracted, I was in awe of James. Preston were in the Second Division and the general standard of football was not the best, but there was a magic and a mystery about James that mesmerised me.

The man behind Preston's capture of James was chairman Jim Taylor, who later signed me and went on to play a major part in my early career.

The son of a railwayman and a native of North Lanarkshire, Alex James was a steelworker when his football talents were first spotted by Raith Rovers in the year of my birth. He earned good money north of the border – £6 in the winter and £4 in the summer – and his form brought the scouts flocking in. Preston were always well served with 'spies' in Scotland and while his short stature and dubious temperament caused a few potential buyers to dither, Jim Taylor was more bullish. In the June of 1925, the chairman went in with a £2,500 bid – an offer later raised to £3,500 to ward off a late inquiry from Leicester City. Taylor had his man and the signing of James proved a masterstroke. The supporters loved him, a fact reflected in the attendances, which rose by around £300 per game. He was box office, the draw card, a player who grabbed your attention and refused to let go.

James was a character off the field, too. He liked clubs – of the night-time variety – owned a car and, by all accounts, enjoyed playing practical jokes on his colleagues. But he was also a perfectionist, a footballer acutely aware of both his ability and his responsibility. The experts scratched their heads about why his talent was being allowed to languish outside the top flight and it wasn't long before Arsenal came in to present him with a bigger stage. He was my first football hero and my role model and when he was transferred to the Gunners I thought I would never get over it.

The kickabouts we had in the fields and on the streets were daily events, sometimes involving dozens and dozens of kids. There were so many bodies around you had to be flippin' good to get a kick. Once you got hold of the ball, you didn't let it go too easily. That's where I first learned about close control and dribbling.

It was a world of make-believe – were children more imaginative in those days? – and although we only had tin cans and school caps for goalposts, it mattered not a jot. In my mind, this basic field was Deepdale and I was the inside-left, Alex James. I tried to look like him, run like him, juggle the ball and body swerve like him. By *being* James, I became more confident in my own game. He never knew it, but Alex James played a major part in my development.

Our Joe always seemed to be on t'other side in those innocent days, but he certainly didn't show any family favour when the ball was there to be won. We played until our legs gave way – scores of

15–13 were not uncommon – and I never stopped running. I tried to make up in enthusiasm what I lacked in physical presence for all the other boys were much bigger than I was, or so it felt.

Football united the kids. You didn't have to call for your mates; simply walking down the street bouncing a ball had the Pied Piper effect. We could all smell a game from 200 yards.

My dad played his football for St Jude's, the parish church that later hosted his funeral, and he and other fathers from the neighbourhood were forever arranging practice matches for us. We were Holme Slack FC and one of our biggest fixtures was against Freckleton. I remember going over to play at their place for the first time. We booked a coach and they laid on a meal afterwards in the village hall. The game ended all square and Dad, most impressed with the hospitality, decided to invite them back for a return match. The only thing he had overlooked was our own acute lack of facilities. We could just about stage a game, but what about changing rooms and the food and drink?

Once again it was left to the Holme Slack community to come to the rescue. One chap let us use his wooden hut to get changed and all the parents took in a Freckleton lad for dinner. The game was played on a Boxing Day morning to allow the parents to go along to North End in the afternoon. I can't honestly remember how we went on, but the occasion itself was a great success and further underlined the sense of spirit and camaraderie that existed. Whenever there was a problem, someone somewhere would come up with a solution. We were never beaten.

I felt I was making decent progress as a footballer; my one concern was my size. I lacked physical strength and in my schooldays I was also hampered by a gland problem in my neck. It appeared as a swelling soon after my mother died and was fairly unsightly. I was conscious of the way it protruded and used to have it wrapped in a bandage.

The hospital doctors put me on what was then termed sunray treatment. It involved two candles placed at either end of a special machine and I had to stand there, stark naked, for an hour at a time. That went on twice a week for eight years until, when I was 14, they decided to operate and remove the gland altogether. It has never bothered me for a single day since.

I wasn't alone in worrying about my frail build. Teachers at Deepdale County Primary School broached the subject with my father but there was little he could do. We had to 'wait until I filled out'. There were no other medical problems and I had more than a healthy appetite, sometimes finishing off not only my own meals but anything that my sisters and brother left on their plates as well.

My early school years were largely uneventful. I felt I did OK without ever threatening to top the class, and I was far too shy ever to give cheek or misbehave. Indeed, had it not been for football, both during PE periods and at break, I would have passed through junior school fairly anonymously.

Things continued in much the same vein when I switched to Deepdale Modern although the teachers suddenly seemed even stricter – you treated 'Sir' with a mixture of respect and fear, not wanting to run the risk of a caning. Corporal punishment was acceptable then, which probably accounts for general discipline levels being a damned sight higher than they appear to be today. If you were caught acting the goat you were punished – the procedure was straightforward and we knew the risks involved if we were daft enough to flout the rules. And there was no point running home crying to your parents, either. Those who tried that one usually finished up getting another thick ear for their pains.

I don't remember getting into trouble too often, but one instance does stand out. I had just gone back to school after recovering from a broken collar bone and one of my classmates, a rough little lad, deliberately knocked my cap off my head and rubbed it into the ground with his dirty shoe. It took a lot to rile me, but I lost my temper completely and really let rip at him. The skirmish was soon over as the bigger lads came to separate us, but we continued to glare at each other and agreed to 'meet after school' to sort things out.

As soon as the bell went we were swapping punches again in someone's backyard. Suddenly, old 'Pop' Wilson, the headmaster, decided to put in a surprise appearance. He frogmarched us back to his office and I remember getting a clip even before he had shut the door. He was furious and seemed particularly annoyed with me for getting involved in a fight so soon after my injury. It all seemed a bit unfair but I have since come to understand that the offended party often comes out worse than the perpetrator.

Deepdale Modern signalled the final whistle as far as playtime football sessions were concerned. The building was of a new design, including some all-glass walls, and football in the yard was not permitted. However, the sports teacher (always felt that was a great job) Bill Tuson was particularly keen on football and seemed to take a shine to me. He put me in the school Under-12 team at inside-left – Alex James's position, where else?

We won our way through to the final of the Dawson Cup, one of three major local school tournaments of the day alongside the LFA Cup and the Ord Cup. To get to the final was joy itself, so imagine my reaction when Mr Tuson told us that the venue for the big game was Deepdale.

In common with many other clubs back then, North End officials were only too pleased to stage school and amateur league finals –

and why not? Those matches pulled in thousands of people, many of them not regular supporters, so it was not only an excellent public relations exercise but a means of attracting potential new support. I can't think of many places where it happens now. The official line is that the clubs don't want to damage the pitches. I consider that both a poor excuse and a terrible shame.

Considering it was 70 years ago, I can remember the Dawson Cup final of 1934 in a fair bit of detail. St Ignatius' School provided our opposition. The game was played at teatime on a midweek night in the spring, the pitch was shortened and narrowed and we used small nets.

Not much schoolwork was done that day as everyone, pupils and teachers alike, prepared for a Deepdale invasion. The team members met at the ground about half an hour before kick-off and were shown into the main changing rooms. That was a tremendous thrill in itself. North End may have been in the doldrums but the first-team players were still stars to us and here we were using their hooks and benches.

A few of the lads who played that day went on to join the North End groundstaff – Eddie Burke, Cookie Eastham, Dickie Finch and Chuck Scales – but I doubt whether anyone enjoyed it more than I did. For one thing, playing at Deepdale was the stuff of fantasy, especially with my family and friends looking on; for another, I was lucky enough to put my name to the winning goal. Funnily enough, the goal is the one aspect of the night I struggle to recall. It came late on and gave us a 2–1 win.

I was chaired from the field a hero. Scenes of jubilation surrounded the presentation and we were greeted by hundreds of smiling faces when we came out of the ground. It seemed that the whole of Deepdale Modern had turned out.

I stayed with my Grandma Finney and Auntie Martha that night. They had been to the game and were determined to carry on the celebrating with a trip down to the pub. The problem was they wanted to take my medal along with them and I wasn't at all happy about that.

'Do you have to, Grandma?' I pleaded, knowing that I was fighting a losing battle.

'Oh, come on now, Tom,' she replied. 'Our friends will love to see the medal and hear all about your goal. We will be careful with it, don't worry.'

But I did worry. In fact, I couldn't get to sleep for worrying. That medal was the most important thing in my life and the thought of it being passed around a pub was cause enough for concern. I lay there until I heard the key in the front door. Then I jumped out of bed and ran to the top of the stairs.

'Grandma, is that you? Have you remembered my medal?'

They had, of course they had. Such was their pride, the medal could not have been in safer hands. My appetite for football and for Deepdale was well and truly whetted.

In 1936, I was chosen in the squad for the Preston Town team in the prestigious All-England Schools' Shield tournament. It was run on a knock-out basis and we won through to the final, not that I could claim much credit. I was a permanent fixture as the reserve, thanks to a fellow called Tommy Hough. Tommy played in my position and was much bigger and stronger than I was. Amazingly, he had held the spot for three years after first getting into what was an Under-14 side as an 11-year-old. History was to repeat itself some years later – Tommy also kept me on the sidelines after we had both signed for North End.

The Shield final was against West Ham at Upton Park and 13 of us went off to London, not just for the final but for a full weekend of sightseeing.

West Ham were firm favourites and no one gave us a chance, but we dug in and managed to force a draw to become joint champions. On returning to Preston, we were given a civic reception and I remember feeling mighty pleased with myself even though I hadn't kicked a ball at any stage. Suddenly, things were happening for me – nice things, positive things, things that made me think I might just find a future in football.

Back in the pre-war days of the late 1930s, and in common with other Lancashire town clubs Blackburn, Blackpool, Bolton and Burnley, Preston North End liked to shop locally for up-and-coming talent. While all of the major clubs had scouts strategically placed around the country (especially in Scotland in North End's case) it was considered extra special to bring a local lad through the system and into the first team. The supporters liked to see one of their own make good and it is my view that they still do, even in these days of the global game. We certainly never had to compete with lads from overseas for a place in the team and while I can see how some foreign players have added glamour to our game, I contend that their arrival has worked against the development of our own lads.

It really comes down to mathematics. Take the Premiership. If every team plays, there are 220 places in the starting line-ups up for grabs, and I would wager that some weeks more than half go to foreigners, a clear obstruction for our own youngsters. I would like to see the international football authorities introduce some sort of limit, similar to cricket, with overseas players restricted to an agreed number per club or team.

It didn't cross my mind that the person who would get in the way of a career in football would be my dad – and that after he had been fundamental in setting up the opportunity.

One night, soon after tea, I spotted an advertisement in the evening paper. Attributed to Preston North End chairman Jim Taylor, it invited any up-and-coming young footballers aged between 14 and 18 to write in for a trial.

Mr Taylor was a huge devotee of youth football, one of the first administrators to put a proper policy in place. He talked of 'nurseries' and established a scouting system that covered not only Preston but took in the nation as a whole. His main focus, though, was the town itself and he managed to persuade his fellow directors to sponsor the Preston and District League for schoolboy soccer to the tune of £250, and put forward four teams under the Preston North End banner.

I could hardly believe the advert. This was it, the chance I had been waiting for. I showed it to Dad who shared my excitement and before I went off to bed we had put a letter together, listing my height, weight, age and all other necessary details, and popped it in the post.

By this time, I had left school and, with further help from Dad, joined a local plumbing firm, Pilkington's. The boss, Harry Pilkington, knew of our family and the struggle we had endured in an effort to stay together and I am convinced he took me on out of sympathy. For all his understanding, however, he wasn't sympathetic enough to jack up the pay and my first wage was a princely 6 shillings (30p) for a 46½-hour week. Overtime came in at a penny an hour.

It might not have been the most lucrative of starts but I liked Harry and valued the chance he had given me. I was also mindful of the fact that while the pay was low, some companies actually charged apprentices a fee for taking them on.

But plumbing was plumbing and football was football. One was work and the other play. The trick now was to make the play part, the pay part; the newspaper advertisement was the first step on the yellow brick road – or so I thought. I was wrong. Perhaps there was an oversight; perhaps the club failed to administer the responses properly. Whatever the reason was, my application didn't even merit a reply. I was devastated.

Dad tried to console me by saying that North End had probably received hundreds of letters and that responding would just take time, but I feared the chance had gone. I blamed the facts and figures in my letter. It was down to my physical build. What would North End want with a 14-year-old who tipped the scales at under 5 stone and stood just 4ft 9ins?

But if I had given up hope, my father was having none of it. He had a plan. He was working part-time as a waiter in The Sumners Hotel near to Deepdale, a pub used occasionally by North End trainer Will Scott. Will became a North End institution, eventually enjoying a glorious period as manager, and he became a close confidant of mine. We shared a similar outlook on life and football and he gained many points in my eyes, not least for his sense of fair play.

One night in the pub, Dad told Will about me and Will suggested I went along for a trial. Despair turned to joy. Will did his bit and within a couple of days I got a letter inviting me to report for a match at Ashton Park.

The events of that summer evening are vivid in my memory. Will pulled all the young hopefuls to one side, explained the rules and selected two teams – the blues and the whites. I was picked at inside-left for the blues but when I got over to where the shirts were laid out on the grass, a much bigger lad had already pulled on the number

10 jersey. I asked him for the shirt but he made it clear he wasn't for parting with it. I was near to tears as one of the fellows running the trial came over to sort things out. He turned to the big lad and said 'Give the kid your shirt, son – he won't be on long anyway.'

But I did stay on, right through to the final whistle, and although I didn't score I was very pleased with my performance. So, too, it seemed were Will Scott and Jim Taylor. As we were getting changed at the side of the pitch afterwards, they came over and asked for a word. The word was did I fancy a job on the Preston North End groundstaff at £2 10s (£2.50) a week. I was speechless. Was I hearing things? Were they serious?

Mr Taylor urged me not to make a quick decision but to go home, talk it through and let him know the following morning. I nodded agreement, but there was nothing to talk about. How could there be any problems? I wanted to be a footballer, Dad wanted me to be a footballer and, beyond my wildest dreams, here was my hometown club offering me the chance to become a footballer.

So my father's reaction amazed me. In fact, it damn near killed me. He said no. He explained – not that I wanted to hear his explanation – that I should concentrate on learning the plumbing trade, continue to play football as an amateur and re-assess the situation in a few years' time. He felt that my joining the groundstaff represented a gamble and it wasn't worth the risk.

I couldn't take it all in and accused him of trying to ruin my life. I cried and cried but it made no difference and the following day I had to tell Mr Taylor that I wouldn't be taking the job.

It was only later that I fully accepted my father's reasoning, having realised that he was, after all, acting in my best interests. When you are young and impressionable with a burning desire and what might as well be a passport to paradise in your hand, it is very difficult to sit down and see sense. He didn't want me to toss aside the chance to build a solid career in plumbing on the off-chance that I might make the grade as a footballer. For him to say no must have crippled him, too; not only because he knew what it meant to me but because he could certainly have made good use of the extra money.

North End accepted my father's decision and I signed amateur forms, which meant I qualified for the B team and was allowed to report for evening training sessions twice a week after work. There was great rivalry between the A and B teams. We were looked upon very much as the poor relations, and everyone assumed that only those in the A team would have any chance of progressing should a senior opportunity arise.

In the season before the Second World War, I managed to win a place in the club's youth team only to find Tommy Hough in the way again. It seemed as though this fellow was determined to make life difficult for me, but I got a lucky break when the right winger, Eddie Burke, pulled out of a midweek home match with Manchester United through injury. I was handed the task of filling in for Eddie, even though putting a left-footed player on the opposite wing was considered quite bizarre. It went well and I set up a couple of goals in a 3–0 win.

I enjoyed the challenge of resisting cutting inside every time, and instead going down to the line to cross the ball with my weaker foot. I was determined that it would not stay weak for long and put in hours and hours of extra practice until I could use both feet to the same standard. Eventually, I was to play the vast majority of my professional games for club and country on the right wing, and it all came about by chance.

Talking of chance, fate is as obvious in football as anywhere else. For instance, few people know that I very nearly became a Blackburn

Rovers player before I had kicked a senior ball for North End. Our Joe had got on with Rovers, training with them in the evenings, and my father thought it made a lot of sense to have us both join the same club. However, before that had a chance to develop further than the idea stage, Preston came up with an offer.

War was a few months old and I was still some way short of my 18th birthday when Miss Simpson, a secretary at Pilkington's, sent for me. I had just got back in from a job and it was no more than a few minutes before we clocked off. She said a Mr Taylor from Preston North End had telephoned and asked that I should not go home at teatime, but instead make my way round to his house. My father had also been invited.

I was a bit puzzled. It all seemed very formal and my first thought was what have I done? When I arrived, still in my overalls, my father was already there and it was clear the news they had for me was anything but alarming. North End wanted me to turn professional on wartime terms of 10 shillings (50p) a game. The paperwork was ready and waiting and I remember trembling as I signed. Your mind races at such times. You can almost hear the roar of the crowd as you make your full debut and score the winning goal.

It later transpired that my father had arrived a good half-hour before me and the deal was already agreed by the time I knocked on the door. I was not unduly concerned; I was too busy celebrating my break into the big-time.

Unfortunately, the war was to prove a most stubborn and difficult opponent for all young footballers across the land. It wasn't for some six years that any of us had the chance to play at full Football League level. The upside, if there can be such a thing in wartime, was that the government deemed that football should continue as an entertainment spectacle even though the Football League had disbanded.

It might have been watered-down fare, but regional wartime football was fine by me. I very much doubt that in normal circumstances I would have started the first game of the 1940–41 season playing for the Preston first team against Liverpool at Anfield.

Also in our team that day was a man who, many years later, was to become a Liverpool legend – *the* Liverpool legend – the great Bill Shankly. If my father was my guiding light in life, Bill Shankly was my football mentor. Has there been anyone with a greater love for the game? If there has, I have yet to meet him.

Shanks was unique, a complete one-off. He caused a great stir when he described football as more important than life or death and, what is more, he meant it. He was the best pal in the world to anyone prepared to eat, sleep and drink football, but a man with no time for those who failed to meet his standards. Extremely fit, his enthusiasm was infectious and the word defeat didn't have a place in his vocabulary. Bill influenced so many and so much, and his contribution to the game cannot be exaggerated – unlike many of the tales about him and his antics.

Shanks first set foot in Deepdale in 1933 and within months, at just 19, he was in the first team. As you may imagine, he wasn't a guy to give up his shirt without a fight and he followed his debut by playing 85 games in a row. He stayed for 17 seasons, eventually returning to Carlisle as manager. During his time at Preston, he won an FA Cup winner's medal, in 1938, and was capped by Scotland; he was also a member of our double-winning wartime side.

He was an established player when I first encountered him during my days as a junior. He invariably popped along to our matches – Bill would stop off anywhere a game of football was being played and, even at that early stage of his career, you knew he would go into coaching and management and make a damn good job of it.

A much better all-round player than some might have you believe, Shanks worked tirelessly to improve. After morning training he was always asking if anyone fancied going back for an extra session or a game of head tennis in the afternoon.

In the dressing room he was the driving force, with the knack of geeing everyone up while at the same time maintaining an air of calm about the place. He liked a laugh and a joke – he used to take great delight in recalling his days as an accomplished amateur boxer in the Air Force by running around in a pair of long johns just before kick-off – but essentially he was deadly serious about his football. He gave you confidence; that was his secret. I am sure all those who played under him at Carlisle, Grimsby, Workington, Huddersfield and particularly during his golden years at Liverpool, would say the same.

It is no secret that we got on famously as footballers and as friends, close friends. Shanks said some wonderful things about me, often introducing me to others as 'my friend, the greatest footballer ever'. It could be very embarrassing, but it was his way and you accepted it. His passing in 1981 left me with a hollow feeling. It would be impossible to put a value on the help he gave me. Along with hundreds of footballers, I owed him a hell of a lot.

For a youngster starting off in the game back in the thirties, there was no better example, and he was a constant source of inspiration. For sure, he could rant and rave and wave his fist around, but he never had a shouting match with me. If you had a good attitude to the game, you got on well with Shanks. If you could play a bit as well, you had a friend for life.

My goodness, in those days you looked upon the senior professionals with awe and trepidation. It was an honour and a privilege to be allowed in the dressing room with them, let alone engage them in conversation. But Bill was different, so obsessed with football that it didn't matter to him whether he was talking to the chairman, his first-team colleagues or a kid from the youth team. So when Jim Taylor decided that the club's future lay in establishing a sound youth policy, it surprised no one that Bill stepped forward even though he had only just turned 20 himself. It was the first rung on the ladder to managerial stardom.

Fear no one was his motto. He used to say, 'No opponent is better than you until he proves it out on the park.' A fitness fanatic, he set the standards and everyone followed. He frowned upon smoking and drinking and had no time for cheats or dodgers, no matter how skilful they might have been as players. Simply being able to play was never enough for Bill; he wanted much more out of you. He demanded that you gave your all, but he was by no means an ogre. The kids loved having Bill around and he was our link with the first team. I remember him coming over to me after one game and saying, 'Well done, Tommy. Carry on like that and you'll make it.' I was lifted to a whole new level.

He made you feel special, damn near unbeatable, and had you believing that all the best players in the country played for Preston. Arsenal or Wolverhampton Wanderers, Stanley Matthews or Peter Doherty, Anfield or Stamford Bridge – it didn't matter who you played against, or where it was, Shanks always believed we could win. More than that, he believed we would win. Even if you were three down with two minutes to go, he would refuse to accept the possibility of losing. Before one particular game, he overheard a few of us chatting about a member of the opposition and how good we thought he was.

'Hang on a bloody minute,' he boomed. 'We won't have any of that bloody talk in here. Whoever he is, he's no better than us until we get out on the pitch.'

With the benefit of hindsight, I suppose it counts as ironic that my first outing as a first-team player with Shanks should be against Liverpool at Anfield.

The Second World War robbed us both of six years but, if anything, it was harder on Bill than it was on me because when the hostilities finished I was still only 24, while he was 32.

I vividly recall Neville Chamberlain's depressing broadcast to the nation on that Sunday morning, 3 September 1939, two days after German forces had invaded Poland. After attending morning service at St Jude's, I called in on a mate of mine, Tommy Johnson, a fellow plumber, and he was glued to the wireless as the news we all dreaded came through.

League football was suspended, players were told that they would be paid up to the end of the week only, and supporters were informed that there would be no refund on season tickets. Andy Beattie, another of North End's 'Great Scots' and a man for whom I held the utmost respect, was due a richly deserved benefit match. The war ensured that didn't materialise. Contracts were effectively cancelled although clubs retained players' registrations.

Preston made strenuous efforts to get players fixed up with jobs – Shanks found employment shovelling sand, George Mutch building aeroplanes and Jack Fairbrother joined up as a policeman. Troops were stationed at Deepdale, and police and military use of the ground continued through until 1946.

Wartime football was no substitute for the real thing but it did serve a purpose. There were restrictions galore and most clubs found their squads decimated through call-ups into the armed services, but the public passion for football won through. Sometimes matches were in doubt right up to kick-off as clubs tried desperately to recruit some guest players, but when the action rolled it was good. Football provided the country with some much-needed escapism and, speaking as a player, it was thoroughly enjoyable – despite the bombs. After we had lost 2–0 at Anfield, our coach-ride home was caught up in an air-raid on Merseyside and that was a frightening experience by any standards.

The 1940–41 season was a shortened affair but Preston United did well. We finished as Northern Section champions, which was some achievement considering the fact that we had struggled at the wrong end of the First Division up to war being declared.

CHAPTER THREE

At 'war' with Matthews – and Hitler!

Stanley Matthews was a footballing genius. A product of the Potteries, Stan became England's favourite sporting son, the game's first true superstar. The maestro played to a supreme standard for 33 years, filled grounds all over the world and didn't retire until he was 50. He was an entertainer extraordinaire, a crowd-pleasing, defender-teasing bundle of tricks for whom the football pitch was a theatre. The English footballing public adored him.

Just imagine what it felt like to be compared with him, to be looked upon as his rival and to be touted as his successor long before he was ready to hang up his boots. Impossible, or what?

Imagine, too, how we both felt, continually reading in the newspapers of a so-called feud between us. Time and time again we tried to put the record straight, but it was almost as if the media didn't want to know. Perhaps the truth would have served only to ruin the stories.

So let's put a few myths to bed. I have waited a long time for this. Stan and I shared a mutual respect and a close friendship and I categorically refute all rumours suggesting any kind of bad blood or friction. More than that, I was one of a quartet of men chosen to provide a guard of honour for Stan's funeral at St Peter Ad Vincula Church in Stoke-on-Trent on Friday, 3 March 2000. No further proof required.

The Potteries came to a complete standstill as thousands of football followers gathered to pay their last respects to a man renowned the world over as a footballer supreme. To be present was a privilege, but to be asked to play an active role was something else. Bobby Charlton, Nat Lofthouse and Gordon Banks were the other three invited to stand beside Stan's coffin on what was a day of deep emotion. We didn't actually carry the coffin, we wheeled it in, and during a very moving service, I remember a particularly excellent address from Jimmy Armfield, who played with Stan at Blackpool.

Inside and outside the church people wept openly, but amid a huge sense of loss, there was an atmosphere of dignified celebration. To see so many spilling out into the streets served to underline Stan's enormous popularity. It was a fitting tribute.

Stoke City officials arranged a reception at the Victoria Ground afterwards and we all took delight in swapping stories about Stan.

I had been told of his passing the previous week in a telephone call with the Press Association and although I was well aware of his age, his death still came as a real shock to me, probably because I had him down as indestructible.

During our playing days together he was a model of professionalism, always careful about his diet and exercise – you don't play football at professional level at 50 if you abuse yourself – and he maintained that respect for his body throughout his later life.

By the time I broke into the England scene he was a recognised international of the highest calibre. He was brilliant, a pleasure both to play alongside and to watch. We both enjoyed the advantage of more space and time than modern-day players but he would still have been a massive star today. He was superb, always rising to the occasion. The bigger it was, the more he liked it. The greatest ball player of our era, he showed no mercy to defenders. I have never seen another player who could take the ball so close to his opponent and still manage to retain possession. It was almost hypnotic as he invited a challenge, but while the full-back dithered and deliberated, Stan would drop a shoulder, wiggle his hips and disappear down the line.

I got to know Stan well, better than most. In fact, we roomed together regularly. In his playing days he was a modest, quiet, unassuming fellow, often preferring to read than to socialise. He had a fantastic love of football, completely enveloping himself in the game. He would chat away for hours about matches, goals and opponents, and his verbal assessments on the strengths and weak-nesses of full-backs bordered on the phenomenal. Yet away from the privacy of a hotel room, he might not utter a dozen words in an afternoon. Some people reckoned he was aloof and stand-offish but his reserved nature was born out of shyness.

His preparation was second to none. He was an excellent trainer and a keep-fit fanatic. A man who lived for football, he could turn games upside down through his trickery on the right wing.

We talked at great length about the game but I can never once recall either of us mentioning the inquest into our respective merits as players. We both knew that a feud did not exist. Stan found it all rather distasteful and unnecessary, and so did I.

Stan was a peerless player, an ageless genius who could turn on the magic at the drop of a hat. If I had been picking an England team at that time, I would have started by putting the name of Matthews against the number 7 shirt and worried about the other positions later. If I could have been born again as any other player, I would undoubtedly have chosen to be Stanley Matthews.

He was seven years my senior, born in February 1915, the third of four sons of barber Jack Matthews and his wife Ada. People tell me that Stan displayed the makings of a footballer from the age of three. I don't know about that, but I can confirm that he fulfilled his potential!

It would be foolish to try to list all the great things I saw Stan do on a football field – I can't recall a game in which his magic didn't play a key role. If I was to select one game, though, it would have to be the England fixture against Belgium in Brussels in the autumn of 1947. I called it the Matthews Match because he was responsible for putting the fear of God up the Belgians and the 'stan' in outstanding!

We won 5–2 and he had a part to play in all five of our goals – I got two – not to mention half-a-dozen other chances that went begging. A typical dribble down the line and a telling cross gave Tommy Lawton the chance to power us in front with a header. Minutes later, Stan did the trick again only this time it was Stan Mortensen who capitalised, shooting home from close range.

Sick and tired of seeing Stan hold the upper hand, the Belgian defenders resorted to tactics of an unpleasant nature. That was not an uncommon occurrence. Forwards, and in particular wingers, were targets of a bit of rough stuff every now and again. I can remember vividly opponents threatening me during games, 'I'll break your !!!**!* legs if you do that again!' being among the more popular calls. It didn't worry me and I don't think it worried Stan, either. In fact, it acted as something of a spur. The more they tried to talk me off my game, or kick me out of it, the more I found encouragement. They thought they were being strong; I considered their actions to be a sign of genuine weakness.

Of course, you looked for protection from the referee and it was frustrating when he failed to intervene. But I was brought up in the school that preached getting the ball down, playing a pass and then moving for the return, trying to outwit your opponent with brain, not brawn. We were taught that good play would invariably triumph over foul, and that is how I tried to see it.

I was never much of a talker during games, certainly not to the opposition. Some players jabbered incessantly but I had enough on my plate concentrating on playing.

As everyone played to a 2-3-5 formation, you became very familiar with your direct opponents, consistently finding yourself up against the same group of defenders. There were a few who left a stud mark or two on my legs, or offered me some verbal advice, but I never let it bother me. I was more concerned when I was confronted with players I admired – Roger Byrne, for instance – because I knew I was in for a difficult time. Ball control, speed and balance – they were the main tricks in my armoury and, for the most part, they served me well.

Like Stan, I suppose, I was a perfectionist. I didn't go into games relying purely on what might or might not happen on the day; I did my homework. On top of the team's masterplan, I always tried to have a plan of my own, which centred around how I proposed to come out on top in my tussle with the opposing full-back.

Stan and I were brothers in this regard; our styles were contrasting but we shared a common understanding of the role of a winger. While history would ultimately list us among the more successful of

English players, it often made us smile when we saw ourselves described as 'natural' footballers, a description that suggested we had received some sort of gift from God and didn't have to work at it. In truth, few footballers worked harder at their game than we did.

Back in Brussels, one of many fouls on Stan brought us a free kick and while he floated it over, I nipped in to head home England's third. So there we were with just 18 minutes showing on the clock, in a foreign land against a decent side, 3–0 up, mainly because we had Stanley Matthews on our side.

The Belgians stormed back at the start of the second half to score twice in quick succession, before Stan decided to break their hearts by waltzing past three challenges to lay on another headed goal for his fellow winger. Another of his pinpoint free kicks produced the fifth, courtesy of a fine header from Tommy Lawton.

No one was stronger in the air than Tommy and how he relished the service provided by Stan. Both of them stand unchallenged in my Hall of Fame. If I were to choose who to play alongside in an England forward line, Stan and Tommy would be two, plus any two from Raich Carter, Wilf Mannion and Stan Mortensen, the best inside-forwards of my generation.

Stan made something of a habit of saving his best for the internationals. All his 54 appearances came on the right wing and although he scored just 11 times at that level, he created dozens of goals for others. He was around the England squad for 23 years – a quite extraordinary statistic. You have to wonder how many caps he would have won had the war not intervened.

We played together for our country on 21 occasions, losing only four, and Tommy Lawton and Stan Mortensen benefited to the tune of 20 goals between them in the first seven games we played together.

At club level, Stan was always the game's trump card and he made

697 league appearances (scoring 71 goals) for Stoke and Blackpool. He was still going strong aged 46, moving back to Stoke from Blackpool in the year after I had retired. Two years later, he scored the goal that clinched promotion for Stoke and so became the oldest player to figure on the scoresheet in a league fixture. I can confidently predict that, whatever else happens in the crazy world of professional football, that is one record that will stand forever.

All those statistics, especially playing at 50, seemed pretty remarkable back then. When you study them now, they are almost beyond belief.

Stan and I met for the first time in 1942, not as colleagues but as opponents, not for Preston and Stoke but for the Football Association and the Royal Air Force. Now there lies a story.

Called up to the Army as Trooper T. Finney 7958274 of the Royal Armoured Corps, I had given up hope of any action in the football sense, aside from the odd unofficial kickabout with the boys. But I was wrong. Football was important and the FA invited me to take part in a game against the RAF at Stoke. My Preston team-mate Jack Fairbrother was in goal and our line-up also included Stan Cullis of Wolves and Billy Liddell of Liverpool.

The RAF was stronger still. Another of our Deepdale top dogs, Bill Shankly, along with George Hardwick and Raich Carter, let alone a certain Mr Matthews, all featured for the opposition. If that wasn't a daunting enough prospect, Eddie Hapgood, the brilliant Arsenal defender, was my direct opponent. Jack Fairbrother and I were the only uncapped players on view but we still managed to chalk up a 4–3 win in a truly wonderful game in which Stan and I both played well. He relied on speed, balance and body swerve while I was more direct. I always maintained that the secret to beating a full-back lay first in close control and then in your knack of selling a dummy, dropping a shoulder or switching balance from one foot to another.

I am often asked how I felt on getting my call-up papers and while I must have experienced the exact same fear and dread as everyone else, I can honestly say I didn't give it too much thought. I had just turned 20 and, along with all the other lads of my age, I knew that a call-up was inevitable. What you might be trained as and where you might end up going didn't really come into it – it was just how it was and you accepted it. Being a conscientious objector may have provided an escape route for some, but it wasn't an option for me.

Like so many of my contemporaries, the war robbed me of years of family life and put my courtship with Elsie Noblett on a sort of permanent hold. We first met in 1938 when we were no more than kids, and innocent kids at that. Elsie was a keen and very capable dancer and we met, surprise surprise, at a dance, held in the parish hall of St Jude's, my local church.

Dancing is what young people did back then. Apart from going to the pictures, there was little else to keep teenagers entertained. Preston had a picture house on every street corner and there were many established ballrooms including Worsley's and the 'AD'. Many parishes held weekend dance nights and St Jude's was among the more popular ones.

It would not have been such a haven for the kids of today. Alcohol was taboo and you had to make do with soft drinks, cakes and biscuits. As for drugs, you got them from the doctor when you were ill. Some of the boys who attended were not easily put off finding a drink or two. They would sneak out to a nearby pub and it was up to the chap on the door to determine whether they were in a fit state to come back in again.

I noticed Elsie, and fancied her, long before I plucked up the courage to ask her out. She was an attractive, bubbly 16-year-old who seemed to spend most of the evening chatting with her pals in between long spells on the dance floor. That didn't help me because I was no great mover. I found it all rather embarrassing to be quite candid. Eventually, though, I managed to catch her eye and let it be known through third parties that I was interested in taking her out.

Elsie was the youngest of four children produced by ex-Navy officer Jim Noblett and his wife Ruth, who lived on Barlow Street in Preston. She had left Moor Park Methodist School at 14 to work as a packer at Margerisons Soap Factory.

I was also aware that Elsie's best friend, Olive Poole, had her eye on me – or so my mate Alf Lorimer reckoned. Funnily enough, when we finally made our move, I ended up with Olive and Alf stood chatting with Elsie. We agreed to go out on a combined date, as a foursome, to see a Greta Garbo film at the Rialto. It was a midweek evening and we were late meeting. By the time we landed at the cinema the film had already started and the place was in darkness. The other people were none too happy, telling us to be quick and get ourselves sat down, and when we did, Elsie finished up next to me in a 'doubles seat' favoured by courting couples. Fate deemed us to be an item and we both seemed happy enough with that arrangement. Our relationship was up and running.

Neither of us was experienced in affairs of the heart. I had known a couple of girls but had never got round to fixing dates, and Elsie was equally backward in coming forward. We were naïve.

We continued to see one another, my dancing improved and we watched lots of films while Elsie even found time to come along to see me in action as a junior footballer. Then came the moment all young men of my day dreaded – the invitation to go along and visit the prospective in-laws. I was on my best behaviour, scrubbed up and smartly turned out and very, very nervous. Elsie was worse than I was, but her parents could not have been more accommodating. The ordeal turned out to be a pleasure.

We courted for about three years but when I received my call-up papers we agreed it was time to take things further. I wanted to get married there and then, but Elsie was influenced by her mother's view that we were far too young so we opted for an engagement. I didn't get down on one knee, nor did I formally ask Mr Noblett for his daughter's hand, but there was never any objection. I liked them and I was sure they liked me.

We went into town to buy a ring. It cost around £15, a fair whack for a young plumber who topped up his weekly earnings through football, and the purchase left my Grandma Finney lost for words. A keen apostle of the Co-op buying philosophy that was so popular then, Gran chirped up, 'You've paid how much? Why on earth didn't you go through the Co-op? That way you would have qualified for a few quid back through the divi. I don't know, more money than sense you youngsters.'

We laughed. The ring and what it stood for was far more important than the cost or what we may or may not have saved. We were in love and there has never been a price ticket on that.

Funnily enough, we didn't go to Elsie's to toast our good news. We met up with a plumbing pal of mine, Bill Shaw, and raised a glass with him and his wife. But the joy of the engagement soon wore off when Elsie and I parted for the first time due to the conflict overseas. It was a wrench to leave your fiancée on the other side of the world but I was not alone and you had to accept the facts and get on with life. We tried to keep in touch but neither of us was a particularly good writer and there was often quite a gap between letters.

I spent the first six weeks training at Tidworth before transferring to Catterick where they told me I was to train as a driver-mechanic. I had no driving experience whatsoever – families with cars were the privileged few back then – and I didn't know my accelerator from my clutch. But Army life teaches you that 'no' and 'can't' are not acceptable responses when tasks are presented to you and, to be fair, I took to the challenge of learning to drive with ease and speed. Within no time, I was quite at home behind a wheel, be it a van, a jeep or a tank. I sailed through the test and was actually starting to half enjoy life at home military camp. The physical training was no problem to me and I found the discipline of square bashing and marching quite rewarding. Pay was not the best – two bob (10p) a day – and I sent half of it back home to Dad, but the spirit and banter between the lads was lively and I felt quite comfortable.

All that changed the minute news came through that many in our section had been granted embarkation leave. Anything with leave involved sounded reasonable until I discovered that we were being allowed home prior to being sent overseas to confront the realities of war head on. In the December of 1942, six months after first joining up, I was trained and ready, and received instructions to join a troop ship, but there was no clue about the destination apart from the issue of tropical kit.

After spending a week or so with Elsie and my family back in Preston, I joined a night train to Scotland, arriving in the pitch black to be greeted by the eerie sight of a huge vessel anchored offshore in the distance. The troop ship turned out to be the converted *Queen Mary* and as they ferried us across – all 7,000 of us – they finally revealed we were bound for Egypt. There were some anxious faces and one young colleague summed up the general feelings when he said, 'Well, at least we know where we're going now – it's for how long and whether we'll ever come back that bothers me.' History proved him right to be apprehensive. Many hundreds of young men who boarded the *Queen Mary* that bitterly cold winter day in 1942 failed to return home.

We were posted to a camp next to the pyramids and, with the desert campaign in full swing, thoughts of football disappeared out of my mind. Tom Finney the footballer was now Tom Finney the soldier, involved in all sorts of military manoeuvres, sometimes for 12- and 15-hour stretches. The physical demands were punishing in the extreme.

We played the occasional game behind the billets, but it was hardly serious stuff until the chance came to go across to Cairo to try out for a specially formed Army team called the Wanderers. The aim of the Wanderers was clear. We had to entertain the troops and there were plenty of top-class footballers in the ranks capable of delivering that brief – Ted Swinburne of Newcastle, for instance, and Mickey Fenton of Middlesbrough and Bolton's Tommy Woodward.

Suddenly, Army life seemed a much more acceptable lot. I made an immediate impression by scoring a hat-trick in the practice match to justify my call-up for the touring squad.

Touring was very much the word for we travelled all over Palestine and Syria, playing Services XIs and Egyptian national representative sides. What an experience that proved to be! Later in my career, I played in front of partisan crowds in Brazil, Italy, Portugal – and Scotland – but few matched the Egyptians for fervour. They were fanatical in every sense of the word; colourful, energetic and loud, they even brought prayer mats just in case the outcome threatened to go the wrong way.

Unit and depot sides named themselves after famous or favourite teams back home. Here we were, miles from home in a war situation, battling in football contests on behalf of Brentford, Arsenal, Huddersfield – even Queen of the South. I was once included in a squad representing little-known Bovington United and we did OK, reaching the final of the Abbassia Zone before losing to Huddersfield.

It was surreal and great fun – so much so that I began to feel a degree of guilt for playing football and thoroughly enjoying myself while others were locked in combat. I needn't have felt too much remorse, however, for my turn would surely come. But the initial contradiction did cause me concern and I sought reassurance from my commanders. They laughed, insisting that I was worrying unduly. Apparently, by playing football I was fulfilling an important role in boosting morale. It seemed fair enough to me.

The Wanderers were the top dogs. We played 13 games in 23 days, calling in on Jerusalem, Haifa, Beirut and Tel Aviv, to name but four, travelling by train and lorry. It may sound glamorous but in truth we roughed it. Conditions were hot and humid, the journeys were long and tiring and the facilities hardly five star. No one complained because we knew that everyone else considered us privileged. We were the lucky ones, the chosen few.

We did well, winning 11, drawing one and losing one and managing to score 10 goals or more in a game on three separate occasions. The standard wasn't half bad, either. Services football was more akin to the professional game than the pub version, with some very decent players involved. But don't be fooled for a minute into thinking that we had it easy. The heat alone was a killer and a combination of hard graft and oppressive conditions often left you totally drained.

Army kits you out for life and I had plenty of time to practise, serving three years before I got my first break and more than four years in total. While doing my duty for my country, I added to the domestic skills I had learned at home with a spell in the cookhouse, not to mention the very real responsibility of looking after myself. I learned a fair bit about butchery, how to slaughter animals and how to prepare and produce substantial meals from limited stock. I washed my own clothes and made my own bed, such as it was with just blankets and three part-cushioned 'biscuits' for pillows. All your jobs had to be completed within a given time and to a stringent standard, and if your efforts failed to pass the inspection of the duty officer, you were handed more tasks or even a spell in detention.

For most of the lads, it was their first taste of life away from the relative comforts of home and some found it very hard to cope. The chores didn't worry me but I would be lying if I said I didn't suffer pangs of homesickness. A regular chance to play football undoubtedly helped and I maintain that I returned from the war not only a better person but a better player. The pitches were bone hard and bumpy but I am convinced that my touch got better playing on them. I certainly gained a yard of pace.

A posting to Italy took me down to Foggia, right at the southern tip. Encouraged by my Egyptian experience, I made moves to set up a team, only to receive a dressing down from the base captain. The officer in question had no time for soccer or the 'dodgers' who played the game, and he wasted no time in despatching me to the 9th Queen's Royal Lancers. The Lancers needed some reinforcements and, along with thousands of others, I got my orders to assist as required.

Within a day of being 'welcomed', I found myself in the firing line, driving with a squadron of Honey tanks in a month of gruelling action with the Eighth Army. Tank driving was my main role although I doubled as a mechanic, and it was terrifying stuff. Often

I found myself serving as a direct replacement for a lad who had been killed the previous day. Danger lay all around and you sensed it, without having the time to panic.

I saw action at close quarters. When the tanks were in combat, the enemy lay just a few hundred yards away, and I had to learn how to cope with fear and to stay cool as the sergeant in command bellowed orders down your headphones. To return to base at night and discover that some of your pals had perished was a disconcerting experience.

Head-on conflict lasted no more than three or four months, thank God, before the Germans finally capitulated. We were operating from the muddied banks of the River Po at the time, and I well recall the overwhelming feeling of relief. As news of the enemy's surrender filtered through, we were instructed to fire our machine guns into the sky in celebration.

For all of the hardship, pain and torment, life in the Army taught me such a lot, not least the value of companionship and friendship. It opened my eyes to reality, the heartache of listening to grown men, hard men, sitting up in bed crying at night; the empty feeling when news of a death was announced.

I have been asked many times whether I emerged from the Services with a grudge against the German soldiers we confronted. The answer is not at all. Like us, they were simply thrust into a conflict they knew little about and forced to act under the instruction of rulers. For the soldiers involved on either side, it was never a matter of choice.

One consolation from a personal perspective was the rise in my fitness levels; when I was de-mobbed I weighed just a pound or two over 10 stones.

I was a decent soldier, nothing more, but my football brought its own rewards. During a period when the Allies had made good progress in Italy, the commanding officers decided to reward the efforts of the men with some relaxation. Comfort packages arrived and football became part of my life once more. Ironically, the man in charge of the Eighth Army side was Andy Beattie, captain of Preston and Scotland, and the line-up had enough star names to warrant an international status all of its own.

I was invited to play alongside Charlie Adam, Beattie and Willie Thornton, one of the greatest players in the history of Glasgow Rangers and a player I was to face later in England versus Scotland internationals. Beattie, a highly successful manager in later life, became a great ally and trusted adviser to me.

When the war was drawing to a close, he would escort us around Italy and Austria to play competitive matches against service sides. I recall playing one particular match in which Matt Busby captained the opposition. It was staged in the Vomero Stadium in Naples and 30,000 turned up to watch. I was named in the CMF (Central Mediterranean Forces) line-up, captained by Beattie and including Bob Pryde (Blackburn) and Bryn Jones (Arsenal). Our opponents, an FA Army XI, were no mugs, with Frank Swift in goal and Everton's Cliff Britton (later to become my boss at Preston) in defence, and Arthur Rowley of Manchester United in attack.

Was it serious? You bet. So much so that the authorities called upon the services of a neutral referee, an American if my memory serves me right. Busby, 13 years my senior and one of the veterans on view, was magnificent for the Army while Billy Strauss, a South African winger who played for Aberdeen, was our star turn. In spite of claiming the lead twice, we had to settle for a 2–2 draw. It was thrill-a-minute stuff, our determination to end the Army's long unbeaten record thwarted by a late goal from John Martin of Aston Villa.

As well as enjoying plenty of football action overseas, I was also fortunate enough to figure in a number of wartime games in England – and not just for Preston. When people refer to Tom Finney as a one-club man, it isn't quite true. During spells of leave, I managed to squeeze in seven or eight appearances for Newcastle United and also played for Bolton Wanderers and Southampton.

Let me explain how things worked back then. Once you knew you were due some leave, you would contact your club to see if any games coincided with your time back home and request to be considered for selection. Preston were always accommodating although they didn't play quite as many matches as other clubs. Deepdale was out of operation for a couple of years – it actually doubled as a prisoner of war camp – and fixtures had to be switched to nearby Leyland Motors. If your club didn't have a game, you were free to guest elsewhere.

During my time stationed at Catterick in the north-east, I would get regular calls from Newcastle and ended up playing alongside Jackie Milburn and Albert Stubbins. It was great experience, especially playing in front of those passionate Geordie supporters. Sometimes there would be more than 40,000 in the ground and they generated a terrific atmosphere.

My appearance for Southampton came against Arsenal, and I played for Bolton against Burnley. There was added excitement in that game because the Bolton public were eager to see a young forward who was being tipped for the top. Nat Lofthouse was just 16 but he looked a superb prospect, scoring a couple of goals and showing great awareness and phenomenal strength. That was the first time I met Nat, who was to become one of my closest footballing friends.

Wartime football had other advantages, not least of a monetary variety. You got paid £2 10s (£2.50) a game – not a bad little bonus for a soldier earning just two bob (10p) a day.

But my most memorable moment as a footballing soldier is beyond debate. It was 1945 and I had just turned out for a Services team in Austria. After all the travelling and the match, I felt weary and was fast asleep almost as soon as my head touched the pillow. My peace was shattered by a guard bursting into the billet with an instruction for me to report to the duty officer.

All sorts of thoughts whizzed through my mind as I pulled on my clothes – was it bad news from home or had I done something wrong? Either way, it had to be serious. The Army wasn't in the habit of waking up soldiers at three o'clock in the morning for something trivial.

The officer in charge looked almost as bleary-eyed as I did. He made me feel pretty bad about disturbing his sleep, so much so that I offered an apology. He seemed to accept that the disturbance was not directly my fault and handed over a telegram from the English Football Association which requested that I should be released to play for England in an unofficial international in Switzerland.

As I wiped the sleep from my eyes, I could hardly take it in. Surely I must be dreaming. Here was I, a footballer without much in the way of experience, stationed in a foreign country miles away from home and family, being told that I was to play for my country. It was absolutely unbelievable.

The officer, Clifford Thornton, was quick to offer me his congratulations.

'Well done, young man,' he said. 'I'm sure you feel proud and excited. I know the news will be very well received back in Preston. It's my hometown, too.'

I lost touch with many of my Army pals once the conflict

had ended, but Clifford and I were to meet again many times, years later.

I journeyed under escort to the Austrian–Italian border where I met Andy Beattie who accompanied me on the first leg of my long haul back to England via a flight from Naples, and then on to Zurich. As Switzerland was a neutral country during the war, we were not permitted to wear uniforms, so the FA provided us with clothing coupons to spend on a civilian suit. That in itself was a delight, to be back in civvies after years in khaki. The main thrust of the trip, however, was to secure a victory for England and put myself in the frame for further international honours in the future.

The game was frustrating. The Swiss were far too organised for us, too fit for us – damn it, they were just too bloody good for us, playing like a team while we played like a team of strangers, which is what we were. We lost 3–1 and although I felt I did OK, the fact that we lost was a big disappointment. Later we found out that while our scratch team had been thrown together as an afterthought, they had been gearing up for close on a month, including having a three-week training camp up in the mountains. It was some sort of consolation, as was beating a Switzerland B team 3–0 a few days later.

After those games, I managed to obtain 14 days' leave – or, more accurately, Joe Mercer managed to wangle it for me. That's Joe Mercer the great Arsenal player who went on to enjoy a wonderful career in management at Manchester City. Joe was the England captain against Switzerland and he took a real interest in my welfare because I was a rookie and the only overseas soldier involved. When he found out that I had never managed to have any leave, he said, 'Tom, I'm going to go and see if I can sort something out for you.' An hour or two later, I got a note from the officer in charge, offering me a two-week return ticket to Preston. Good old Joe, I thought – a friend for life! In fact, Joe and his wife Nora did become very close friends of ours. I held Joe in the highest regard. Few knew football better and what a lovely gentle and caring man into the bargain.

Going home was a strange feeling. Everything was three years on and I didn't quite know what to expect after so long away from family life. I needn't have worried. Little had changed although life in the harsh days of rationing was far from easy. It was just great to see Elsie again. She managed to take a few days off work and we took ourselves out on a few trips, chatting almost non-stop as we caught up with all the news. I was popular, too, because I had managed to smuggle back some goodies, mainly clothes and material, after trading in my cigarette allowance.

I found time to show my face down at Deepdale, to make sure they hadn't forgotten me. It was the close season so the place was largely deserted, but that didn't worry me. I got my fix just by standing out on the pitch staring around the empty stadium.

Once my leave expired, I returned to a sort of no man's land. The Army was at a loss about how to employ me. Sent back to a transit camp in Folkestone, I built up hopes of a home posting, but my luck was out and I was sent back to Italy where I re-joined my old unit. There, I was handed a new job – and a good one at that.

The CMF had established a sports control body and I was named among the football coaches. We gave demonstrations on ball control, team play and tactical awareness and finished off the sessions with a five-a-side knockout competition. The 'school', as we called it, was invited all over Italy. Wherever and whenever we went, we were guaranteed a great reception. It was tough, but someone had to do it!

Elsie and I had talked long and hard about getting married and during my spell of leave, which was now not hard to get, we turned the plan into reality. In the November of 1945, we were married at Emmanuel Church, Brook Street, Preston. Elsie was 22 and I was 23.

Elsie looked after all the arrangements while I was left to secure a temporary release on matrimonial grounds and four days before the wedding I embarked on the most tiring journey of my life. I jumped aboard a three tonner, a huge covered-wagon-type vehicle with wooden forms for seats in the back. We felt every bump as we journeyed from Italy through France and up to Calais for the sailing across to the transit camp in Folkestone. After a welcome overnight stay on a half-decent camp bed, it was off by train to Lancashire. Arriving at Preston station my weariness gave way to euphoria. I was shattered, but I was back home, back with Elsie, and I could not have been happier.

The wedding service wasn't a fancy do and very few people attended. I hardly knew the vicar and was short of a best man. Most of my close pals were away in the Services, so I drafted in John Pilkington, son of my plumbing boss Harry, to do the honours. Olive Poole, the girl I jilted in favour of Elsie, proved there were no hard feelings by being a bridesmaid. Preston North End chairman Jim Taylor, big in the pottery business, sent us a decorative tea service.

With the formalities done and dusted, we headed off to the Grapes Hotel in the village of Goosnargh for an equally low-key reception. Next stop was Blackpool – well, Bispham to be precise – for a three-day honeymoon. It was not an uninterrupted three days, mind – I had an appointment at Maine Road against Manchester City on the Saturday! Elsie came to watch and afterwards we went back to the seaside for part two.

Then it was back to Italy for me. Although, thankfully, the fighting had ceased, it was still considered necessary for our troops to have a presence overseas until our commanders were completely confident that peace was for the long term. I went to the posting station in Preston where the chap behind the counter asked, 'Why have you been home and where are you heading now?'

'I've been back to get married, Sir,' I replied. 'And as for the second part of the question, I was sort of hoping that you would enlighten me.'

This resulted in much muttering and checking before it was deemed that I should head for Italy – via Folkestone and France, of course. Elsie came to wave me off not knowing whether it would be days, weeks or months before we would be together again.

In the event, it was about seven months before, at long, long last, my days as a soldier were numbered and I secured an exit through the B Release regulation. Builders and plumbers were in great demand in England and I was allowed to return home on the strict understanding that I took up immediate employment at my old firm, Pilkington's. So by day I was a plumber and on two evenings a week I reported for training with Preston North End.

Preston missed more than its footballers during the war years. An estimated 5,000 of the town's menfolk saw active service in the forces. Many did not return. Sadly, four North End players were among the number who gave their lives in the protection of their country – David Willacy and Tommy Taylor, who had both made the senior side, Eddie Gore and Jack Owens. But it soon became clear that the end of the great conflict would trigger a football boom.

CHAPTER FOUR

Back and booming

The late summer of 1946 was just about the most exciting time of my footballing life – a sweeping statement but I daresay every single player and fan across the land felt the same.

Desperate for a return to some sort of normality, just about everyone in Preston threw out their arms to welcome the re-formation of North End and the resumption of the Football League. This is what we had all dreamed about. It was certainly one of the things that had kept me going during the dark days of conflict as I watched the clock tick away on a career that had threatened to end before it had started. Just imagine asking David Beckham or Michael Owen or any other modern young starlet to work tirelessly towards a professional debut and then put it on hold for four years. Beckham had close on 50 England caps when he was 24 – at the same age, I was still waiting for my official debut. But the wait was about to end.

Preston's average home attendance, which had stood at 22,000 in 1938, shot up to 26,500 during the first post-war campaign. It rose by a further 6,000 to top 33,000 two years later. Football was massively popular nationwide and on one afternoon in the 1948–49 season the total attendance figure across the land reached a staggering four million. Cash rolled in through the turnstiles – and stayed there.

Nowadays, clubs need phenomenal levels of income just to meet players' wages, but that was not the case back then, anything but. We were operating under the maximum-wage system while all this was going on. Preston North End, along with most clubs in the land, were able to announce profits increasing year on year. Some of the profit went towards team strengthening, of course, and there was a degree of investment in ground development, but whether that accounted for it all remains unclear.

But such cynicism was far from my mind on 31 August 1946 when we got the league ball rolling again with a Deepdale date against Leeds United. I smile now as I look back and recall the sense of frenzy around the famous old ground that afternoon. There was a special buzz on the terraces and a healthy sort of nervousness in the dressing room. You would have thought we hadn't seen each other for seven years, such was the anticipation, even among seniors such as Andy Beattie and Bill Shankly. We were so eager to get out there and perform that the minutes leading up to kick-off seemed to take an eternity to tick by. This is when Shanks came into his own. He'd been with the club for 13 years and, aged 32, he knew his way around the game.

'Listen, son,' he said, pulling me to one side. 'This is a big day for you and for us all, a day we have waited for very patiently for some considerable time, but we must not let the occasion turn our heads.'

I nodded. His wisdom did not need an answer in words but in actions. Bill was determined that we should not allow all the hype and excitement to get in the way of our professionalism. There was a job to be done.

Football supporters like entertainment – and at Preston it was imperative that we played in an attractive style – but they adore winning. I would never criticise the supporters of Preston – they were nothing but magnificent to me throughout my career – but they demanded a lot from their team and let it be known whenever we fell short of the required standard. They turned up in numbers to support us so we could never complain if they occasionally voiced their protests. Let's just say the club's long and distinguished history has sometimes raised expectancy levels close to the unachievable.

Thankfully, we did hit the spot against Leeds and, although I say so myself, I had a fairly decent game on what was, after all, my First Division debut. A goal, something of a solo effort, too, completed my perfect day.

I was made to feel very special during the week of the game. Without wanting to appear boastful, the pre-match build-up had me as the pivotal figure, largely because the football-watching people of Preston had heard much but seen little of Tom Finney. Apart from the few games I'd played while on leave, I had been out of sight for more than four years, but not out of the news. During the war, many national newspaper correspondents filed regular stories about the progress of the British footballers stationed overseas and I got more than my share of headlines and acclaim. That coverage un-doubtedly whetted the appetite of North End followers. Jim Taylor, chairman and team selector, was quick to make contact when I got back to base in Preston, making it abundantly clear that my place in the first game against Leeds was assured.

My dad came, as did Elsie, although Joe couldn't be there because of his own playing commitments. Deepdale looked a picture. The crescendo of sound when we stepped out will live with me for the rest of my life. It is at such moments that you realise you are precisely where you want to be, where you ought to be and where you intend to be.

Four members of our starting line-up – Andy Beattie, Bill Shankly, Bobby Beattie and Jimmy Dougal – had played league football for the club before the war, which meant seven were debutants. One of them was big-money signing Willie McIntosh for whom Jim Taylor had agreed to pay St Johnstone the princely sum of £4,750. Willie had been recruited to score goals and, like me, he was ultra keen to find the net on this historic afternoon.

Leeds, a strong and physical outfit, made the early running and our defence found life a touch uncomfortable with Bill Shankly, of all people, looking particularly vulnerable in his new role at centre-half.

Our supporters' initial concern over a dithering back line was soon replaced by joy. With our first attack of note, we shook the Yorkshiremen by snatching the lead. Ken Horton found me with a fine pass and I played the ball across the goalmouth for Willie McIntosh to take possession in his stride and shoot home. Deepdale's decibel level went off the scale. What a start!

We went two up on 18 minutes when I got in on the scoring act with a goal that gave me immense satisfaction. Leeds pulled one back, with former North Ender Bob Batey involved in the move, but Jimmy Dougal made the game safe in the 75th minute with our third. Although Leeds grabbed a second late on, our victory was very much deserved and very well received. It was great to have won and Shanks was one of the first to say well done.

Media coverage was more than complimentary. While I was pleased with my own performance, Viator in the *Post*, went a little over the top. He wrote:

Finney's composure, mastery, artifice and tantalising finesse made his match-winning scheming the talk of the town. Being an artist he will suffer many tumbles through being unfairly tackled, that being the regrettable penalty for beating a man with adroitness and ease. He is a ready-made successor to Stanley Matthews.

We were in home action again on the Wednesday night, against Sheffield United, and the crowd figure rose by a couple of hundred. That made it more than 50,000 people through the turnstiles in four days. This time, though, it was a disappointment and our enthusiasm was blunted as the Blades ran out 2–1 winners.

Maximum points and eight goals in successive victories over Grimsby away and Charlton at home soon got things back on track and Deepdale had a new hero in Willie McIntosh. Not only did he manage a hat-trick at Blundell Park, he followed it up with another one against Charlton. With seven goals in his first four games, it looked as though Willie was worth every farthing of his transfer fee.

It took me more than two months to get my second goal, in a 2–2 draw with Derby, but our form was very consistent. We lost only five times before the end of January and we stayed up among the title contenders. But then we lost three games in a row, to Middlesbrough, Stoke City and Blackpool, conceding 10 goals and not managing a solitary reply.

We also lost an FA Cup sixth-round tie at Charlton and the season petered out, although to finish seventh – Liverpool were the champions – represented a decent all-round effort. More than half a million spectators enjoyed some cracking entertainment at Deepdale and the place was packed full (40,167) for a Boxing Day draw with Chelsea.

Willie McIntosh had 32 reasons (his total league and Cup goal haul) to look back with pride on his first term, while goalkeeper Jack Fairbrother was another star performer.

We had a squad of 36 seniors with which to tackle the 1947–48 season although one promising youngster was shown the door. Football is a game of opinions and decisions, and in the case of Ronnie Clayton it must be said that the footballing judges at Deepdale formed the wrong opinion and made a poor decision. They reckoned that Ronnie was too small to make it and announced his release. By going on to set an appearances record for Blackburn Rovers, captain England and play in the World Cup, I think it is fair to say that he proved North End wrong. I played with him at international level and against him in some ding-dong tussles between our two clubs and I will tell you this – I would much sooner have had him on our side than on the opposition's.

We gave our supporters plenty to cheer in those early weeks and five wins in a row put us in a lofty position even though there was much chopping and changing. Perhaps that should read 'Mutch' chopping and changing because George Mutch, the goalscoring Cup hero of 1938, was allowed to join Bury. Jimmy Dougal, also in his mid 30s, was transferred to Carlisle for the princely sum of £1,750 and it was left to Willie McIntosh and me to share the responsibility for goal gathering.

But nothing that occurred during the first few weeks – and most of it was good – could have prepared us for the events of 6 December and the visit of Derby County, locked with us in third place. That fixture always had the makings of a tasty game but this time it produced what can only be described as a match-of-a-lifetime. Many Deepdale diehards still rate it as the best they have seen and I wouldn't argue.

The Rams were a talented team and their talisman, Raich Carter, was a superstar in every sense of the word. They hit us like a whirlwind; mentally, some of our lads were still in the dressing room as Derby eased into a two-goal lead, fashioned by the mesmerising Carter. We looked at one another and faced up to the options. Either we carried on in our disjointed state and faced a humiliation or we got stuck in and launched a fightback.

We chose the latter. Bill Shankly kept his head and converted a penalty after Harry Anders had been brought down, and the game was suddenly alive. We attacked them, they attacked us, the football flowed and chance after chance kept the 34,000 crowd on pins. Further goals were inevitable. We struck next to equalise when Andy McClaren timed a run to perfection and scored with a copybook header from my corner.

On the half hour, Derby edged back in front. Angus Morrison, whose superb performance later earned him a move to Deepdale, beat two defenders before drawing Jimmy Gooch off his line to shoot into an empty net. On the stroke of half-time, we hit back to level again, thanks to the persistence of Shankly.

In games like these, the second half regularly fails to live up to the events of the first. This was not one such case. Derby pushed their noses ahead yet again, Morrison capitalising on a rare error of defensive judgement by Shankly to complete his hat-trick.

I was getting plenty of the ball and managed to create an

equaliser for Beattie. I still get a tingle when I recall the atmosphere with the match at 4–4, but it was to get even better – better for us at any rate. The home supporters were delirious when Willie McIntosh broke loose in the 75th minute to give us the lead for the first time. I think they heard the roar at Blackpool Pier when he added number six after a goalmouth scramble. The match was won, but there was just enough time for me to have the final say with a goal to put Preston into seventh heaven.

To come from behind three times and then to win by three clear goals was truly amazing – even the famous radio commentator Raymond Glendenning, on hand to give a blow-by-blow account, was for once lost for words.

So was it the best game of my North End career? For thrill-a-minute, action-packed, non-stop excitement – not to mention 11 goals – I would have to say yes it was. Funnily enough, although I don't remember too much laughing at the time, my worst league experience came just a few months later, and they really were roaring on the piers of Blackpool this time.

Finish on a high and make sure you give your local rivals a going over at home. Those two objectives feature high on any football club's 'must do' list, so it is fair to say that we fell some way short on the closing day of the 1947–48 campaign. The final fixture was staged on May Day and this was certainly a distress signal! To lose it 0–7 was bad enough but to surrender, and surrender is precisely what we did, to the old enemy from Blackpool bordered on unbearable. To top it all, five of the goals came from a former North Ender, Jimmy McIntosh. Not many North End followers wore the club colours with pride down on the seaside promenade that summer, I can tell you! It was a shocker, a result as unbelievable as it was unexpected.

It was not as though we were having a poor season – the final First Division league table, printed later that afternoon, had us in seventh spot, behind Wolves and Aston Villa on goal average. We were not in a poor run of form, either, having won two of our previous three matches 3–0, against Everton and Manchester City. There was no injury crisis or illness epidemic although we might just have been suffering from a little travel fatigue.

In the week leading up to the Blackpool match we had embarked on a short tour of Scotland. Yes, that's right, in between two Saturday league fixtures the Preston hierarchy had decided to organise a couple of games north of the border. So, after losing at Derby County on 24 April, we played at Falkirk on the Monday, where we drew 1–1, and St Johnstone on the Wednesday, where we won 3–0.

Why did we go? Don't ask me. Tours and friendlies in the middle of the season were not uncommon for North End back then and the players didn't ask questions, they just did what they were told. I can only think that such games were undertaken for financial reasons – what other possible purpose could there be?

The wear and tear on players certainly didn't seem to be a concern. Footballers were used as and when the club thought fit. Take the holiday seasons – we always played on Christmas Day and Boxing Day, and had three matches in four days over Easter. When you compare it with now, it was an amazing state of affairs.

There was one occasion when I was really glad the club opted to play a friendly north of the border. It was 11 February 1950 up at Dens Park, home of Dundee, and I did something for the first and last time in a North End shirt. I scored a hat-trick! The feat eluded me at league level so I have always looked back with fondness on our visit to the fair city of Dundee. The result, a 6–2 triumph, came at a good time; we'd managed just one win from our previous seven outings and had scored one goal in our last five league matches. I was struggling as much as anyone to find the net; apart from penalties, I had only five to my name all season.

A shock FA Cup exit against Watford left us with a free weekend so we headed for Dens Park with new recruit Joe Marston, an Australian centre-half, in our ranks. An enthusiastic crowd of around 12,000 – police had to come on to the field to disperse the eager young autograph hunters – watched a goal feast.

Paddy Waters gifted the Scots the lead with an own goal but a foul on Eddie Brown gave me the chance to claim my opening goal from the penalty spot. Midway through the second half I added a second and ten minutes from time came my golden moment. I don't think I bothered going in search of the match ball, probably thinking there would be many more hat-tricks to come, but I wish I had. It would have been a collector's piece!

Incidentally, I only have myself to blame for not scoring a hat-trick during my league career, as anyone who watched Preston's First Division game against Leicester City at Filbert Street on 29 March 1958 will testify. I scored in our 4–1 win but had the misfortune to miss not one penalty, but two.

However, back in 1948, despite the trek to Scotland, we went into the match with Blackpool on something of a high. A few rungs down the ladder from us, they had wholesale and well-documented injury problems and when it was announced that Stanley Matthews, Stanley Mortensen and Harry Johnstone, to all intents and purposes their best three players, would all be missing, we rubbed our hands in anticipation.

Whether we were guilty of being overconfident, thinking Blackpool's 'reserves' at home would present no problem, or merely complacent, I don't know. What I can say is that it turned out to be a complete and utter shambles. The fact that our goalkeeper, Willie Hall, was a bag of nerves and gifted Blackpool four of their goals on a plate didn't help matters, but it would not be fair to hang Willie alone.

Willie had come through the ranks. He was a local lad, born down the road in Walton-le-Dale, and he had struggled to push open the first-team door due to the consistency of first Jack Fairbrother and later Jimmy Gooch. An injury to Gooch finally gave him an opportunity and he kept a clean sheet on his debut in a 2–0 win at Sunderland. His form stayed fairly sound, but Willie's world crumbled against Blackpool.

No one relished Willie's uncertainty more than Jimmy McIntosh, who had been on North End's books before the war. Jimmy made his bow in the 1937–38 season, playing four times without scoring. He played 23 games the following season and scored just three times. He fared better in some 70 plus appearances during the war years but whatever his ability – and against us he looked a world beater – he could never have been termed a prolific goalscorer. To see him return to Deepdale in the tangerine shirt and help himself to five – another record – was quite astonishing.

The evening paper didn't beat about the bush, Viator reflecting the thoughts of the majority in a crowd of 26,610. The fact that I was offered up as a saving grace was some consolation:

> It will be a long time before Preston live down the reproach and humiliation of such a hiding and, frankly, the team's sluggish, uninspiring display, colourless in the extreme, offered little in extenuation . . . There was scarcely a redeeming feature apart from Finney's efforts to put some life and method into the attack.

The hiding was comfortably the club's heaviest home reverse, beating the 0–5 losses against Middlesbrough and Aston Villa in 1935 and 1900 respectively. Our demoralised line-up read: Hall, Walton, Scott, Horton, Waters, Dougall, Finney, McLaren, Jackson, Hannah and McClure.

Willie Hall became the sacrificial lamb and his North End career was effectively over just seven games in. He never featured again for the first team, banished to the reserves until his career was given a new start in the summer of 1949 when he was signed – by Blackpool! He struggled to make an impact at Bloomfield Road with just 16 appearances, and after joining Reading he broke his arm, an injury that was to force him into retirement.

Just for the record, Preston had lost 0–7 just once before – away to Nottingham Forest during the April of a Second Division season in 1926–27 when the great Alex James was listed in the line-up. If Alex felt half as bad after that match as I felt after Blackpool, he must have squirmed.

CHAPTER FIVE

Offered football's first bung

Top footballers crave the big stage. Nothing gets the heart pounding faster than the opportunity to parade your skills in front of a capacity crowd. I always relished the prospect of a big match, be it for club or country, and was lucky enough to sample some truly great occasions at home and abroad. To trot out of the tunnel at Deepdale or Wembley, Highbury or Rio, Hampden Park or Lisbon, with the crowd cheering in eager anticipation, was a fantastic experience, the ultimate buzz.

When you have tasted the high life, how can you possibly be expected to cope with anything less? That was precisely why I put my career on temporary hold in the summer of 1949.

There was considerable talk, most of it media-driven, of me leaving Preston following the club's relegation to the Second Division. If you believed all the stories, Manchester United and

Arsenal were both 'monitoring my situation', while Blackpool were waiting in the wings with chequebook open and pen poised. I cannot pretend that the newspaper stories were total fabrication. I must concede that I was unsettled at Deepdale. The previous season, 1948–49, had been dreadful and I spent half the time watching in frustration from the sidelines.

We had started full of hope, having signed Bobby Langton from Blackburn Rovers for a then club record fee of £14,500. He finished up our top scorer. But we never got out of first gear and by Christmas found ourselves in the bottom three with just six wins to our name. We were staring straight down the barrel of the relegation gun.

Plagued by niggling injuries, I had to sit and suffer as we stumbled from one heavy defeat to another. If losing 4–1 at Everton was bad enough, imagine what it felt like to crash 6–1 to Manchester United on our own midden. It was more painful than breaking my jaw in an FA Cup fourth-round defeat against Leicester City at Filbert Street!

We brought in Angus Morrison from Derby, but our problems stemmed from indifferent defending and although things improved a little in April after Will Scott returned to the club in a supervisory coaching role, our fate was to rest on the events of the very last day.

Huddersfield, a point above us in third-bottom spot with an inferior goal average, entertained Manchester City while we had the little matter of trying to get a positive result at Anfield to contend with. Against the odds, we won quite comfortably, 2–0, and then had to face up to the agony of waiting for the result to filter through from Leeds Road. For some reason that escapes me now, Huddersfield's match had been delayed by 15 minutes. When the news finally reached us, it was not good. Huddersfield, a team we had beaten home and away with an aggregate score of 4–0, were safe. We were relegated. Going down sent shockwaves through the club and the town.

The tailend of that season included one of the most nerve-racking experiences of my football career. It didn't come in a match situation and neither was it played on a pitch; it did, however, involve a ball, a net and an enthusiastic crowd. Not for the first or last time, the action also centred around Stanley Matthews. We both accepted an invitation to appear at the Palace Theatre in Preston for a six-night run of a unique production.

Stan was in his pomp at Blackpool and I was doing my bit for North End and the media just loved to build up the rivalry. They did not have to try too hard. Blackpool versus Preston fixtures were always spicy affairs and we could turn an average season into a satisfactory one simply by beating the Seasiders home and away. Stan and I were invariably used to stoke up the pre-match fire and the inquests afterwards usually centred around which of us had fared best.

The rivalry was to be taken to new heights thanks to a north-west impresario by the name of Tom Moss. A bright and progressive man who was steeped in showbusiness, Tom was constantly exploring new ways of attracting paying punters into local theatres. His inventive notions consistently captured the public's imagination, but he surpassed himself when he came up with the idea of pitching Stan and I head-to-head in a live show.

Tom approached us to ask if we would be prepared to play a one-against-one game of 'football tennis', an exercise in ball-control skills used extensively by clubs as part of training sessions. It is a sort of no-hands volleyball. Stan and I both enjoyed the game and Tom was offering a decent fee, so we decided to accept the invitation provided our respective managers agreed. No objections were raised, both clubs deciding that the risk of injury was minimal (strange that, considering North End's predicament) so the Matthews v. Finney show was declared very much on.

When word got out, interest rocketed. So much so that Tom had to re-think his plans and what was initially to be a one-night stand suddenly became a week-long affair. Just to add to the anticipation, Tom timed the shows to open on the Monday night following the Saturday of Preston's First Division match with Blackpool at Bloomfield Road.

Well, that was the plan. Unfortunately, it didn't quite go as Tom had hoped. At the eleventh hour there was something of a hitch – my co-star had to pull out through injury. To make matters worse, Stan suffered the knock after being on the receiving end of what can only be described as a brute of a tackle from North End centre-half Paddy Waters. The fact that Paddy's ferocious challenge was rather out of character did little to quell the furore. I still have a vivid picture of Stan lying prostrate on the cinder track clutching his leg with the crowd jeering disapproval. The Blackpool players were equally incensed. I had never seen Harry Johnstone, the Seasiders' skipper, so wound up.

I admired Harry as a player and as a person. He and his wife Marjorie were among our closest friends. Harry and Marjorie and their son David lived around the back of Blackpool, near to Stanley Park, and many a time we would pop across to see them. The friendship, born out of footballing rivalry, blossomed to such an extent that we went on family holidays together. We stayed in close contact after our playing days ended. Like me, Harry got involved with the media and spent many years touring the country covering games for the *People*. Elsie and I were devastated to lose them both,

Harry after a short fight against cancer and Marjorie following a long and painful illness.

A footballing defender who loved to get the ball down and play, Harry's talent took him to the top of the tree with England and he played in that historic international at Wembley against the revolutionary Hungarians. That experience left a mark on Harry – he was not alone in that – and he had strong beliefs on how the game should be played.

So, you can imagine that Harry was not best pleased about the way Paddy Waters had 'marked' Stanley Matthews. Friend or no friend, Harry was determined to vent his anger on someone and who better than the opposing captain – me. He had a couple of false front teeth, which he took out for matches, and he presented a fearsome figure as he sprinted across the field.

'What was that?' he boomed, not really expecting or wanting an answer. 'Bloody disgraceful, that's what it was and what are you going to do about it?'

This time he paused for breath and did seem to require a response.

'Harry, I'm sorry about it and I'll certainly be having a word with Paddy,' I said – a rather weak reply, perhaps, but what else could I say? The challenge was a bad one. Had it taken place in today's tackle-free game, it would certainly have merited a yellow card, possibly a straight red. But football in those days involved much more physical contact than it does now. Rough stuff like shoulder charging was part and parcel of the game and defenders were considered quite within their rights to tackle you from behind. Tommy Docherty has gone on record saying that if today's referees had officiated in the forties and fifties, most games would have ended up as five-a-side contests!

Although Stan did manage to get back on his feet and re-join the action, he was clearly a passenger. The game ended 2–2, a decent point for us in a desperate season. Bobby Beattie and Bobby Langton, who finished the campaign with a combined tally of 22 goals, were our marksmen, but the big talking point was Stan's injury.

It soon became apparent that the great man would need a few days' rest and treatment before resuming football duties. Tom Moss contacted me in a state of some agitation. Tom tried to sound genuinely concerned about Stan's well-being, but it was obvious that he was far more flustered by the potential damage to his show. But, disaster or no disaster, Tom was a showbusiness man and in time-honoured fashion he vowed that the show must go on.

'It's just too unlucky for words. I really can't believe it. Stan has no chance of making the first night and probably won't be able to go on at all,' said Tom. 'It's a terribly disappointing state of affairs, but I have managed to get a stand-in if you are happy to give it a go.'

I said I was quite happy to proceed and Tom revealed that the deputy was Jack Matthews, Stanley's brother. Crafty old Tom not only saved the day, but fulfilled his promise of putting Matthews and Finney on the stage.

The Palace was probably Preston's premier theatre. All the big-name stars appeared there. Elsie and I knew it well. We both enjoyed live entertainment and there was never any problem getting tickets because we were issued 'comps' through the football club. But while I was familiar with the Palace from the audience's side, I had never imagined what it would be like up there on stage doing the entertaining as top of the bill with a host of friends looking on. Standing backstage, first-night nerves kicked in and I know Jack felt much the same, but once the curtain went up we were fine. It helped that we weren't the only attractions. Comedian Wee Georgie Wood was also booked to appear.

The audiences were really enthusiastic and I will not pretend that it was anything other than great fun. Stan turned up to watch and to offer his brother moral support and I thoroughly enjoyed myself. On the final night I was presented with a silver salver, personally signed by Stanley Matthews, Wee Georgie Wood and Tom Moss. Some 54 years on, it still stands on a display unit in our lounge.

Demotion to the Second Division was a catastrophe for the club and there was bound to be some bloodletting. Bill Shankly was an early casualty and he was not happy about his release. His exit typified the way in which clubs treated players in those times. It didn't seem to matter who you were or how much service you had given, the manner of departure was unsatisfactory.

The retained list would be pinned on the dressing-room door and it was up to the players to go along to see whether they figured in future plans or not. The lucky ones were called in to see the manager one by one and told something along the lines of, 'Well done, you've had a good season and so we are offering you the same terms for another twelve months. Sign just here.' You would sign a blank form, the club officials insisting that they would fill in the details later on.

With a service record stretching over 17 seasons, from joining at 19 to departing at 36, perhaps Bill was right to feel aggrieved, especially as he felt in his own mind that he could have played on. Whether he was right in that regard is debatable. Although he remained as enthusiastic as ever, he was hampered more and more by injuries and found it harder and harder to retain the fitness levels he demanded of himself. He featured just half-a-dozen times during the relegation campaign.

After being released by North End, he saw the light and retired, eventually taking his first managerial job back at Carlisle. But not being retained by Preston, cast aside, unwanted, was very hard for him to take and it took a while for him to recover. As you might expect, he did not go quietly, voicing his annoyance in the public arena. But it changed nothing and the club made it even worse by withholding his benefit money of around £150 a year. It would not happen today – and quite right, too – but in the football world of post-war England, all the power lay with the clubs.

I was very sad to see Bill go. The prospect of a stint outside the top flight hardly filled me with euphoria, either. It wasn't that by becoming an international I had suddenly got an inflated impression of my standing at the club, or that I had simply decided it was time to move on just for the hell of it. My attitude centred squarely on one main factor – how would playing in the Second Division hamper my chances with England?

So, when Preston presented me with the terms of re-engagement for the 1949–50 season, I delayed putting my signature to the contract. As we all know, there is no such thing as a secret in football and when word of me not re-signing leaked into the public domain, the rumour factory worked overtime. I was at loggerheads with the club; there must have been a row; I wanted more money and was ready to choose between a host of clubs keen to recruit me – and so it went on.

But I never once asked North End for a transfer, nor did the club invite offers for me. While all hell was allegedly breaking loose on the outside, all that actually happened internally was that I met with Jim Taylor. He listened to my concerns and gave me the chance to sound off about the plight of the club. Then, in his calm and considered way, he convinced me within minutes that plans were afoot to make our stint outside the First Division a short one. He promised new signings and said that the aim was to build the revival around me. If I left, it would make the goal harder to achieve, and he asked me to put the interests of the club first.

That was a clever ploy because he knew what I felt in my heart for Preston North End. I would have found it difficult, if not impossible, to turn my back on the club, particularly with them in the doldrums.

Then I just mentioned the little matter of an unofficial offer of £2,000 from an agent. It was my first – and last – experience of an illegal approach and it came in the most unlikely setting of a local park while I was out for a walk one afternoon.

I noticed a chap making a beeline for me and I genuinely thought I had seen him somewhere before, perhaps through general football connections or maybe he was just a keen North End follower. He expressed his sadness at our relegation and asked me outright whether I fancied moving on. He told me, in whispered tones, that if I got myself on the transfer list, he had a club ready, willing and more than able to buy me and throw two grand my way as a tax-free payment.

'There's really nothing to it,' he went on. 'You say the word and I'll sort out the detail and the cash, and it will be in cash.'

I must have looked totally bemused so he repeated the offer, and I have to admit that he seemed certain he could deliver on his wild promise. I was stumped. Was I interested? Well, yes, I suppose so. When you are on £10 a week, £2,000 represents a small fortune.

When I threw the outline of the story into my meeting with the chairman, it was a little like throwing a match into a box of fireworks

– he just exploded. Red in the face, Jim went absolutely berserk, demanding I should reveal the man's identity so that he could track him down and bring him and his club into the public arena for a flogging.

'Tom, you must say who it is. We have got to stamp out this sort of behaviour. It's just not on.'

However, as I had not had the presence of mind to ask for the chap's name, the chapter closed without further comment.

Jim settled down and got back to the pressing issue of my future with Preston North End. He didn't go so far as to talk about rats and sinking ships, but I got the message, and when he pushed a contract under my nose, I smiled at him and signed.

I came away from that chat feeling satisfied that the club's ambitions matched my own, and more than a little relieved to be staying. Playing for Preston was always so special to me. From the first time I watched a game from the terraces I was in love with the place. It was – and still is – a proud club, reflecting a proud town, now a proud city.

Someone once wrote that you could tell Preston was a true footballing town from the profusion of chimney pots. Perhaps you have to be a northerner to understand such a sentiment. It means that the great game originated and prospered in places where people lived back-to-back in terraced properties next to mills – Preston, Blackburn, Bolton, Burnley, Accrington. There were 12 founder members of the Football League back in 1888, and those towns accounted for five of them. Of the other seven, Aston Villa were located the furthest south, so to all intents and purposes, football was a northern game and, in spite of claims from elsewhere, it remains the hotbed.

During those formative years, Preston were the big noise. The club took the first-ever championship, without losing a single

This is the earliest photograph in my collection, I was about four years old and we were on a day trip to Blackpool.

My mother, Margaret, who was so tragically taken from us at the age of 32 – how I wish I could have got to know her.

With granddad Mitchell, my brother Joe's wife Beatrice and their first baby, Joe. It was taken in the garden of granddad's Preston house in 1939.

Being a choirboy you often got involved in street processions and carnivals – here I am one Whitsuntide, right at the front, aged 12.

My guard and my guide. My dad, Alf, was the biggest single influence on my early life and we stayed very close.

My first medal for football. Our school team from Deepdale Modern lifted the Dawson Cup at Deepdale – I scored the winning goal! – and shortly after this studio photograph was taken.

Football pitches weren't quite as good back then! This was Holme Slack, the council estate in Preston where I, and hundreds of other young hopefuls, first experienced the joy of a match.

Pick up thy bed. On the march in Klagenfort, Austria, in 1945.

This portrait of me in uniform was sent to Elsie by my stepmother, Mary.

War-time football abroad – I had some great times with The Wanderers and here I am, bottom left, in action in Egypt.

Our wedding day at Emmanuel Church, Preston, on 1 November 1945. I had received temporary release from the war – on matrimonial grounds. Olive Poole, far left, was a bridesmaid.

Elsie was always a keen dancer – we met at a dance – and while I was never great, I did improve with practice.

Daughter Barbara models a new pair of shorts for Elsie and me in our garden.

Passing on a few tips to our Brian.

On holiday in Greece in the early 1960s – we hadn't managed many family holidays during my playing career, for I was invariably involved with an England tour, but we made up for lost time later.

We always enjoyed cruising and had several holidays with PNE physio Des Coupe and his wife Alice. Here we are aboard RMS *Alcantara* in 1953, heading for the Med.

Steps in the right direction. This snap was taken in 1946 after I was demobbed. I was never frightened of getting my hands dirty and I remained actively involved in plumbing long after my football career had become established. (*Lancashire Evening Post*)

My other life: running the Preston plumbing and electrical business which my brother Joe and I started soon after the war. (*Lancashire Evening Post*)

In the Preston Council Chamber in 1979 when I was made a Freeman of the Borough. It was one of my proudest moments. (*Lancashire Evening Post*)

After being awarded the CBE. (*Lancashire Evening Post*)

game, and won the FA Cup, without conceding a goal, eventually beating Wolverhampton Wanderers 3–0 at the Kennington Oval. The championship stayed with North End – by now tagged the Old Invincibles – the following year, but runners-up spot had to suffice for the next three seasons.

The success of the football club served to lift the spirits of a community used to hard graft and an oversized share of misfortune. The town topped a different sort of table in the latter years of the nineteenth century – the league of infant mortality. Just two years after Preston North End FC was formed and five years before the birth of the Football League, a quarter of every thousand Preston infants died.

Cotton was to blame. While the cotton boom was clearly welcome, the town could not cope with the industry's rate of expansion. Cotton lords demanded too much of their workforces, poor housing prevailed and public health was not an item for discussion. Consequently, epidemics of infectious diseases brought tragic loss of life. Looking back, it is hard to comprehend what some families with young children must have gone through, the cramped and often squalid living conditions, the all-work-no-play philosophy of the mill tyrants, the fear of disease and death.

I am not a particularly political or religious man, but I do have a deep regard for the welfare of my fellow human beings. Once again, it probably stems back to my childhood and the lessons I learned from my father. We were encouraged to look out for one another and care for those less fortunate than ourselves. Maybe that was why, in the mid 1980s, I agreed to take on the role of chairman of the Preston Health Authority. The offer came right out of the blue, as have many other things that have happened to me, and I found the job challenging, enlightening, rewarding and, at times, distressing. Over a hectic four-year period, I got a better grasp of the intricate workings of a major public organisation and I treated it not just as a position of great responsibility but also as a chance to bring about change. Good health is something to be treasured. You don't have to look very far to see someone suffering.

The health problems of a hundred or so years ago were clearly evident, but alongside them, a new society was developing. While some people struggled in poverty, others flourished. Employment was high and for those with decent jobs, things got better and better. The emergence of a definite class structure was plain to see.

Football was quickly becoming the pastime of the masses and the central figure in the formation of Preston North End FC was a certain William Suddell. He was, I suppose, the Jim Taylor of his day. The Suddell clan were extremely well known around Lancashire, cloth traders with links not only in Preston but also in Blackburn.

William, though, was a true Prestonian. Born in the town – two of his antecedents had worn the Preston mayoral chain of office – he returned from a private education in Cheshire to take up a post with one of the leading cotton lords, John Goodair. By all accounts he did well although 'accounts' did threaten his good name when, in 1895, he appeared in court charged with embezzling various sums of money and falsifying the books of the firm.

William's defence was football. As the man most responsible for getting the club off the ground, William Suddell, complete with long beard and top hat, was Mr Preston North End. He claimed that he did not 'cook the company books' for any personal gain but simply to further the developing interests of North End.

An accomplished sportsman – he won prizes for swimming, cricket and cycling – William also found time to become Preston's first football manager. More than a century later he still stands as the club's most successful, having led them to that glorious first double. His place in Preston North End history is guaranteed and, along with thousands and thousands of others, I have much to thank him for.

I was always deeply conscious of the sense of a rich and illustrious past whenever I pulled on a Preston shirt. You felt you belonged to something special and I don't mind admitting that I still experience that reaction whenever I go along to Deepdale as a spectator.

CHAPTER SIX

Out of the limelight – but not for long

J im Taylor was a man of honour and a highly respected football administrator. He was also a dictator. His enemies dubbed him the 'Stalin of English Football' and Bill Shankly once claimed to have absorbed many of Taylor's qualities into his own persona. You knew on first meeting Jim that he was both chairman and boss.

I once asked him if the club would consider giving me a rise. He dismissed the claim out of hand, telling me I was getting a bit too big for my boots.

'Just get on with your football, Tom,' he said. 'That's what you should be concentrating on, nothing else.'

Jim Taylor first joined the board at the end of the First World War. He resigned briefly and later became the top man during an outstanding and lengthy period of service. Few people did more to promote the good name of Preston North End and we shared a mutual respect and a love for the club. He helped me a lot and for many years he was my next-door neighbour in Victoria Road.

His finest hour came in 1938 when North End lifted the FA Cup thanks to a controversial penalty from George Mutch against the mighty Huddersfield. The club came within a whisker of a second double; the 1937–38 campaign was the club's most successful in the twentieth century.

Jim orchestrated a revolution at Deepdale. As well as possessing a shrewd business brain, he was no fool when it came to weighing up football and, more significantly, footballers.

When the country was on the verge of the Second World War, with Hitler's warnings sending a chill of fear across the land, Jim Taylor was preoccupied with football matters. There were those who thought he lived at the ground, such was his commitment. He even made a bold bid to land a player I was to get to know rather well and with whom I was often compared – a certain Stanley Matthews. Anxious to build on the Cup triumph, the chairman reported to the board that he had heard Matthews had been made available for transfer by Stoke. Preston agreed to pursue the matter but were finally told 'nothing doing'.

Jim Taylor was nothing if not adventurous and ambitious and although he liked – no, demanded – his own way, you always felt he had the best interests of the club at heart. He was still in the chair when we had our 'clear the air' talks on my future in 1949 although it was abundantly clear that he could not be expected to carry on for much longer. His health had deteriorated in tandem with his ailing club. Part way through the relegation season he had a seizure and underwent a critical operation in hospital. In the spring of 1950, aged 75, he finally admitted defeat and stepped down. But Jim saw to it that all his promises to me were fulfilled and it wasn't long after our fall from grace that the re-building began and the new recruits came marching in.

The number included two Scots who were to become North End legends, full-back Willie Cunningham and half-back Tommy Docherty, plus defender Willie Forbes and inside-forward Eddie Quigley. If we had previously lacked a little in the never-say-die stakes, Willie Cunningham and Tommy soon changed all of that. Small in stature but a giant in terms of heart and desire, former coalminer Willie was as hard as granite while Tommy, a fresh-faced kid from the Gorbals who tackled as though his life depended on it, didn't know what losing meant.

Quigley cost North End £26,500 from Sheffield Wednesday, not just a club record but a British one to boot. In fact, it was just £3,000 under the world transfer record of the day, the £29,500 paid by Italian giants Inter for Amedio Amatel.

Quigley was the golden boy of Hillsborough where regular crowds of 60,000 watched him become their top scorer. When the Yorkshire outfit decided to cash in, they were not short of takers. Eddie could have gone to Wolves or Everton, but opted for Preston because he was a native of Bury and his family wanted to get back to Lancashire. He also fancied living near the seaside.

I had a lot of time for Eddie despite what the newspapers tried to make people believe. The alleged feud wasn't quite of Stanley Matthews proportions, but the stories were distressing all the same. It was claimed that I was not happy about seeing another 'star' in the dressing room and that I made moves to get Quigley out of the picture.

It was not true, of course. For one thing, it was not in my nature to try to make anyone feel unwelcome; for another, it was me who had gone to the chairman and requested some new faces. I was striving to instigate an improvement in our playing fortunes and that would hardly involve signing people who were not as good as those we already had. When I first heard we were chasing Quigley, I was delighted. It was a statement of North End's positive intent for the future. But the back pages threatened to cause upset and unrest, so much so that Eddie eventually talked of asking for a move. If Eddie was below par in a game, I got the blame; if he failed to get on the end of a pass, it was because I had deliberately under-hit or over-hit the ball; if he didn't score, it was due to poor service from the wings. Newspapers were crammed with letters, the majority supporting Quigley, others siding with me.

It was an absurd state of affairs and I didn't know whether to feel livid or upset. Once again, I turned to the chairman for guidance. 'I find the situation intolerable,' I told him. 'All this stuff in the papers about a row between Eddie and me, where is it coming from? It's not true and very damaging. I'm getting to the stage where my own form is suffering and perhaps the best thing all round is for me to move on.' I could not believe I had suggested leaving, but it was an indication of how down I had become.

Jim was very sympathetic. He dismissed my leaving theory out of hand and made it his business to approach the editors of the newspapers involved. I don't know what he did or said, but the whole thing finally settled down.

Eddie was a stoutly built inside-forward with a good touch and a reputation for long-range passing and shooting. I have not seen many strike a dead ball with such ferocity and accuracy. We spent hours practising free kicks together, but I could never match him for sheer power.

In all the fuss that surrounded the eventual capture of Quigley, Preston's signing of Willie Forbes got a little lost, but at £18,000, it was another substantial deal. Close on half the total spend was recovered through the sale of Bobby Langton to Bolton Wanderers but, nevertheless, people were starting to sit up and take note of this clearly ambitious Second Division club.

Ready to bounce back at the first attempt, we discovered two harsh realities of football life – money doesn't always guarantee success and good teams take time to mould together. Our first taste of life outside the highest level was not a disaster but it was hardly a success either. The team did show genuine signs of promise, but it was not promising enough for the shareholders. They were up in arms when we couldn't manage better than sixth and finished six points off the second promotion position – occupied by Sheffield Wednesday of all clubs. The annual general meeting hit out at the ridiculous amount of money 'wasted on players who had not improved the team'. One shareholder termed it the road to ruin, but I thought that rather unfair.

I believe much of the turbulence was prompted by our lack of firepower. Eddie Quigley had not settled as quickly as he – or we – would have liked and managed just five goals. Our collective total of 60 was two less than in the relegation season. The answer? Easy. Sell the top scorer! Sounds bizarre, but that's what happened.

Just a few weeks in to the 1950–51 season, Eddie Brown, who had reached a dozen goals in just 24 matches, was traded off in a deal that brought in Charlie Wayman from Southampton. Now, with all due respect to Eddie, a fine footballer and a forward with an impressive goalscoring record at a number of clubs, Wayman's arrival was a turning point, catapulting Preston North End back into the big time. That may be a sweeping statement, but it is an undeniable fact. Charlie was the goal poacher supreme and he bagged 27 league goals in 34 starts as we took the Second Division by the throat, setting all sorts of records along the way to the title and playing some wonderful attacking football in the process.

The season had not got off to the best of starts. I took a little time to get going after a pre-season appendix operation, missing the first five games, and Eddie Quigley and Harry Anders were both sidelined through injury. We lost the opening game, 2–4 at home to Manchester City, and not many people who saw the match that day would have put money on us winning the championship. The supporters were not quite ready to boo, but the widespread feeling of dissatisfaction was almost tangible.

For the next few weeks our form was scratchy. Willie Cunningham was struggling to establish himself, as was Joe Marston, a young centre-half from Australia, goalkeeper Jimmy Gooch looked decidedly ill at ease, and we didn't look menacing enough up front. Enter Charlie Wayman. Although the little man found himself on the losing side in early clashes with Barnsley and Blackburn Rovers, it wasn't long before his craft and guile, coupled with clinical finishing, triggered off a remarkable revival.

It all started in November with a 5–1 win over Swansea at Deepdale. Charlie scored two, I got one as did Ken Horton (a replacement for tonsillitis victim Eddie Quigley) and Swansea helped our cause with an own goal. By March, we had taken our unbeaten record to 20 games by drawing 3–3 at Southampton, Charlie marking his return to the Dell with a brace and Ken Horton getting the other.

During that wonderful spell of nearly five months we not only equalled Bristol City's record of 14 successive wins (nine of ours away from home) but beat the Preston North End Invincibles' record of 13 successive wins. In the process, we established a new club record of eight successive away wins in the League – and all this in the

Second Division. By the close of the campaign we had also put our names to new club records for points gained in a season (57) and most wins in a season (26).

The supporters – who had never had any doubts right from day one! – turned up in their droves and our average crowd topped 31,000. What is it they say about people always following winning teams?

The 14-match winning run started at QPR when Charlie Wayman was our only scorer in a 4–1 triumph. It continued like this: QPR (home) 1–0; Cardiff (away) 2–0; Birmingham (home) 1–0; Grimsby (away) 4–0; Notts County (home) 3–1; Bradford City (away) 4–2; Luton (home) 1–0; Leeds (away) 3–0; Barnsley (home) 7–0; Sheffield United (away) 3–2; Blackburn Rovers (home) 3–0; Leicester (home) 3–2; Leicester (away) 3–2. That gave us the maximum 28 points (2 for a win in those days), with 42 goals scored and just 10 conceded. I scored seven of them, Ken Horton grabbed 11 and Charlie Wayman averaged better than a goal a game with 15. The run finally ended with that 3–3 draw at Southampton, but there was major consolation in the point proving enough to guarantee promotion with five games left to play.

Our next outing ended in defeat against West Ham, ironically the last team to beat us prior to the great run getting under way, but we would have ended up sharing the spoils had Willie Cunningham not fluffed a penalty five minutes from time.

We didn't hold it against Willie who had been a key figure in our promotion drive. He was rugged and determined, and forwards always knew he was around. Not an easy man to get to know, he was a great buddy when you finally managed it. He proved himself to be a team player with a heart as big as Heart of Midlothian! His name was still on the teamsheet a decade later. He was 37 when the book closed after more than 400 appearances and he continued to live within a full-back's clearance of the ground.

And then there was the Doc! Tommy came to Preston as a raw prospect, clearly talented and tenacious, but with a lot to learn. For all that, he was a kid you couldn't help but like. His enthusiasm mirrored that of Bill Shankly and many actually reckoned he was brought in as a belated replacement for his fellow countryman.

Away from football, Tommy lived life to the full. He was a character in every sense and there was never a dull moment when he was around. As quick with the wit as he was in the tackle, Doc was marvellous company, especially when we went away.

For trips to London, the itinerary rarely varied. We usually travelled by lunchtime train. Preston to Euston was a direct line. On arrival we would usually spend a few minutes signing autographs – the kids knew that Euston was a good place not only for train spotting but for footballer spotting, particularly on Friday afternoons – and then board a coach bound for our hotel. I roomed with Ken Horton. He and I had come through the schoolboy ranks together and we became close friends. Later, he came to work in the plumbing business and stayed for 30 years. After a light meal, we took in the first house at the Palladium. There was no choice; everyone in the party, players, management and directors, went along. We saw a succession of top-line stars down the years, but often our best entertainment came via the Doc . . .

Once, he volunteered to represent the club on a television quiz show called 'The Memory Man'. We all egged him on, of course, because we thought it would be a laugh. It was a laugh all right and the Doc had the last one – he won the show hands down!

He helped to encourage the best of team spirits. Everyone seemed to get on famously (often the case in winning teams) and arguments and disputes were very few. As skipper, I did little but call 'heads' at the toss and choose ends; the players around me were dedicated to their jobs and played together for the good of the team as a whole. Full of nervous energy, the Doc was one of those players who could not keep quiet. He was always a bit chirpy with referees and, occasionally, a mixture of his over-enthusiastic tackling and backchat got him into hot water. Sendings-off were rare – I can remember only a handful – but the Doc was definitely one.

He became a fixture in the team, playing through to the 1957–58 season. In our Second Division title campaign and the first season back in the big-time, he did not miss a single match.

He eventually moved on to Arsenal after failing to hit it off with manager Cliff Britton, a strict disciplinarian who didn't care for those who liked to partake of a drop of alcohol. It didn't bother me, but it bothered Tommy who was many things but not a teetotaller or interested in learning how to become one. Britton's intense training regime and strict discipline all round made life uncomfortable for Tommy. After a bid of £15,000 from Everton had been rejected, Arsenal met Preston's £20,000 asking price, and off he went to Highbury.

As with Bill Shankly, the other great character of my Deepdale career, I was terribly sorry to see him go. The fame and success he went on to enjoy as a manager certainly came as no surprise to me; nor did the fact that all his teams put the emphasis on good football – fun was always the name of the Doc's game. We have remained good friends and whenever we meet up at matches or functions, he is exactly the same bloke I remember from our marvellous days together in the North End dressing room.

He is always joking (at least, I take it as a joke) that but for the quality of his passes I would not have been half the player he turned out to be. I don't know about that, but Tommy Docherty was a very talented and underestimated footballer and Preston only fully appreciated him after he had gone.

As players, particularly when he played right-half and I was on the right wing, we had a good understanding of each other's game and Tom was always keen to bring me into play. It was alleged that he considered part of his role was to be my guardian angel but that was not the case. Thanks all the same but I didn't want or need a protector on the field; a good strong pair of shinguards pushed down your socks and a quick turn of pace usually did the trick when the defenders came hunting.

I didn't always escape and a kick on the leg from an evil-minded opponent wearing hard toe-capped boots would test the cool of any player. We had players in our team who didn't take many prisoners – and you can include Tommy Docherty among them. He knew how to rough things up and having faced him in training I know, believe me I know!

Some of the rough stuff was limited to hard talk. I recall many a full-back whispering sweet nothings in my ear about how far he would go to stop me. In one particular game at Chelsea, two of the home defenders came over with a message about 'getting shot of the ball a bit quicker next time or else', but they were wasting their breath.

On the subject of kit, I took great personal pride in my appearance as a player, something that was instilled into me at an early age. I would never have dreamed of representing Preston or England in need of a haircut or a shave and I always believed that I should be suitably dressed. My standard matchday kit was a strong jockstrap, shirt, shorts and stockings. Contrary to popular belief, we were not padded out with all sorts of vests and undergarments although many players, myself included on occasions, did use bandages to strap up their ankles. The club insisted on blazer and flannels or a suit and a club tie for away trips. No one ever objected – pony tails and earrings had no place in a footballer's attire back then – and the uniform helped to encourage the feeling of being part of a team.

We tended to do a lot of things as a unit – even down to sharing a bath. The big plunge baths had pride of place in every dressing room. After the match everyone jumped in together, perhaps not the most hygienic of activities but an integral part of football life.

The dressing room was where we did our talking and our laughing, sometimes our shouting and occasionally our crying, but what went on in there stayed in there. It was not a kiss-and-tell era and much the better for that. I have no intention of breaking that pact now. I did see and hear some strange goings on although some of the stories doing the rounds back then were the stuff of fantasy. If any player ever scoffed a late lunch on his knee, half stripped, minutes before going out for the game, or turned up looking more than a little worse for wear through over-indulgence the previous night, it didn't happen in our dressing room. But I remember quite a few players locking themselves in the toilets shortly before games to have a quiet fag.

I was one of the less animated of the Preston squad, but that didn't mean I kept my feelings bottled up. I enjoyed the chitchat with the other players and the tactical briefings from the manager. It has never been my nature to seek the spotlight, and I was happy to leave the gag-telling and the practical joking to those who did it best. That's probably why I have always fought shy of appearances on the after-dinner circuit.

The return to the First Division in 1951 was a blessed relief, an absolute joy and a fearsome challenge. The big boys were ready to take us down a peg or two after the headline-grabbing, record-breaking way we had gone about walking away with the Second Division.

We opened up with a win at Fulham, fielding the precise position-by-position line-up with which we had finished the previous season – I bet that hasn't happened too often – and followed it up with a 3–0 win over Charlton. Then it all threatened to turn sour. We managed just three points from a possible 15 and there was a degree of apprehension as we approached the big local derby with Blackpool.

Interest was at an absolute maximum. Preston experienced what the media dubbed the area's biggest post-war traffic jam as hundreds of coaches and cars converged on Deepdale. Every available policeman in the borough was summoned for traffic and crowd-control duty, with support from mounted officers. The streets in and around Deepdale could not cope as traffic, two deep and nose to nose, came to a standstill. Buses carrying hundreds of eager football followers were delayed in the gridlock.

The gates were closed an hour before kick-off with the ground packed to the rafters and we discovered later that the attendance of 40,809 on that September evening was a record for a midweek fixture. The traffic chaos worsened when news spread that the full signs had gone up outside the turnstiles. Some people tried to turn around and head home while others simply abandoned their vehicles and ran to the ground in the vain hope of getting in somehow. A stampede of angry supporters hammered on gates and climbed boundary walls. Those of a more understanding nature accepted their fate and settled down in nearby Moor Park with the flasks of soup and packs of sandwiches they had hoped to eat while watching the match.

Down in the dressing room we were protected from the pandemonium, but we knew there were problems because several of Blackpool's reserve team players and staff failed to arrive on time. Some didn't get there at all.

The police allowed a number of fans to climb over from the Paddock into the Spion Kop in order to create more breathing space and avoid any chance of anyone getting injured in the crush. This was football fever and Deepdale simply wasn't big enough; later, the authorities revealed that up to 8,000 people had been turned away.

It was our first home date with Blackpool for three years and the fans were keen to make up for lost time. We were keen to put the record straight, too. The last time we hosted Blackpool we had lost 3–1 and the time before it was 7–0, our record home reverse. We wanted revenge and we got it. The 3–1 scoreline did not do justice to our performance. Had it not been for the heroics of George Farm in the Blackpool goal, we too might have scored seven.

Derby games, while always high on excitement, sometimes fall short on quality. This was an exception as we produced some vintage pass-and-move football, fashioned in a manner that must have delighted a delegation from the Scottish FA who had come along to watch the eight Scots on parade.

We won with a bit to spare and everyone made a decisive contribution. You know when managers talk about getting individuals playing to their maximum for the collective cause? Well, this was the dream in reality, a triumph for teamwork. Even the two opposing Stans, Matthews and Mortensen, were helpless although Morty did give his side misplaced hope with an early goal. Our attacking was just too much for them, and Bobby Beattie, Eddie Quigley and Angus Morrison got the all-important goals. Whenever I look back on my playing days, that win over Blackpool stands among the highlights.

Five days later we made the short trip to Bloomfield Road for the return. Our line-up was identical in terms of personnel, the crowd figure just 4,000 down and the result an even better 3–0. A couple of own goals from the Seasiders, John Crosland and Eric Hayward the guilty men, plus a fine effort from Eddie Quigley, made it more straightforward than we had dared hope.

Charlie Wayman, who somehow missed out in both derby wins, continued knocking in the goals with stunning regularity and I got my share, but there was great debate over the respective claims of Ken Horton and Eddie Quigley. Ken was finding First Division defences less generous than those in the Second, while Eddie simply couldn't grasp the chances when they came along. There was little doubt that Eddie was the more accomplished all-round player, even Ken would have acknowledged that fact, but he just didn't fit in to our style.

Given the strong Scottish connection with North End – an association that has carried through to the present day with former Scotland manager Craig Brown succeeding former Celtic defender David Moyes in the manager's chair – it was no surprise that we adopted a Scottish method of play. It revolved around possession, passing and movement. When we got it right, it flowed, but it required a high level of close control and agility and everyone had to feel comfortable and able to join in.

We rarely played what later became dubbed the long-ball game and our front players needed to be quick in both eye and feet. I believe that is why Charlie Wayman did so well while Eddie Quigley floundered. Charlie lacked both height and weight, but he had great touch and awareness in and around the box where space is so tight, and he had the happy knack of losing his marker. Always on the move, switching positions, drifting out to the wings and ready and willing to chase and hassle, Charlie was a handful. Considering that goalscorers were always man-marked in those days, it would amaze me just how often he had time and space aplenty when a scoring opportunity fell his way.

Some said he was just lucky, that his goals were often scrappy and that he had overachieved by dropping into a good side at the right time. That assessment was inaccurate and unfair. To score 20 goals or more every season for four seasons in a row required a bit more than luck, and who said it mattered what sort of goals forwards scored providing they scored? I recall him netting a hat-trick at Highbury, successive hat-tricks against Middlesbrough and Wolves, and scoring four at QPR – not to mention scoring in every round of the 1954 FA Cup, including the final. Yes, he was lucky all right!

As for dropping into a good side at the right time, I thought the opposite. Charlie made us a force by coming in just when a prolific scorer was top of our priorities.

Eddie preferred the more accepted route, either playing balls through for the centre-forward to run on to or hitting 60-yard cross-field passes. He was a class act, no doubt about that, but something of a square peg in a round hole.

Blackburn Rovers decided they needed someone to halt their slide towards the Third Division and made a £12,500 bid for Eddie, which North End accepted. His form improved with immediate effect and he went on to become something of a folk hero at Ewood Park, much later taking over as manager.

Apart from the double over Blackpool – a feat which in itself constitutes a good season in the eyes of many North End fans – we enjoyed some memorable results, putting five past both Middlesbrough and Huddersfield and scoring a Christmas Day victory at Burnley. Then there was the 4–0 drubbing of Liverpool on the final afternoon of the season. We finished in seventh spot and had gone some way towards re-establishing the club as a force.

The hullabaloo over my possible move to Palermo dominated the scene during the summer of 1952, but when we returned for pre-season training, I sensed a real belief within the squad. We had surprised ourselves with the positive and relatively trouble-free way we had adapted to life back in the First Division. No one said it in as many words, but we felt we were a team on the rise, a team ready for the next stage – a crack at the championship. Little did we know just how close we would come!

The build-up to what was to be Will Scott's final season at the helm went like a dream. Not all players like pre-season, some positively detest it, but I enjoyed training and Will always tried to make the session interesting.

I was lucky in that I never had to fight a constant battle with the scales. During my entire playing career my weight of around 10 stone varied by just two or three pounds. I didn't drink – not because I objected to alcohol but because I didn't like the taste – and although I could eat like a horse, I found it easy to burn off the fat. Not everyone was so fortunate and the dreaded weigh-in on the first day back after summer was positively feared in some quarters. For those who had allowed extra pounds to creep on, there was a fine to pay. But that was nothing compared to the other part of the punishment, a few trips to the boiler house, the place where the kit was hung to dry. Many a player was banished there, often wrapped in two or three heavy sweaters, until a satisfactory weight loss was recorded.

At Preston, we had the distinct advantage of a training ground, complete with grass playing surface, right next door to Deepdale. A typical training day, lasting around three hours, went like this. We would report in for 10 a.m. and start by lapping the pitch eight or nine times to loosen our limbs. Then we had to do a variety of running exercises, stop-start and sprinting, under the watchful eye of trainer Hughie Ross. The ball was never far away and all the players were encouraged to fine-tune their control or take part in shooting sessions for half-an-hour or so prior to the main event, the full-scale practice match. That was a competitive affair, especially when the first-team defence was asked to cope with the first-team attack. Tommy Docherty and Willie Cunningham sometimes went a little over the top!

Then it was up to the gymnasium for some supervised exercises and a game of head tennis. We were free to leave at around 1 p.m., but when I wasn't due in at the business, I was among a group of players who stayed on for extra training in the afternoon.

Our squad was bolstered when cigarette-smoking Jimmy Baxter, yet another Scot, arrived from Barnsley. Jimmy was no great athlete, you could say he didn't even have the look of a footballer about him, but he was an instinctive inside-forward who could spot the telling pass. He emerged as an important element in our game plan and soon earned himself a special place in the hearts of the North End faithful.

Arsenal were the title favourites, but we managed to run them close, incredibly close in fact, losing on goal average. That didn't seem a likely outcome at the beginning of the season, though. We opened with three draws and managed just two wins from the first nine games – hardly the sort of form associated with would-be champions. When we conceded 10 goals in losing back-to-back games with Chelsea and Manchester United, we were looking more towards the bottom of the table than the top. That was in October and a wonderful mid-season run that yielded 15 points out of a possible 16 got things moving in the right direction. At the final count, both Arsenal and ourselves returned 21 wins, 12 draws and 9 losses from 42 matches to total 54 points apiece. Unfortunately, the Gunners had done better in the scoring stakes and, although we had conceded fewer goals, the glory was with them.

But with two games each left to play, we did give them one hell of a fright. They held a two-point lead and the next fixture up? Arsenal at Deepdale! It was the biggest league game of my career, played out in front of close on 40,000, and it came at a time when I was arguably producing my very best form. I think they call it peaking. The Gunners needed only to avoid defeat to claim the title and a record seventh championship success; a win for us would take the race to the wire. So the Pretenders entertained the Aristocrats with the world watching. The atmosphere inside Deepdale was electric and the media reckoned much hinged on whether Arsenal full-back Lionel Smith could put the shackles on me.

I remember it being a bright and sunny day, if somewhat windy, and the pitch had been watered just before kick-off to make control of the ball a touch easier. The visiting fans released dozens of red and white balloons to greet their team, adding to the carnival feel. It was one of the first occasions I can recall seeing that happen at a football match.

The early part of the first half was a bit like a game of chess, with both teams asking questions of each other and neither really gaining the upper hand. We managed to go ahead via the penalty spot and I was both the victim and the scorer. I had got past Smith and was shaping to shoot when the full-back came at me with what can only be described as a desperate lunge, a man-or-ball challenge from behind. It was a clear penalty and I converted with a left-foot shot beyond the reach of George Swindin.

When we got the stiff breeze behind us after the break, though, it was a different story. Arsenal were on the back foot and they looked distinctly vulnerable. For once – and it didn't happen very often – Arsenal's famed regimented defensive drill was absent. Smith lost his cool and played right into my lap. On another day I might have scored that elusive hat-trick from the penalty spot. The more I teased and tormented, the more rattled he became, and he was not alone as Arsenal relied on aggressive tactics to try to keep us out.

They looked a tired and beaten side long before Charlie Wayman scored a truly magnificent goal, a rasping left-foot shot from a Jimmy Baxter cross. Goal celebrations were quite subdued back then compared with today, but the quality of the goal and its importance proved too much for Charlie. In his delight he jumped straight into Angus Morrison's arms.

The result meant that all attention switched to the final fixtures, Arsenal versus Burnley and Derby County versus Preston North End.

But I had a problem. For the past week or two, a tightening in my groin had steadily worsened. Such pulls and strains usually respond best to a period of rest, but Preston were hardly likely to suggest that and, even if they had, I would probably have declined. Both parties agreed that the summer would provide me with all the rest I needed. I had to play at Derby no matter what.

While I was right behind this particular decision, there were other occasions when I played when I was nowhere near full fitness. Pain-killing injections made it possible. I smile when I hear people refer to them as a new phenomenon in football. They were around in my day – I know, I had them. Was it wise? Was it safe? Was it ethical? I am not medically qualified to pass judgement but I have read that doctors have suggested that players who were injected frequently ran the risk of long-term damage in later life.

Preston never forced me to turn out when injured, but there were

occasions when I felt under pressure to play. I got a lot of strains –
players who rely on a quick turn of pace are particularly susceptible
– and I was 'in doubt' leading up to a fair number of matches. More
often than not I came through to 'pass a late fitness test' although I
sometimes operated at 75 per cent capacity.

It didn't always work. Once, against Burnley, I was talked into
playing when unfit only for the plan to backfire. The injury flared
up within minutes of the kick-off and I spent the remainder of the
match as little more than a passenger. These were pre-substitute days
and I had to stay on the pitch, hobbling around in discomfort and
unable to make any worthwhile contribution. All I could do was
stay out on the wing and try to follow the manager's instructions to
'make a bloody nuisance of myself'.

For all of that, there was no way I was going to sit in the stands
at the Baseball Ground. When the whistle blew on that tense
Wednesday night in the East Midlands, I forgot all about my groin
strain and got cracking with the job in hand. If we could beat
Derby, a team rooted at the bottom of the table and already
destined to spend the following season in the Second Division,
perhaps our neighbours could produce a shock result at Turf Moor
two days later.

We did our bit, although Derby didn't half make us work. Indeed,
it was as hard a match as we had faced all season with the Rams'
kick-and-dash tactics putting us under long spells of pressure.
Encouraged by their biggest crowd of the campaign, Derby really
came at us and Hugh McLaren missed a couple of glorious chances
as we relied largely on the bravery of goalkeeper George Thompson.

I was well below par. Although determined of mind, I was
unable to rely on my body to produce either long runs or sudden
bursts of speed. However, I was certainly in the thick of things in

terms of the game's only goal. I was brought down in the box just before half-time and a penalty was duly awarded. It seemed clear cut to me, but Derby's defenders thought otherwise. When the protests subsided, I kept a clear head and converted. We then spent long spells defending stoutly to record a priceless win and move two points clear at the top.

The First Division championship – unanimously rated the biggest league prize in world football – was in our sights. There was nothing else for us to do but watch and wait. It all came down to whether Arsenal could win at Burnley.

There was no doubting the size of the task. Burnley were a good all-round side; a last-day victory would have put them fourth, just four points behind us. The Gunners would also have nerves to contend with and their confidence had taken a bashing after losing at our place.

But Arsenal did what Arsenal always seem to do – rise to the challenge and win when it matters. They took the game 3–2 although Burnley put up a tremendous show by all accounts and were so on top in the closing minutes that the Gunners boss, Tom Whittaker, couldn't watch any longer and sought refuge in the dressing room. The Burnley lads later told us they felt that Arsenal had been lucky – now where have I heard that before?

But championships are never won or lost on the last game of a season. Decided maybe, but over a 42-game campaign you finish where you deserve to finish.

When you go so close to glory, you invariably track back through the preceding weeks and months to find where you might have turned a draw into a win, or a defeat into a draw, analysing how a goal here or a save there might have made all the difference. We could cite many such examples – drawing our first three matches and managing just three wins from the opening dozen games; losing by the odd goal in seven at Newcastle; being held to a 0–0 draw at relegated Stoke City (the only goalless fixture of the season); a surprise home defeat by Aston Villa; and as for the 5–0 Deepdale disaster against Manchester United, well, the least said the better, especially as United, swimming around in the safe waters of mid-table, went nap against us again at Old Trafford a few weeks later.

Set against all of that were the occasions when we picked up points against the odds. I recall particularly a rumbustious afternoon with Tottenham Hotspur at White Hart Lane. It finished 4–4 and it could have been 8–8. Three weeks earlier we had lost an FA Cup fourth-round replay at the Lane and there was a clear sense of revenge in our camp. Tommy Docherty seemed particularly fired up: 'We slipped up in the Cup, lads, should never have lost that one – let's have no mistakes this time, eh.'

With people like the Doc around you never went into a game anything less than fired up, so I shudder to imagine what was going through his head after just eight minutes when Spurs were two goals to the good. He threw a withering glare or two the way of our hapless defenders and was clearly of a mind that they could have done better in their attempts to keep our goal intact, but this was not a time for recriminations. Not that we ever fell out much; internal squabbling on the pitch was never a good idea in my opinion. I always believed that you knew better than anyone when you had made a mistake and the last thing you needed was a dressing down. Negative situations demanded positive remedies and the Preston North End players of that era were resilient and purposeful. Attack had long been considered our best form of defence. On occasions, we probably tended to overindulge, but this time it worked a treat and we silenced the Spurs crowd with some superb football.

I pulled a goal back and Charlie Wayman grabbed an equaliser. For a 15-minute spell it seemed as though we could score as and when we pleased. But football does not award points for entertainment or the number of chances a team conjures up and we were rocked when Spurs scored twice in the last minute of the first half.

Our dressing room was a bemused place. We all sat there, staring into our teacups, with no one able to explain how we found ourselves two goals adrift. There was only one answer – get out there and get after them. A rare error by Alf Ramsey enabled Angus Morrison to collect a pass from Charlie Wayman and rifle a shot beyond Ted Ditchburn, before young Derek Lewis continued his rich vein of scoring form (he had notched five in his previous seven matches) with the game's final goal.

More than 50,000 crammed into the famous North London stadium that day for a game I count among my most memorable. The performance epitomised the team and the style of play we adopted. You don't score 85 goals by being defensive. It won us friends across the land. The Deepdale turnstiles certainly didn't need oiling that season as we averaged 30,586 – something approaching a quarter of the town's population.

Among the other highlights of the season were a 6–2 win over Manchester City; putting nine past Portsmouth over the two fixtures; a New Year's Day mauling of Blackpool; and a goal apiece for Charlie Wayman and me in a 2–1 win over Charlton Athletic on 29 November, the club's 2,000th league game.

It was heartbreaking to come within a decimal point or two of the biggest prize – you didn't even get a medal for being a runner-up – and the fact that we had played a major role in a thrilling finale to a magnificent season was little consolation. It was heartbreaking, but not tragic. We got to understand the true definition of tragedy twice during that campaign. Our young inside-forward Derek Lewis died after a brain haemorrhage in the early summer of 1953, and a playing accident resulted in Sheffield Wednesday forward Derek Dooley having to have his right leg amputated.

Lewis had joined us in February 1952 from Gillingham, a decent player and popular lad. He scored twice in eight starts in his first season and followed up with 12 in 29 in his second before tragedy struck and put our playing disappointment into some sort of perspective.

Dooley was a fearless forward, a typically blunt and down-to-earth Yorkshireman who never shirked a challenge. But on 14 February at Deepdale, his promising football career came to an abrupt end and his life changed forever. He was involved in a collision with our goalkeeper, George Thompson, while chasing a loose ball. Both men got there at about the same time and some spectators behind the goal said they actually heard the crack. It was quite sickening.

We knew immediately that Derek was badly injured; he was rushed to Preston Royal Infirmary and a fracture was diagnosed. That was bad enough, but far worse followed when complications arose, gangrene set in and the leg had to be removed. The club contacted me at home the day after the game with the terrible news. Seemingly, as well as being broken, Derek's leg had been cut quite badly and the open wound had become infected, possibly by some substance from the soil on the pitch. It all seemed so unnecessary and had happened so quickly, all I could think about was Derek and the dreadful way his life and career had been turned upside down. Good God, he was only 23. It was too shocking for words.

Derek Dooley was not someone I knew well, but his outstanding form for Wednesday, something like a goal a game over 60 matches, had thrown his name up as a future England international and he was clearly a player of real promise.

Bob Gardener, the specialist who carried out the operation, had sorted out one or two minor problems for me down the years and was a medical man of sound reputation.

Along with several other members of the North End team, I was a regular visitor to the hospital over the next week or so. You never know quite what to say in such circumstances, but Derek made it easy for us and the way he kept his spirits up was quite inspirational.

The story dominated the news for some time and poor old George Thompson, as honest as the day is long, was in deep shock. No blame was ever attached to George. He was rightly cleared of all responsibility and he showed great strength of character by playing in the following weekend's game at Tottenham and by being ever-present for the remainder of the season.

George, who appeared as a special guest when Derek Dooley was the subject of television show 'This Is Your Life', took great encouragement from a wonderful gesture made by Derek and his club. A telegram arrived for George before our next match carrying the following message: 'Best of luck – don't worry, keep smiling.'

This was also the season Deepdale waved a tearful farewell to Harry Anders, the winger who had for so long lived patiently in my shadow. Harry was a cracking little player in his own right and after six years of playing the role of understudy, he went in search of regular first-team football at Manchester City. Everyone was sorry to see Harry leave and I was at the front of that particular queue. Between 1947 and 1953 he pulled on his size four boots just six dozen times at first-team level, and when his chances came the crowd hardly gave him much in the way of encouragement – in fact, they booed him.

Whenever I was out through injury, the North End management went to great lengths to keep the fact a secret. The local newspaper was asked not to mention any possibility of me being absent when they ran their preview pieces or, at best, they should have me down as 'doubtful'. The team line-up was not announced publicly until just minutes before the kick-off, by which time all the supporters had paid their admission money and taken their places. Consequently, when the Tannoy system rang out, 'For number seven, read Anders, not Finney', the crowd jeered their disapproval. Harry, down in the dressing room getting stripped in preparation for the game, was able to hear all of that kicking off outside and it could hardly have been a source of inspiration for him.

Luckily, he had the perfect temperament and never let the crowd reaction get him down. He went about his business in a most professional and friendly manner, never bearing a grudge and always asking about my welfare whenever I was injured. When I told him I expected to be back for the next match he was genuinely pleased – or so he said.

CHAPTER SEVEN

1954
and all that

Schoolboys dream, and so they should. From as far back as my memory can take me, my wildest dreams always involved football – I fantasised about playing for Preston North End, playing for England, playing at Wembley, playing in cup finals and scoring goals, great goals, loads of goals. And in 1954 all my dreams came true.

I was 32, and according to those whose opinions I respected, I was at the peak of my powers as a player. But that wasn't the half of it. Just take a glance at this little lot: I was named Footballer of the Year; I was playing in a multi-talented Preston team that had finished First Division runners-up to Arsenal the previous season; I captained North End all the way to the FA Cup final at Wembley; I was selected in the England squad for the World Cup in Switzerland; I starred in a famous international win over

Scotland in front of 134,000 at Hampden Park; I won my 50th England cap.

On paper, 1954 was unquestionably Tom Finney's year. However, while it would be churlish to moan and groan after all that happened to me in that momentous year, some of the events that promised so much failed to deliver. At club level we performed indifferently to finish mid-table, my display in the FA Cup final against West Bromwich Albion at Wembley was my worst in a North End shirt, England underachieved in the World Cup and I struggled with injury.

If I had to select the biggest blot on the landscape it would have to be the Cup final. Funny that, because Wembley usually smiled so kindly on me. At international level, I had the privilege of representing England under the famous twin towers on 16 occasions, finishing a winner 13 times and a loser just twice (both against Scotland). The stadium played host to some of my greatest moments and provided me with a treasure chest crammed full of memories that I will take with me to my grave. Forget what others might say, Wembley always stood proud as the home of world football. But – there is always a 'but' – it was also the scene of my biggest downer.

The 1954 FA Cup final was billed as my big day. My great friend and rival Stanley Matthews had shone like a beacon when the chance had fallen his way the previous year with a virtuoso performance for Blackpool against Bolton. The Matthews Final has remained one of the FA Cup stories of all time, perhaps *the* FA Cup story of all time. Now it was my turn to lead Preston North End to glory at the expense of West Bromwich Albion.

The heavyweight soccer scribes reckoned Albion were to play no more than a supporting role despite finishing runners-up to Wolves in the league. To a man they were sure that I would captain my hometown club to glory in English soccer's showpiece. To all intents and purposes, it was inevitable. It would be the pinnacle of my achievements they said, my finest hour they said, it was written in the book they said. They almost convinced me.

But I am nothing if not a realist and the trouble is football isn't played in a book. It turned out to be an unmitigated disaster and a complete embarrassment. The day was a collective and personal disaster. We played poorly, lost 2–3 and I had a stinker. I could blame the pressure and, heaven knows, there was enough of that. Apart from the build-up, there was the little matter of the events of the night before when I was guest of honour at the Football Writers' Association annual bash. On the agenda at this most illustrious occasion was the presenting of the Footballer of the Year award, and Association chairman Jack Orange presented the famous statuette to me.

It is one of the top domestic honours and the hairs stood up on the back of my neck as I went forward to receive it (as they did four years later when I was awarded it again). At such moments one tends to reflect; not a bad effort, I thought, for a lad who learned his football on the back fields of Holme Slack to be named the year's top footballer on the eve of leading his team out in the FA Cup final.

Before I take you chapter and verse through the big day – big flop more like – let me first run through how we had got to Wembley.

Our third-round opponents were Derby County and the tie at the Baseball Ground marked my return after an eight-week absence with a groin strain. Charlie Wayman and I got the goals in a hard-fought 2–0 win, but I picked up a training injury and didn't figure again until the fourth-round date at Lincoln. The same scoreline prevailed and the tie was also memorable for Charlie's 100th goal for Preston and a superb penalty save by George Thompson.

Ipswich Town had never taken Preston on in a senior fixture until they came out of the hat as our fifth-round opponents at Deepdale. How they must have wished they could have delayed meeting us a little longer. A crowd north of 35,000 – were the fans starting to dream of Wembley? – saw us hit top form that afternoon, scoring six times and conceding only one. The Ipswich defenders lost their composure more than once – usually at my expense – but it made no difference. I got one and had a hand in a few of the others shared between Charlie Wayman (two), Jimmy Baxter (two) and Angus Morrison.

It had been fairly plain sailing so far, but the quarter-final against Leicester was anything but straightforward. It turned out to be an epic. A goal from Angus Morrison earned us a 1–1 draw at Filbert Street and Angus was on the mark again, as was Charlie, in the 2–2 replay at Deepdale. Close on 80,000 people watched the two games and paid each club record receipts totalling close on £14,000.

There were no penalties or golden goal deciders back then and we all trooped off to Hillsborough to try to find a solution. We emerged victorious, 3–1, and I found a place on the scoresheet alongside Jimmy Baxter and Bobby Foster.

Injuries continued to cause me concern, the latest a pulled muscle, and our manager, Scott Symon, made no secret of the fact that he intended to nurse me through in what amounted to the ultimate footballing contradiction – we were concentrating on the Cup. I reckon Scott sensed a real chance of some silverware in his first season and thought that such an achievement would read well on his CV. He was disliked by the media, tagged 'awkward' and 'pompous' when, in actuality, all he was doing was giving his team the best chance of succeeding.

Our long-drawn-out saga with Leicester meant our preparations for the semi-final date with Sheffield Wednesday at Maine Road were restricted to just five days. It was touch and go whether I played in the semi-final. Had it been a league match I feel sure the manager would have opted for caution, but he hadn't got this far to miss out through being careful – and neither, for that matter, had I. I was not fully fit, but what the hell! How could you sit out a match of such importance, a match that captured the imagination of a capacity 75,000 crowd?

The mood in our dressing room beforehand was one of 'this is not the time to falter, lads. One last jump and we have made it to Utopia'.

While West Brom, on that very day standing two points clear of the field in the championship race, were clear favourites to beat the Cup's surprise package, Third Division (North) leaders Port Vale, we had a much bigger challenge on our plate. Wednesday, just a point and a couple of places below us in the First Division, had players of real quality, men of the calibre of inside-forwards Albert Quixall and Jackie Sewell. Their right winger wasn't bad either – an England Under-23 star by the name of Finney, Alan Finney.

They had beaten their local rivals Sheffield United, Everton and Bolton, but we did hold something of an advantage, having thumped them 6–0 in the league back in August.

We had played the same line-up in all our previous six Cup outings, but that changed when Willie Cunningham, who had complained of a heavy cold and a temperature the previous day, was instructed to stay at home. Willie was a big miss for us although in Harry Mattinson we had a very competent replacement who had deputised with aplomb earlier in the season after Tommy Docherty broke a leg.

We started like a train with Wednesday's goal enjoying a charmed life until Charlie Wayman and I combined for the opening goal. I picked up a mishit clearance and my first-time cross was headed home by our goalscorer-in-chief.

The Yorkshiremen rarely threatened to equalise, especially after Sewell had been carried off on a stretcher following a fierce tackle from Tommy Docherty. Sewell did manage to come back on, his leg heavily strapped and his movement clearly restricted, but his contribution was minimal.

Jimmy Baxter, who had scored a hat-trick in the league rout at Deepdale, got our second goal to secure as straightforward a semi-final victory as you could wish for.

Was there a noisier place in Manchester than our dressing room? I doubt it. There certainly wasn't a happier place. We had fired Preston into the FA Cup final for the first time in 16 years and we were ready to party.

Some reckon it was one of my best games for North End and while it is always difficult to judge your own performance, I felt I did more than OK. I was flavour of the month, the darling of the media. One football journalist went so far as to proclaim that our run to the final had been so much a one-man show that I should be allowed to claim tax relief for my 10 dependants! That was flattering and embarrassing and it just wasn't true. No one player can dictate the success of a team to that extent. I played some good stuff during the Cup run, but one-man shows happen only at the theatre. We reached the final because we had some excellent individuals, a united determination and, more than anything, we played exceptionally well. The record of 18 goals for and just five against said it all.

And so to the final itself – oh, if only! Call me naïve, but I wasn't prepared for the pandemonium leading up to 1 May. With hindsight, I would have made up some excuse and locked myself away in a cupboard during the intervening five weeks. Life was not worth living. The telephone never stopped ringing as hundreds of people, many of them complete strangers, got in touch to try to beg, borrow or steal a ticket. I had a handful to give out and my main concern was to make sure Elsie and the kids, my dad and brother Joe and sister-in-law Beatrice were all taken care of. I also got a couple of complimentaries, as was the practice for all games, and the club found me a few more when the demand on me became apparent, but I had to disappoint an awful lot of people.

The way the powers-that-be allocate tickets for Cup finals has always rankled. If the two clubs involved can sell out – and in this case that was not a question even worth asking – they should get the lot.

Then there was all the media attention. Would I turn up for a photo-shoot here, an interview there, sometimes several in the same day? Perhaps I was too agreeable; perhaps I just got carried away with the euphoria of it all. Anyway, I expected too much of myself; something had to give. This is not meant to sound like an excuse, just a reason. I remain convinced even now that the build-up caught up with me on the day of the game.

As captain and the local boy, I was the top target – even my colleagues added to the burden by asking me to speak to the chairman about a possible bonus for reaching Wembley. I didn't tend to fare too well in one-to-ones with Nat Buck and I didn't upset the form book on this one.

'A bonus?' said the chairman. 'As you and the other players know, Tom, all of that has been sorted out already – you will get £25 per man if we win.'

I explained that I appreciated that fact and while we were ever so grateful I was really inquiring about whether there would be anything extra. Nat was not for budging. He shook his head.

'Sorry, Tom,' he said, 'that's your lot.'

The players were not happy, even though £25 was a decent amount. We were earning £14 per week at the time. Talking of pay, I can recall wages rising three times in my career. On the resumption of the Football League after the Second World War I was on £12 in the winter and £10 in the summer. A couple of years later it rose to £14 and £12 and then £17 and £14 before peaking at £20 and £17. That's a grand total rise of £8 in 14 years although we did get top-up money, £2 for a win and £1 for a draw. I once asked the chair-man why they felt it necessary to reduce the wages during the close season. 'Because you're on your bloody holidays, that's why!' was the response. The Preston officials of 1954 did soften in the days leading up to Wembley – they bought all the players' wives a new handbag apiece.

The final was an anti-climax, not because we lost, but because neither side lived up to its reputation for free-flowing football. There were five goals, but the overall standard of play was distinctly second class. I don't know what the special guests, including Her Majesty Queen Elizabeth the Queen Mother, made of it, but the sun-soaked fans must have been hard pressed to stay awake as the lush surface took its toll on the players' legs at the end of a gruelling season.

Unlike most of my team-mates, I had experienced the feel of Wembley before, but if they looked to me for help and guidance they were wasting their time. In the dressing room and walking out from the tunnel I was fine; it was just when the match started that my problems took hold and didn't let go.

Ronnie Allen, an England international, was Albion's star turn. He wasn't the biggest centre-forward in the world, but a player with great awareness and movement who often drifted out to the wings to find space. Any centre-half who shadowed Ronnie ran a few miles during the course of a game, I can tell you. He had netted a hat-trick in a fifth-round win over Newcastle, converted a penalty in the semi-final defeat of his old club Port Vale and it was he who accepted the easiest of opportunities to give Albion an early lead against us.

We weren't behind for long. Inside a minute, with Albion still cheering, Angus Morrison met a Tommy Docherty cross to head an equaliser.

Albion's 33-year-old captain Len Millard, a player I had fared well against down the years, was keeping me on a tight rein, but I finally managed to escape his attention to help set up a goal for Charlie Wayman. It preserved Charlie's record of scoring in every round. Albion's defenders were furious, insisting that Charlie was way offside and I reckon they had a case. Nevertheless, we were in front with one hand on the Cup.

If that goal prompted debate in the stands, there was even more controversy about the penalty award from which Albion drew level, Tommy Docherty rather harshly adjudged to have pulled down Ray Barlow. Allen converted.

We were on the back foot as Albion surged forward and with two minutes to go we capitulated when George Thompson misjudged a shot from Frank Griffin to concede a soft winner.

I was heavy-legged and weary as I made my way back to the sanctuary of the dressing room after the formalities were over, puzzling over why I had played so badly. Some journalists and supporters – I even heard our officials joining in – reckoned I had been carrying an injury. 'Nonsense,' I thought, 'I'm a hundred per cent fit.' But although my body was fine, as good as it had felt all season to be honest, whether my mental state matched up was highly questionable. Perhaps a lack of careful preparation cost me – where were my agents, my advisers and my management team when I needed them!

The atmosphere in our dressing room was flat. We needed cheering up and, in fairness to North End, every effort was made to get us smiling again. The directors might have resisted upping our bonuses beforehand, but they didn't skimp on the after-match do. Along with our wives and families we were whisked off to The Savoy, then London's top hotel with a tariff way beyond the reach of humble footballers, for a truly lavish reception. We were treated like royalty, tucking in to a banquet before sitting back to be entertained by Norman Wisdom and The Bachelors. The club also arranged for us all to stay overnight before returning to Preston by train on the Sunday morning.

The post-mortems went on for months although there was some respite at the official homecoming. We didn't feel we had much to celebrate but the supporters had other ideas and they generated a party mood. Just as they had at Wembley when 25,000 made the journey by car, coach, train and plane – the return airfare was £6 12s 6d (£6.63) – they cheered until they were hoarse. They danced and sang to 'Keep Right On To The End Of The Road' and many others and, just like The Savoy, they put on a reception fit to set before winners.

But, much as I tried, I felt what I was – a loser – and I had a medal to prove it.

CHAPTER EIGHT

Getting into bed with the press

They can make you and they can break you, but there is never anything to be gained by becoming their enemy. I refer, of course, to the gentlemen of the press.

If we agree that the way the game is played has changed, what about the way the game is covered in the newspapers? Football reporters in my day reported on football. It was that simple. Praise and criticism was directed at your public performance out on the pitch on a matchday. Your private life was left untouched and press intrusion was not an expression we heard at all in the 1950s. Match reporting was a mix of fact and opinion – the facts from the action and the opinion from the writer. I do not remember journalists ganging up afterwards to put a manager or a player on the spot like they do now.

I think it is deplorable the way a manager is expected to face a grilling from the media within minutes, sometimes seconds, of the final whistle. And you can bet your bottom dollar that the tone of the questioning will often relate to matters of so-called controversy – a particular decision from the referee, a mistake by a player, an off-the-ball incident, the reaction of the withdrawn party at a substitution.

Sometimes you pick up a Sunday tabloid to read about a match and end up little wiser by the time you have waded through paragraph after paragraph of manager speak. In my day, you rarely, if ever, read a manager sounding off about his team or individuals; what a manager had to say and to whom stayed within the confines of the dressing room.

At local level, you got to know your club reporter quite well and at Preston we were lucky to have a genuine gentleman to deal with. Walter Pilkington covered the playing affairs of North End for the *Post* for the duration of my career, and for a few years either side. A fine upstanding fellow, Walter was someone you could trust. He cared passionately for the club but still managed to retain an independent opinion.

Walter travelled on the team bus with us to away games, hearing and seeing everything that went on, but there was never the slightest problem or fear that he may betray a confidence or two. Perhaps that had something to do with the fact that we never got up to anything untoward. Our behaviour levels were extremely high, the club demanded that it should be so, and I cannot recall any unsavoury incidents or scandals. There may have been the occasional row but nothing more.

As for late-night boozy sessions or groups of players going off to nightclubs or messing about with girls or dentist's chairs – well, on away trips we had to be tucked up in bed by 9.30 on Friday nights and the trainer would do the rounds to make sure we were. When he knocked on your door it wasn't enough to shout back 'we're fine', you had to open it and let him see in for himself.

Walter lived outside that rule. He would often stay up and enjoy a drink or two with the official party. If memory serves me, Walter was quite keen on a drink – he certainly seemed to have no problem sleeping, when he eventually found his way to bed. Sometimes, a few of the lads would pop into his room during the early evening and make his bed up in such a way that it was hard to get in. Many a time we would stay awake until the early hours to listen out for the thud as he rolled off the blankets and on to the bedroom floor. We would pull his leg about it in the morning and he always seemed to see the funny side.

But if he was occasionally muddled on Friday nights – perhaps the directors plied him with drinks to keep him onside – his mind was always very clear when it came to reporting on Saturday afternoons. He was an intellectual chap with a good knowledge of the game, and he held very defined ideas on how it should be played with the emphasis on entertainment.

I got to know him as well as anyone, not just because of my long-service at Deepdale, but also because he regularly came along to international matches to give a 'local slant' by reporting on my form with England. In the main, he treated me well and we became quite good friends. I always had a strong affinity with the *Post* and for many years after my retirement I contributed a column to the Saturday football edition.

But not all the players fared so favourably. Walter could dish it out when he thought it necessary and consistently argued that he 'reported as he saw it'. On occasions, one or two of my colleagues took exception to Walter's opinions and sentiments. He must have had a knack of upsetting goalkeepers because I twice recall Jimmy Gooch and Malcolm Newlands taking him to task over his comments in match reports. Once Jimmy, normally quite a placid guy, got a little hot under the collar.

'Hey you, a word!' he bellowed on seeing Walter outside the ground. 'What was all that in the paper about my poor handling and accusing me of vital mistakes? Do you know the damage it can do? When was the last time you did any goalkeeping and how come you're such an expert all of a sudden?'

Walter stood there unmoved, clutching a closed notebook, and waiting for Jimmy to get his anger off his chest.

'Jimmy, calm down. The answer to your question is quite simple. I wrote it that way because that was the way I saw it. I have nothing against you, nothing at all. It was just my opinion.'

Jimmy had to accept the explanation. Arguing with journalists after the story has appeared is usually futile, a bit like contesting a referee's decision – only rarely can you demand or expect a retraction. My policy on these matters never wavered – if I felt I had played badly, I didn't read the papers.

To object to someone's opinion over how you played is one thing, but worse still is the dreaded misquote. It happened to me on a couple of occasions, none worse than an incident in January 1952 when a reporter really dropped me in it. Preston had drawn Bristol Rovers in the FA Cup third round and I was struggling to get fit after missing the previous First Division game at Newcastle with a strain. I travelled down with the team as usual and it was touch and go whether I played. In the end, the management decided that I should sit it out and let Gordon Kaile continue as my replacement in attack. They explained that they wanted to make sure I was fit and well for the following weekend's local derby with Bolton

Wanderers. Without appearing arrogant on behalf of those who made the decision, I think it is fair to say that they thought we could see off Rovers without my assistance. They were, after all, a team from the Third Division and even with home advantage few would have offered them much hope of progress.

But you know what they say about the Cup. We were over-powered by the West Country side who played beyond their limits and survived a clear-cut penalty claim against them to win 2–0 and send a crowd of more than 30,000 into raptures. Even allowing for a great show by Rovers, it was a pretty feeble effort on our part and we were all fairly subdued on the long coach journey back north.

The following morning I was astounded to read a Sunday newspaper article in which I was quoted as saying how poorly we had played. The account went on to say that I didn't feel we should have had a penalty and that we fully deserved to lose the match. It alleged that the interview had taken place in the Eastville boardroom. I was livid. For one thing I would never have said any of that about my team – not in public at any rate – and for another thing I hadn't taken part in any post-match interview. I had never set foot in the boardroom, having watched the game from the stand, gone down to the dressing room and then boarded the coach.

There are times when it is perhaps best advised to let things pass, but this was not one of them. My club, my colleagues and the people of Preston were not amused. They clearly felt that I had no right to turn on the team in that way and they would have been quite right had the information been correct.

I didn't know where to turn. The more I denied the story, the more people seemed to think it was true. I opted for a legal solution and consulted my solicitor who suggested I should contact the newspaper concerned and let my feelings be known.

The editor listened to my story – all of it factual – and went away to speak with the reporter involved. When he rang back the editor said he was prepared to publish an apology even though his reporter stood by the initial piece and was adamant that he had interviewed me. He said it was probably a case of mistaken identity. I had little option but to accept the apology and the reasoning although I never did find out who was masquerading as my double that day in Bristol.

Many footballers have suffered in similar circumstances and it is a wonder there are not more legal actions flying around. I firmly believe many of the football stories we read day in and day out are totally manufactured. Take the transfer gossip columns that appear in half the Sunday tabloids to feed the insatiable hunger of the fanatics. Suchabody is linked with a move to so-and-so. They talk about fees and sometimes get a quote or two from some 'spokesman' or 'source close to the club'. There can be twenty or thirty of these stories in each paper, but does anyone ever track back to see how much of the speculation turns into fact? You don't need to because when a paper gets one right, it flags it up with 'as we told you last week' in the following weekend's issue.

The papers are in close contact with agents and I daresay many a player is deliberately linked with a particular club in the hope of prompting a move. I'm sure managers are aware of it, too. I heard of one occasion when the manager of North End contacted a journalist at the *Post* to ask if he had any contacts on Fleet Street. He wanted to get a piece in the Sunday gossip columns about a First Division club being interested in one of his young starlets. There was no truth whatsoever in the story but the manager was hoping that by getting the 'information' into the public domain it would alert other top clubs and start an auction. With that example in mind, those within football cannot lay the blame for all the falsehoods that appear at the feet of the press.

I suppose the whole thing is a game not to be taken too seriously, but it is difficult when you find yourself on the receiving end.

I feel I can talk with some authority on media matters, having spent more than 14 seasons in press boxes across the land as a match analyst for the *News of the World*. As well as covering the big games of the time, including England internationals, I was also contracted to submit a weekly column. I had not been retired long when *News of the World* sports editor Frank Butler, a respected national journalist whom I knew well from my England days, contacted me about the possibility of signing on as a guest writer. The idea had immediate appeal, not least because it served as perfect vehicle for retaining an active contact with the game and the players.

'Oh, I'm so pleased,' said Frank. He sounded relieved because he had been trying to find a successor to his original star columnist, Frank Swift. 'The main column will be ghosted and we will send you along to a different First Division game every Saturday, accompanied by a writer from our desk who will get your views on the game and ghost the report. Can you start right away?'

A fee was agreed, from memory it was about £30 a week, which was decent money and 50 per cent more than my last pay packet as a player.

So between 1961 and 1975, I toured the major football venues of the North of England, watching top-level football and being paid for the privilege. Don Evans, a key figure at the *News of the World*, often acted as my personal scribe at the games. We would meet at the ground about an hour before kick-off, chat about some of the likely talking points and then digest the action. Don would fire a few questions at me before phoning the report to the copy desk in

Manchester. The system worked well and Don was also the guy who helped me compile my weekly column, coming over to our house to discuss the big stories and personalities of the day.

Although I have never been, and will never be, frightened of airing my views and opinions, I didn't go out of the way to be deliberately controversial and always steered well clear of over-the-top criticism. But if it needed saying, I wasn't afraid to speak out. Come on, you cannot be a national newspaper columnist and sit on the fence, can you? That said, I would have resigned from the post had there been any pressure to rubbish someone for the sake of it or to put my name to something I didn't believe. Not everyone agreed with my views – what a boring place the world would be if there were no differences of opinion – but rarely did I get called to task.

But there was one occasion when a player took great exception to what I had said about him in print. The player in question was Rodney Marsh, then of Manchester City, a tremendously talented player who also enjoyed playing the role of showman. On this particular afternoon, I felt that he had overdone the skylarking and wrote that he would be better advised to concentrate on playing and to cut out the tomfoolery. It was an honest opinion, but Rodney was far from pleased and not prepared to let the matter rest until he had found a suitable platform from which to respond. He was rattled and, sure enough, a few days later a follow-up story appeared with Rodney claiming I was way out of order and calling me old-fashioned.

Such instances of retaliation were few and far between and I thoroughly enjoyed my time as a sports reporter. In fact, I was very disappointed when the chapter closed. It wasn't a decision of my making; it was brought about by a trade union dispute. Frank Butler rang me to say that he was under pressure from members of the

National Union of Journalists who felt that I was operating outside the system.

'I'm sorry, Tom,' he said, 'but the union boys have got quite hot under the collar on this. They claim that you should become a member by training as a journalist – otherwise we won't be able to keep you on.'

Frank said that he would be happy to send me on a block-release journalism course in London, but I told him it was a non-starter. I could not afford the time away from my business.

'Fair dos, Tom,' he said. 'Thanks for all you have done.' I said much the same in response.

Walter Pilkington stayed local and always seemed to enjoy his job – so he should have done because short of being paid for playing, being paid for watching was an enviable way of earning a living.

Walter covered North End during the period generally regarded as the best in the club's long history. Although we probably never quite realised our true potential – slide-rule runners-up in the league and beaten finalists in the FA Cup – we did play our football with a certain panache. We were crowd pleasers and many opponents noticed above-average attendances when North End visited.

Attacking with zest and scoring goals was never much of a problem, but our general form did suffer and in season 1955–56 we went within a point of relegation. We still managed to find the net 73 times – more than Arsenal who finished fifth and 21 and 19 more than Aston Villa and Huddersfield who both finished just one point beneath us – and that after scoring superman Charlie Wayman had left. Luckily, the club had found a replacement forward of at least equal ability and effectiveness in front of goal.

Tommy Thompson, signed from Aston Villa, made his intentions known from the word go, turning in a brilliant debut performance, and scoring, as we thumped Everton 4–0 at Goodison Park. I benefited from Tommy's presence and grabbed a brace. He scored in the next two matches as well, wins over Luton Town and Newcastle United. That autumn of 1955, our instant-hit of a partnership ran and ran and ran. Tommy could read my game and I could read his. When the league tables were published, we were top dogs and would have laughed to a man if someone had dared forecast that a long winter fighting for survival lay in wait.

Even up to the turn of the year we seemed comfortable, if a little inconsistent, the main highlight coming at the seaside with a 6–2 triumph at Blackpool, but an FA Cup thrashing at West Ham was quickly followed by a run of five straight defeats. The warning signs were obvious.

Two months separated wins over Manchester United and Portsmouth. The win over United, the season's eventual champions, was a major result with Tommy Docherty particularly impressive as our driving force. After accounting for Pompey, we pulled off two good results against London opponents over Easter, winning 4–0 at Spurs and then, just 24 hours later, 1–0 at Chelsea courtesy of my successful penalty.

On the journey home to Lancashire there was a real sense of relief even though Willie Cunningham and Tommy Docherty were determined to keep our focus. One player, I can't remember who it was, made the mistake of suggesting that it was time to relax a bit. Let's just say Willie disagreed.

Some of the players clearly didn't take heed of Willie's warning and we made our supporters sweat until the death by losing our last three games. The directors clearly found the experience far too unpleasant to risk a repeat performance and promptly removed Frank Hill from the manager's office.

Tommy Thompson was one member of the senior side who could look back with satisfaction on his efforts, 23 goals – including one to remember back at Villa Park – and an ever-present record more than justifying his recruitment.

During the course of the campaign there was a period of great sadness for the club as a whole and for me as an individual with the passing of Jim Taylor. He might not have endeared himself to everyone all of the time and he certainly made mistakes and enemies, but no one could dispute his massive contribution to the cause of Preston North End. I was one of three players, along with Joe Walton and Harry Mattinson, invited to carry his coffin and I was proud to do so.

CHAPTER NINE

Striker light – a new role at 34

Bill Shankly could always embarrass me, even when he claimed he didn't mean to. Shanks certainly turned my face a bright shade of crimson when he said on television that I would have been a star player no matter in which position I had played. It was a tremendous compliment – he obviously never saw me in goal! He reckoned that all the truly great and gifted footballers were adaptable and flexible, able to perform to the highest standards irrespective of the circumstances or conditions.

I knew what he meant, but I always believed I was a right winger. In my day, right wingers played on the right wing against the opposing left full-back and the centre-half marked the centre-forward and so on. Utility players, such as midfield wingers, were products of the seventies and eighties when, from a positional sense, the game grew increasingly complex.

I was often commended for my versatility and the fact that I played for England in three different positions along the forward line has always given me a real sense of achievement. I switched to playing as an out-and-out centre-forward in the autumn of 1956 – the autumn of my career. I was 34 years old, the age when most players who endure the physical battering involved in leading the line head for the safety of the wings or 'retire' into defence. Yet here was I, several hundred games and many injuries down the line, about to do the opposite.

So how did it come about? Well, it is high time the facts were rolled out in full. Cliff Britton has been credited with moving me into the middle of the front line, but that's wrong. Jimmy Milne, then the North End trainer, instigated the switch before Cliff took over as manager.

Jimmy was in temporary charge of team affairs while the club looked for a successor to Frank Hill. Jimmy started the 1956–57 season with me in my usual right-wing slot. Dennis Hatsell wore the number 9 jersey, Angus Morrison was on the left and Jimmy Baxter and Tommy Thompson were the inside-forwards. The first two results were disastrous, a 4–1 drubbing at the hands of Tottenham Hotspur and a 3–1 beating by Manchester United, both at Deepdale. We went to Chelsea on the second Saturday with our chins on our chests and nothing much happened to ease our pain. We lost 1–0.

On the face of it, there was nothing particularly notable about that visit to Stamford Bridge, or so I thought. However, as it turned out, that was the afternoon when one of the most famous football pictures of all time was taken. Entitled 'The Splash', it was chosen as the national sports photograph of the year in 1956 and print sales now run into many thousands.

An incredible cloudburst just prior to kick-off – I have never seen rain like it before or since – left spectators soaked to the skin and the pitch so waterlogged you struggled to see the grass. The running tracks encircling Stamford Bridge were like rivers and, as we squelched around during the kick-in, Willie Cunningham made his feelings plain.

'It's going to be bloody hard going,' said Willie. 'So be on your toes, lads, right from the first whistle.'

The centre circle itself was a water hazard and every time you clashed with an opponent there was spray. Conditions were farcical and the game would never have gone ahead today.

The match-winning goal came after just six minutes when young Ron Tindall, a surprise choice over England star Roy Bentley, made the most of indecision in our defence to score from four yards.

The rain finally relented, but the playing surface hardly improved at all and I remember being left with water dripping off me more than once after challenges from Wally Bellett. I think, although it is difficult to tell, that Wally is the Chelsea defender featured in the photograph. He is partially covered by a huge spray of water as I try to keep my balance while sliding diagonally down the wing near to the corner flag. The photograph, which appeared on the football pages of most of the following day's national newspapers, was taken by John Horton, who lived in London and covered football matches across the capital on behalf of the Press Association.

I suppose I became synonymous with the photograph and I was most flattered when, in 2001, 'The Splash' was turned into a magnificent life-sized bronze statue and placed inside the main entrance of the National Football museum, which is housed at Deepdale. Many of my old team-mates came along to the official unveiling, including a trio of survivors from the Chelsea match – Fred Else, Sammy Taylor and Tommy Docherty. We talked for hours about the old days but little was said about that wet and miserable day at the Bridge. Our performance was so poor that the media started talking of us as clear relegation candidates. Walter Pilkington did not mince his words:

> After three games only six of the 92 clubs are pointless and Preston are one of them. Unless there is a radical and sustained improvement on the pathetic display at Chelsea there can be only one eventual outcome. Watching leaden-footed North End splashing around on a miniature lake was a truly depressing experience – they cannot hope to win matches by playing in this lackadaisical, disjointed and aimless fashion.

About ten minutes from time, Jimmy Milne had decided that desperate situations required desperate measures and he shouted for me to move to centre-forward. Although my positional switch didn't affect the outcome, I must admit that I enjoyed the cut and thrust of the role and I twice went close to scoring an equaliser. During the train ride home, Jimmy came over to sit with me. Sensing the seriousness of his tone and noticing the frown etched across his brow, I gave Jimmy my undivided attention. What he said went something like this:

'Tom, I need to ask your opinion on something. Three defeats in a row puts us in a grave situation and we have to find a way of getting out of this mess. I've been giving matters considerable thought and I wonder if you would have a go at centre-forward – it might just give us the spark we need.'

Now Jimmy Milne was at a great advantage here because I liked him. He was a super chap who served North End loyally and faithfully in every role imaginable, including a later spell as manager.

If there was ever a man for whom you would go the extra mile it was Jimmy. That is probably why I agreed to accept his challenge even before I had given myself any reasonable thinking time.

Was it wise to be switching roles so late in my career? How would it affect my England prospects? Would it work and what if it didn't? Was I putting my reputation on the line? All those doubts and questions came into my mind only after I had said, 'Yes, that sounds OK by me – we'll give it a go.'

Jimmy went off to offer up his brainwave to the mercy of the directors – just as Sir Alex Ferguson would do today, I don't think! – and they gave it the green light. Luckily, it was a fairly straightforward start – Manchester United, the reigning champions, at Old Trafford!

It was a midweek fixture and all the talk in Preston during the build-up centred round the arrival of our new manager but Cliff Britton was conspicuous by his absence in the dressing room beforehand. It was not until afterwards that he came to introduce himself, or 'announce himself', to the players.

A re-shuffled team, with Les Campbell taking my place on the right, put up a very spirited show. I scored with a penalty and we were unfortunate to lose by the odd goal in five. I felt I had adapted well to the new position even though I wondered whether my lack of inches and frail physique would hamper me over the long term. The manager did not share those concerns and his decision to stick with it for the next match paid a rich dividend as I scored twice in a 6–0 rout of Cardiff City.

It was at this point that my partnership with Tommy Thompson really began to blossom. When he didn't score, which was rare, I did and very often we both found the net in the same game. Statistics tell the story – Tommy bagged 26 league goals and I got 22; if you include the FA Cup, we shared 57 between us. It was just a wonderful friendship. Apart from becoming best mates off the park, we also enjoyed a very successful outing with an FA XI against the Army. Maine Road was the venue and Tommy and I were selected to start. We won 7–3, I scored two and Tommy, or 'Topper' as he had become known, hit a hat-trick.

Our partnership was not going unnoticed. On 6 April 1957 we were both picked for the England team to face Scotland at Hampden Park in the Home Championship. Tommy found himself in direct opposition to a certain Tommy Docherty in what must have amounted to a 'first' for Preston North End. I doubt whether Preston had ever had three players starting an England–Scotland encounter, let alone three players with the same first name.

It was an important international for me because I was asked to play down the middle in spite of a few people starting to get on my back. I am still puzzled about why. There was no obvious reason. I was playing to a high standard at club level and scoring plenty of goals, and I felt I was doing more than enough to justify my England place. But the media always needs a story and no footballer is allowed to go through a career without facing the critics. I lost count of the number of times Stanley Matthews was written off and now it was my turn. There was only one way to silence the doubters and that was to play well, and that's what I did in our 2–1 win. In the space of 90 minutes I was a hero again.

Scotland rocked us by scoring in the very first minute, not the best of starts for our debutant goalkeeper Alan Hodgkinson. Another first starter, Derek Kevan, pulled us level before a wonder goal from young Duncan Edwards brought the house down.

In spite of the absence of three top players on international duty, North End had to muster a team to play Wolves (cancellations because of call-ups were unheard of back then), and won 1–0 thanks to a goal from Jimmy Baxter.

Manchester United went on to retain their title. Surprisingly, our team included not one but two players who would later manage at Old Trafford. Apart from the Doc we had Frank O'Farrell, who was recruited from West Ham and who didn't sample the bitterness of defeat until his 17th game. Overall we had a hell of a season – a 16-match undefeated run, six goals against Cardiff, six more against Sunderland and then seven against Portsmouth, home crowds of knocking-on 40,000 and a third-place finish.

My new role as a centre-forward was heralded as a great triumph by the media and Cliff Britton was happy to accept the plaudits. The following season was better still. Topper and I ran riot to share 60 league goals – Tommy's 34 from 41 outings is still a club best – and the team hit the magical 100 figure, finishing runners-up to Wolves. We didn't run the Molineux men as close as we had run Arsenal five years earlier, but I bet the supporters enjoyed this season more, much more. I certainly did.

Ask me for a highlight and it must be our 8–0 trouncing of Birmingham. Tommy scored a hat-trick, as did Sammy Taylor, and I got the other two. Pop into a Preston pub and mention Birmingham City and, even today, someone will say, 'Oh yes, 8–0. What a bloody match that was!'

Our 'ton' goal came against the Gunners in a last-day 3–0 win, and it was only right and proper that Tommy should get it. He had a run of scoring in 11 consecutive games (17 in total) and those doubters who had feared there could be no goalscoring life after Charlie Wayman had to eat extra large helpings of humble pie. It would be smug of me to say I never questioned the wisdom of selling Charlie. At the time, it appeared nonsensical, but we counted without Tommy – a Preston North End great in every sense of the word.

Tommy and I chatted a lot about the game. One night he said, 'Tom, I never thought moving to Preston would turn out to be such a dream for me.'

'Well, I've never known football away from Deepdale,' I replied, 'so I've nothing to compare it with, but all I will say is that it feels pretty damn good to me, too.' And it did.

I was voted Footballer of the Year again, the prize rated so highly among the players. I still maintain that winning it for the second time was the biggest single thrill of my career.

I was the darling of the media; even I could not believe some of the things I read. I had assumed a status well beyond what felt comfortable and some of the headlines and platitudes made me cringe. My old friend Walter Pilkington wrote: 'Great is the football glory of Tom Finney, the artificer and designer who can so magically turn his tormenting skill into the finished product bearing the master stamp.' At 36, I was enjoying an Indian summer, playing top-flight football as captain of Preston, and World Cup football for England. If Tommy Thompson couldn't believe his luck, where did it leave me?

Deep down, I knew it couldn't last. The good times are temporary in football and the 1958–59 season proved to be the beginning of the end for me. For starters, I moved out to outside-left, which I always rated my least effective position, and I was dogged by injury managing to play in just 16 league matches and score only six times. We never threatened to retain our top-three position and eventually did well to finish halfway.

Genuine optimism at the outset proved grossly misplaced. We had lost Tommy Docherty to Arsenal, Tommy Thompson had needed knee surgery during the close season and there was a feeling that an excellent team was past its best. However, the players were anxious to turn their superb football over the past couple of years into a tangible return. For all our entertaining, we continued to stand on the outside of football's major honours and, believe me, it gets a little wearying, always occupying the role of nearly men. When we lost just twice in the first dozen games, we started to believe this could be our year at long last. I started 11 of them, missing a goalless draw at Bolton, but injury again struck me down and I featured in just five more games.

The team's form dipped alarmingly, and we crashed to heavy defeats at Birmingham (1–5), Blackpool (2–4) and Blackburn Rovers (1–4) and at home to Burnley (0–4) and Nottingham Forest (3–5). I made an abortive attempt at a comeback in that Christmas Day defeat at Blackpool when our line-up included 16-year-old goalkeeper John 'Boy' Barton. Classed as an amateur, John had made his debut five days earlier in a magnificent 2–1 win over Arsenal at Highbury, receiving rave reviews. He pulled off a series of stunning second-half saves to keep Arsenal at bay, including a late header from a certain Tommy Docherty.

The Doc's replacement in the North End line-up proved to be one of the season's successes. Gordon Milne, son of North End stalwart Jimmy, was born close to Deepdale but had found his first-team chances strictly limited. As a half-back, he was up against the likes of Docherty and Jimmy Baxter who were looked upon as automatic choices. Gordon's progress at club level was also handicapped by National Service, but he was a regular in the British Army XI and played in representative matches against France in Paris and Scotland in Glasgow.

He featured in 30 games for North End during the 1958–59

season but was later sold to Liverpool in a most peculiar deal. Bill Shankly was the Anfield boss who paid £17,000 for Gordon, and Jimmy Milne was the North End manager who agreed to sell his son to his former team-mate.

Gordon had a sound career at Liverpool, playing 300 games before ending his playing days with Blackpool. Like his father, he was a deep thinker on the tactical side of the game and he moved into management with great success. He cut his teeth with Wigan Athletic, and spells at Coventry City and Leicester City preceded a distinguished spell in Turkey with Besiktas.

While our league form was disappointing in the extreme, there was hope among the fans that another Wembley date might be on the cards in the FA Cup as we swept past Derby County and Bradford City to set up a fifth-round date with Bolton Wanderers. But this wasn't a Cup tie – more a mini series. The first meeting ended all square at 2–2, the replay 1–1 and by the time we reached a second replay at Ewood Park, the fans were breathless and I was among their number, nursing injury, as we lost 1–0.

I frequently use that Cup marathon as an example of football's huge popularity in those days; the aggregate attendance for the three matches topped 146,000.

Being sidelined for so long allowed plenty of time for thinking. My international career was at an end and for the first time I was beginning to ask serious questions of myself. I could hear the door creaking shut and it was not a pleasant sound.

CHAPTER TEN

Bowing out

It was ironic that my best season for appearances should also by my last – it was also the only season that I was top scorer. Injuries interrupted my career consistently – there was an occasion when I came close to packing it in altogether – and I was never able to claim an ever-present prize. A variety of strains and sprains, coupled with international calls, accounted for the fact that my appearances average during 14 seasons was 31 games out of the standard 42. But in my farewell season of 1959–60, I managed to play in all but five matches and also helped myself to 17 goals (21 if you count the FA Cup) – not bad for a fellow deemed to be on his last legs.

It was a reasonably satisfactory season all round. We won more than we lost and finished ninth, only 11 points adrift of champions Burnley. We had the pleasure of beating them at Deepdale in the

September, courtesy of one of my goals. We also reached the sixth round of the Cup, eventually dipping out to Aston Villa, and were involved in one of the most remarkable matches imaginable against Chelsea at our place.

Chelsea had provided our opening-day opposition. It finished 4–4 and could not have been bettered in terms of sheer entertainment, or so we thought. But the return meeting on the last Saturday before Christmas went one better – one goal better, or worse, depending on your allegiance. We lost 4–5 in what was an epic.

We were flying high as Chelsea arrived on the back of four straight defeats, just ripe for a good hiding. It was a gloomy afternoon, more like a night match with the floodlights on from the start, but the standard of play was electric. The ball was in either one penalty box or the other for the duration. Ultimately, we had to doff our caps to the goal-scoring brilliance of a certain Jimmy Greaves. A hat-trick hero in the first meeting, this time he helped himself to all five.

Jimmy got the ball rolling with Chelsea's opener before Tommy Thompson and then Dave Sneddon put us 2–1 up. But ace poacher Jimmy was not to be outdone and he scored twice in a frantic three-minute spell, the first a truly superb solo effort. He was far from finished and added two more before we responded with a stirring late fightback. Tommy added another couple for his hat-trick, but we couldn't quite find the equaliser.

The only disappointment came in the size of the crowd. Just over 15,000 side-stepped the festive shopping expedition and braved the elements. The estimated 10,000 stay-aways really missed their way that day.

Deepdale was packed to the rafters on the following 30 April for what was to be my last game at professional level. I can recall that emotion-charged afternoon as though it happened last week. I was sad, not just for me it seemed, but for Preston the town and Preston North End the football club.

The announcement of my retirement, while not totally unexpected, still came as a shock to the people of Preston. I had played through the pain barrier more than once, but found one groin strain increasingly troublesome and decided to consult the experts. The doctors were unanimous. I knew what they were saying was right but that didn't make it any easier. No one prepares you for 'hang up your boots' time. I felt sick.

Elsie and I talked things over, not focusing so much on whether I should stop playing, that was already decided, but how to go about it. Indeed, if Elsie had been the decision-maker supreme, my football career would have ended long before this – five years earlier to be precise.

I had developed a mystery back problem during the 1954–55 season, a nagging ache that travelled down through my thigh and caused extreme discomfort. I still don't know the cause but it certainly affected my performance on the park. Although I struggled through 30 games, I was well below par in the majority of them and managed only seven goals. When I ran it hurt, when I turned it hurt, even when I rested it hurt; and when I got home after training, it nagged and nagged so much that I fell into depression. I tried all sorts of remedies, even buying a special cushion, but nothing worked. Without wishing to sound a martyr, I kept going for the good of the team; we were in a relegation dogfight. It was only at Easter, when our position appeared relatively safe, that I opted out and took a rest.

Rightly or wrongly, I was dogged by guilt whenever an injury flared up. I knew my value to the team cause and North End officials always let it be known that they would prefer it if I was able to play, to forget the pain for 90 minutes and give it my best shot. With the benefit of hindsight, I was daft to be goaded into turning out unfit and having all those pain-killing injections. The consequences could have been severe. I was lucky – I got away with it.

Internationally, I won just one cap that season – against Germany at Wembley – and it was more than I deserved. I felt I was selected on reputation rather than current form and that frustrated and annoyed me.

After we had drawn with Bolton, I decided the time had come to say 'enough is enough' and I asked to meet with manager Frank Hill. Frank was under pressure and it was not the news he wanted to hear, but he did me proud, agreeing that if I was unfit I should withdraw from competitive action and seek the best advice.

The club booked me a check-up at Preston Royal Infirmary to try to get to the root of the problem. However, as any fellow-sufferers will testify, back pain is sometimes impossible to diagnose and so it was with me. The consultants carried out tests, pushed and poked and prodded and examined numerous X-rays but were unable to find a way forward apart from recommending a period of rest and relaxation. 'Wear a surgical corset, get your feet up and follow an exercise plan' was about the top and bottom of it although I still had my doubts. Something felt very wrong. I could hardly walk for the stiffness and pain. I felt like a cripple.

Elsie was equally perturbed and she was all for me quitting football. I remember one day she came into the living room to hear me grumbling about the pain and said, 'Tom, this is crazy. You can't carry on playing like this. Think of the damage you might do for later in life. North End will just have to manage without you – your health is all that matters.'

In the summer of 1955, with my future still up in the air

(privately, at least), I pulled out of an England tour to the Continent and a Preston tour to Scotland. Instead, Elsie, Brian, Barbara and I headed for Rhodesia for a coaching trip organised for me by the Football Association. Prior to departure we received some welcome news. A top city specialist informed me that my back problem was being caused by a sciatic nerve and by following a course of intense treatment it would eventually sort itself out.

Thankfully, he was dead right. During six weeks in Rhodesia, I improved enough not only to take an active part in coaching sessions but also to play in some exhibition matches – and pick up £200 in fees. The career I feared was over was suddenly back on track as the pain simply disappeared. I even agreed to play in a couple of games in Kenya on the way home.

But football catches up with every player. The Stanley Matthews of this world are not rare – apart from the man himself, they are non-existent. He was unique. So during the 1959–60 campaign, I decided it was time to bite the bullet and retire. I managed to play the first 22 games in a row, which was not bad for a veteran player operating at the sharp end of the team with a body that many said could let me down at any time. In fact, I played in 37 of the 42 league matches and in all six of our Cup outings. Only goalkeeper Fred Else, Dave Sneddon, Joe Walton and Gordon Milne could better that appearance record.

Suggestions that I was in failing physical order were clearly misplaced although I must concede that I often played while feeling the effects of strains, and it was starting to take me longer and longer to recover after matches. Elsie saw this at first hand and did not need much persuading when I broached the subject of retirement. I wrote the following letter to chairman Nat Buck and handed it to the manager, Cliff Britton:

Dear Mr Buck,

I find this letter difficult to write but it is only a reflection of the problems that have confronted me in arriving at one of the major decisions in my life.

I have decided to retire from football, at least in the active sense, as from the end of this current season. I have given a lot of thought to this problem. I have discussed it with my wife and family and my business associates and I have had quite a few sleepless nights before making up my mind.

I came straight into North End's first team more than 20 years ago. I have remained in it ever since and want to go out while still in good health, physical condition and playing ability. I do not want to drift out due to either deterioration arising from increasing age or the ever-present possibility of serious injury, which could have a lasting effect on my future fitness.

As you know, I had a lot of trouble with my groin injury last season, which fortunately has not as yet recurred. Nevertheless, I have had one or two twinges of pain which remind me that the possibility of a recurrence is still there and reinforced my desire not to tempt providence any further.

Football has provided me with a long, happy and enjoyable career not without its material benefits. It has allowed me to travel all over the world and to meet people from all walks of life whom, apart from football, I should never have had the opportunity of knowing. I want to go out with these memories and recollections untarnished.

I should like in this letter to say thank you to you, your predecessor Mr Jim Taylor, your directors and all who have assisted in the management of the club in the 21 years I have been associated with it.

Thank you for your help and assistance throughout that period and the happy relationship that has always existed between us.

Comment is frequently made in the Press about a player remaining loyal to one club throughout his career, but in so far as it takes two to make a bargain, a relationship such as ours is reciprocal. It reflects loyalty on the part of the directorate and management to me and it is for this that I most want to express my appreciation.

There is one other point on which I should like to comment. It may be a presumption on my part to imagine that efforts may be made to bring about a change in my decision but I would prefer that this should not be done and that my decision should be treated as irrevocable.

As I said earlier in this letter, it has not been easy to contemplate retirement. It has taken me a long time to make up my mind. I have vacillated quite a lot and do not want to go through a similar period of indecision again.

Finally, although retiring in the active sense, I would not like to think that I was severing my connection with football, the game that has given me so much enjoyment and to which I owe so much. Nor would I like to think that my association with my one and only club was coming to an end. If, therefore, I can continue to serve the interests of the club in any capacity whatsoever, I shall be only too happy to do so.

Yours very sincerely,

Tom Finney

Mr Buck called the board to an emergency meeting on the Monday night, 25 April. I don't know what went on or what was said but I do know that Preston's directors played ball with me. They took notice of my views and accepted my decision without trying for a moment to impose any pressure. Within a couple of days I received a letter in which the directors expressed their shock but said that they accepted my motives and my decision.

However, that official response, while very prompt, did not reach my door before news of my intention reached the public domain. The *Lancashire Evening Post* were tipped off and the Tuesday night edition was full of it. Football, or any sport for that matter, was always at the back end of the paper but this time the editor made an exception. Walter Pilkington, who obviously had good contacts within the Deepdale hierarchy, contacted me, and a photographer was dispatched to my business for an on-the-day picture. That photograph underneath the headline 'The end of an era' was given prime spot on the front page.

Walter was clearly shocked. 'Tom, I'm sad to hear you're calling it a day,' he said. 'What's prompted all this?'

'Walter, you've seen me more than anyone over the years and you will appreciate just what a wrench it is,' I replied. 'I probably won't realise the scale of the decision for some time, but I always knew the day would arrive and I didn't want to end up on the scrap heap. I never fancied the idea of being in and out of the side, constantly resting to get fit again and all of that – being chosen on reputation rather than on merit or value to the team.

'Rest assured that this is no snap decision. I've been giving it serious thought for months, and I've also been getting twinges from my groin again, which has reinforced my resolve to quit.'

The *Post*, not known for sensationalism, reckoned the news

would rock the sporting world and they gave the story prominence over the main national news of the day – one of Britain's biggest trade unions, the Shop, Distributive and Allied Workers (USDAW), revolting against Prime Minister Harold Macmillan's atom bomb policy.

Well, without wanting to sound flippant, it was as though a bomb had dropped on Preston. The reaction left me speechless. There was an outcry across the town as Preston's supporters made it clear that they would not let me go without a fight.

Letters poured in to the newspaper, people stopped me in the street or tried to contact me at home and it seemed that everyone had an opinion. Stanley Matthews, who knew a thing or two about footballing longevity and fitness, said he was both disappointed and surprised. I will never forget reading his article in the paper, not least because he referred to me as 'the greatest player in the world'. Have I ever received a bigger compliment? No. Stan thought that the way I had been playing that particular season would have delayed any retirement decision. He actually thought I could have played on for three more years.

Funnily enough, Stan and I were both due to go to South Africa that summer to do some coaching and play games in the newly formed semi-professional league. In the end, I couldn't go but Stan still went. At 45, thoughts of retirement had not even entered his head.

Stan called for me to be handed a role with the FA and the Football League, but the debate on whether I was finishing too early went on for several days. A few people accepted my decision but the main thrust centred around getting me to have a change of heart.

I was flattered but unmoved. No amount of pressure would get me to reverse my decision. I just couldn't afford it to. I had to have my say and took the opportunity in my regular column in the *Post*:

This has been such a difficult decision. In reaching it I experienced many nagging doubts and sleepless nights. There were many things to consider and over them all lay the question of the possible recurrence of my groin injury. I want to go out of football while I am at the top rather than when the game has finished with me. Football has provided me with a grand life and I have never once had a regret over taking up the game as a career, but now I must look ahead. With the plumbing business, my future might be said to be assured, but I have spent almost a lifetime in football and it is not something I can turn off like a tap. I would dearly love to put something back in to football and have already told Preston that if they feel I can be of service then I will be only too happy to assist. I think I would get most satisfaction in trying to help the younger players as a coach rather than dealing with men who are already established. If the opportunity to manage a club arose, then I would consider it, even though it would mean leaving both my family business and my native town. Given the precarious nature of such a job, however, I would have to think about it very deeply.

After that, people suddenly seemed to begin to understand my motives. Walter did me a huge favour in calling my retirement 'sensible . . . considering all circumstances' in a lengthy article underlining the facts, some of which even came as news to me. The atmosphere changed and all the talk centred around my final appearance and what the club and the town would do to mark my career. Another front-page story talked of the public rising up to demand a testimonial game.

The mayor of Preston, Alderman Mrs Florrie Hoskin, said that the council offices had been besieged by calls asking what plan was in place. She did a neat body swerve to buy a bit of time, saying, 'Our stance will be announced at the appropriate time, but it is a little premature as Tom Finney's contract with Preston North End does not run out until the end of June.'

Although I was considered a fixture in the Preston team for 14 years, and had never been dropped or played for the reserves, it transpired that I had missed 155 league matches during that period. Over 90 per cent of those absences were injury or illness related.

It is fair to say that in the early part of that traumatic week, my mind was not exactly focused on our final fixture at home to bottom club Luton Town. For one thing there was the retirement and for another there was injury! In a 2–1 defeat by Manchester City at Maine Road the previous Saturday, I had damaged my heel and aggravated my groin. The headlines changed to 'Finney may already have played his last match'.

I was absolutely determined that would not prove to be the case and spent hour upon hour having treatment. I knew I wouldn't be 100 per cent and so did Cliff Britton, but we both accepted how important it was for me to lead the team out against Luton. I think he also saw it as an excuse to make some experimental changes. In the event, only Gordon Milne and I survived from the front five who had played against City seven days earlier. In fairness to the manager, he was very understanding and he even agreed to my request to play on the right wing, wearing the number 7 shirt for the 214th time.

Although our indifferent form had caused attendances to slump and there was nothing particularly inspiring about an otherwise meaningless end-of-season fixture, close on 30,000 people turned out to wave me off into the sunset. It was a strange atmosphere, jubilant to start with and very tearful later on. The matchday programme carried a message from the board in which they placed on record their 'abiding appreciation and heartfelt thanks' for my career with the club.

I tried to go about my business in the normal way, but I was deeply conscious of this being anything but a normal occasion. Simple things I had done dozens, no hundreds, of times were different. Walking to the ground, getting changed, chatting with the other players – it all seemed odd, very odd.

Then there were all the letters, calls and messages that arrived from all over the country and from overseas. Some were from friends, some from strangers. They came from fellow players, football managers, including my old pals Bill Shankly and Andy Beattie, and various notables within the game. Joe Richards and Alan Hardaker, the respective President and Secretary of the Football League, both sent telegrams. Hundreds and hundreds of well-wishers thanked me for my efforts and the pleasure I had given them over the years. It was a humbling experience, very moving.

Goalkeeper Fred Else and defender Joe Dunn were among those who took it upon themselves to help me through it all, but there was no escaping the reality and the reality was churning me up inside. We walked down the tunnel to be greeted by warm sunshine and a red-hot reception. The applause was deafening. People had arrived at the ground very early; estimates suggest close on 20,000 were in place half-an-hour before kick-off, and some of them had travelled long distances, including a pal of mine, Fred Varley, who had come from Rhodesia.

I almost broke down when the two sets of players lined up in a train of honour. Cliff Britton, Nat Buck and the other eight directors stood side by side on the touchline as the crowd, led by the Brindle

Prize Band, sang 'Keep Right On To The End Of The Road' and 'He's A Jolly Good Fellow'. After a pause for the cheering to subside, the ceremony continued as the players and officials joined hands in traditional fashion to sing 'Auld Lang Syne'. It was time for a stiff upper lip. I was enjoying the unique pre-match entertainment, but I was also looking forward to getting the game under way although I had rarely felt less able to play.

Eventually we got on with warming up and Luton skipper Allan Brown and I were summoned by the referee for the usual formalities. I won the toss and elected to kick towards the Town End, hoping to benefit from a stiffish breeze at our backs.

Quite honestly, I do not recall enough about the match to give a verdict on it. People later told me it was no great shakes but that I had played well. The general standard of play was fairly uninspiring – two carefree teams with little to play for on a dry and bumpy pitch. I also believe that all the hype beforehand coupled with the warm spring conditions left all those present emotionally drained – no one more so than me. Everyone was quick to make excuses and some reckoned the occasion itself had beaten both teams. The newspaper reports were kind to me although much praise was handed to Luton's full-back Alan Daniel for his performance as my direct opponent. For all that, I did manage to bow out a winner thanks to goals from my replacement at centre-forward, young Alec Alston, and our consistent left-half Jim Smith.

Alec put us ahead just after the half-hour mark when Luton centre-half Terry Kelly was caught in two minds over whether to clear or pass back. After earlier missing an open goal, Alec nipped in to place a shot beyond Ron Baynham. The goal served as a real boost, not least to Alec who orchestrated our second decisive strike just two minutes after the break. His energetic running created space and I turned his cross into the path of Jim Smith who converted from ten yards.

It was a satisfactory afternoon's work but, though I say so myself, the goal the crowd really wanted never materialised. It wasn't that I didn't have any chances. I did and I really should have done better after working an opening for myself late on only to fluff my shot.

Come the final whistle, amid the cheers and tears, many supporters ran on to the pitch to slap me on the back and shake my hand. I was handed a microphone and hoisted on to a platform to make a speech.

'I hardly know what to say,' I managed to get out. 'It's such a sad, sad day for me. I would like to thank you all for the wonderful support I have enjoyed during my time here. Also for the many marvellous tributes paid to me in letters from all over England. I would like to thank the North End directors and my colleagues for making it such a wonderful time while I have been at Deepdale. It is sad but today is a day I will remember for ever and thank you all for making it so grand.'

After the match I was invited up to the boardroom for a private ceremony. That was a genuine break from custom because it was the very first time that a North End player had set foot in the boardoom. My family, who were club guests for the day, were there too and Nat Buck paid me a tribute on behalf of the club while Mayor Hoskins did likewise on behalf of the town.

Then I went to shake a few more hands before Elsie and I headed for home, pleased that the day I had dreaded had gone so well and mighty relieved that it was all over. Tom Finney the player was now history.

That fact was brought home on the Monday night when the *Post*'s main back-page sports story talked of North End's plans for the future, revealing that six players, Dennis Hatsell, Harry Mattinson, Les Campbell, Alex Farrall, Ken Hayes and Johnny Byrne were to be transfer listed. It recorded that for the first time in 20 years the name Tom Finney did not feature upon the Preston North End retained list and that, having retired, I was now a free agent and no longer registered with the Football League. All of it was true, but I still found the reality hard to take. It may sound extreme but it was a bit like reading your own obituary.

So I had finished playing football for Preston North End – well, not quite. The club had arranged an end-of-season tour to Switzerland, a country we visited regularly, but I never thought for a moment that I would be either invited or involved. Along with Stanley Matthews, I had accepted an offer to play a few games in South Africa, but I had counted without Cliff Britton. The manager made his feelings plain.

'We have planned this on the understanding that you will be part of the squad,' he told me bluntly. He was not for wavering either, even though I explained in detail that as a retired player I considered myself free to make my own choices and that I had given certain assurances to the South Africa football authorities.

'Look here,' he said in a tone that suggested no compromise. 'The simple fact is that we have promised that you will go and if you back out the trip is off.' With that he turned away, but not before reminding me that I was contractually linked to the club until the end of June. There was little to be gained in having a stand-up row and I accepted my fate.

'Fair enough, then,' I said. 'If that's how it is, that's how it is.'

My contacts in South Africa were very understanding when I rang them. They told me not to worry and that the offer stood. 'Get here when you can' was the gist of their stance and I appreciated it.

I did manage to get over for a much-shortened visit later in the summer and enjoyed every minute.

The trip with North End went well, too. Switzerland is a beautiful country and we stayed for about ten days, playing just two games against Servette and Chaux De Fonds. We beat Servette 2–1, Alec Alston and I the marksmen, and did even better against Chaux De Fonds, winning 4–1 thanks to goals from Alec and Dave Sneddon and a couple from me. So those who reckon that it was a shame that I failed to mark my last appearance for North End with a goal were mistaken – I actually signed off with a brace.

It would be misleading to say that retirement came easy; it didn't. There were times when I wanted to reverse the decision and make a comeback. That feeling could come over me anywhere and at anytime. I could be driving the car or watching the television or be out on site on a plumbing assignment when suddenly I would think, 'Have I done the right thing?' I did have doubts and more than once I could have been talked into playing again.

It's at times like this that you need a partner with inner strength and common sense. Elsie was not for hearing such nonsense and stood firm. While I fantasised about the romance of a return to playing, she pointed out all the disadvantages, reminding me of the many reasons why I had taken the option to quit in the first place.

'Be glad you're still in one piece,' she said. 'You've had your footballer career, Tom, and enjoyed every minute of it, but that chapter is closed now. It's time to move on.'

How right she was.

CHAPTER ELEVEN

My battle of Britton

Few people who knew me as a footballer would ever cast me in the role of troublemaker or rebel. I had opinions and wasn't afraid to voice them, but it took an awful lot to get my back up, as I think my disciplinary record illustrates. In all honesty, I cannot recall seriously falling out with any of my colleagues – club or country – or any opponents for that matter. Even those ruthless full-backs who spent winter afternoons kicking me up hill and down dale were always offered a hand to shake come the final whistle. I never understood the point of bearing a grudge. I was something of a retiring individual off the field, too, a peace lover who liked the quiet life.

But there was one individual with whom I had more than one bust-up – Clifford Samuel Britton, the Preston manager for the final four years of my playing career.

Cliff Britton had been a great player. In a distinguished career he had made more than 200 appearances for Everton, and he was part of that majestic England half-back line alongside Joe Mercer and Stan Cullis. Later he became manager of Burnley, leading them to promotion to the First Division and the FA Cup final. His impressive record at Turf Moor earned him the managerial seat back at Everton, but he resigned after a clash with the directors and, in 1956, took charge at Deepdale. It was reported that he decided he could not continue at Goodison Park because of 'interference' and that the board had not given him the 'freedom to manage in my own way'.

He was obviously power mad. I didn't care for him and couldn't tolerate the ridiculously overstrict and unsympathetic way in which he dealt with players. I am the first to advocate discipline within football. Clubs must impose, and players must adhere to, a code of conduct, but it is important to know when to relax the rules. Cliff just didn't know how to ease off and it led to some almighty rows.

A few examples spring to mind. On one occasion I was accused of setting the worst sort of example to my team-mates, and on another I openly defied his instructions.

The first confrontation occurred on the train back from an away game. I cannot for the life of me remember whom we had been playing or the result, but the manager was adamant that none of the players should be permitted an alcoholic drink. He had even gone so far as to inform the head waiter of this instruction and I thought it was just plain silly. Out of devilment, and in view of the manager's on-going miserable attitude, I ordered a glass of beer. That was unheard of because I didn't drink and when the lads saw what the skipper was doing they followed suit.

On the Monday morning I was hauled into the manager's office to be told in no uncertain terms that I had let him down, the club

The wartime PNE first team line-up of 1941 – I am to the far left of the front row.

Through the mist Billy Wright, that fine half-back with whom I shared many an England international, tries to intercept a shot from me during a First Division match with Wolverhampton Wanderers in 1947.

Greeting Bobby Langton as the winger arrives from neighbours Blackburn Rovers in August 1948. Dubbed the flying machine, Bobby, with whom I played for England, didn't stay long, just over a season, before moving to Bolton. (*Lancashire Evening Post*)

Just about managed to keep this one in. Crossing from the right touchline at Deepdale.

Bill Scott gives us a team talk in the unlikely setting of the Bull and Royal hotel in Preston town centre. I am fifth from the left in the back row, Malcolm Newlands is to my right and Joe Walton to my left. Bobby Langton is seated in front of us.

Signing autographs was part and parcel of daily life – I tried never to refuse and still don't. Here I am with a few 'hunters' after a training session at Deepdale.

Getting in a cross during the FA Cup final in 1954 – it was one of my most disappointing performances at Wembley. (*Colorsport*)

That losing feeling. A long walk back to the dressing room at Wembley after we had lost to West Bromwich Albion in the Cup final. L-r: Charlie Wayman, Bobby Foster, Joe Marston, me, Angus Morrison and Tommy Docherty. (*Lancashire Evening Post*)

Raising a glass to defeat after the Cup final are: Tommy Docherty, Harry Mattinson, Willie Cunningham, me, Charlie Wayman, Jimmy Baxter, Willie Forbes and Joe Marston.

Norman Wisdom was the guest entertainer at a party held at the Savoy hotel in London after the Cup final. My brother Joe, his wife Beatrice and Elsie and I are pictured with Norman.

Addressing the thousands of Prestonians who greeted us when we made a public appearance on the Town Hall steps after the FA Cup final. As captain it was up to me to say a few words – of apology!

Left: Training conditions could be tough in the middle of an English winter. I manage to negotiate a difficult surface to get beyond Harry Mattinson and fire a shot towards Fred Else. (*Lancashire Evening Post*) Right: I always enjoyed training and particularly liked the fitness sessions in the gymnasium at Deepdale where we were encouraged to build up our physical strength. (*Lancashire Evening Post*)

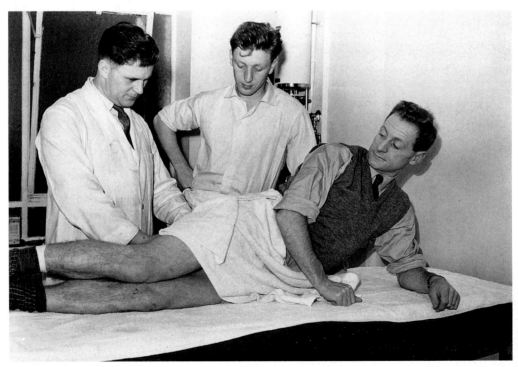

I can't imagine many modern-day players keeping their ties on while they had treatment. Des Coupe gets to work watched by PNE team-mate Dennis Hatsell.

Forward Tommy Thompson arrived at Deepdale late in my career, but we enjoyed a fine spell together and scored many goals between us. We also became firm friends and next-door neighbours, and here we are talking about football as we relax in the garden at Regent's Drive.

I was very fortunate to win the prestigious Footballer of the Year award twice, here in 1954 and again in 1957. (*Lancashire Evening Post*)

Perhaps the saddest moment in my career. Walking off the hallowed turf of Deepdale after my final appearance for Preston against Luton on 30 April 1960. I still get a lump in my throat when I see this photograph and recall that amazing day. (*Lancashire Evening Post*)

My testimonial match at Deepdale was a wonderful affair, more than 33,000 watching some of the true greats share a 13-goal feast. I scored twice, including this headed effort with Alex Parker of Everton looking on. (*Lancashire Evening Post*)

down, the players down and myself down and that I could consider myself fortunate to retain the captaincy. I responded by telling him that he had gone too far, that the senior players could be trusted to be sensible in matters relating to drink and that, if anything, his policies were more likely to create problems than solve any.

But if I was annoyed over that, I was positively livid when he tried to stand in the way of a commercial opportunity. One of the major London stores had approached me about making a personal appearance. They had checked our fixture list, spotted we were due to play an evening match at Arsenal and asked whether I would be able to spare some time to call in. Our travelling arrangements for evening away games were tight – 11 a.m. train from Preston, 3.30 p.m. into Euston and on to the ground for a 7 p.m. kick-off. I wrote back to explain, but told them I would make time by catching an earlier train.

Unfortunately, Cliff Britton didn't seem to think that was such a good idea. He basically asked me what I thought I was playing at, and said that he didn't want me in a shop when I should be resting and that it was all out of the question. His condescending attitude and his clear lack of faith in my judgement infuriated me more than I could ever tell you. He refused to budge and so, rightly or wrongly, I chose to ignore him and went down to London to honour the engagement. He wasn't very pleased about it but no further action was taken.

Few players had Cliff Britton down as their ideal boss. Tommy Docherty left because of him. It was a great shame really because he had a lot of sound ideas and a good football brain. He fell down in perhaps the most important area of them all – man-management.

He was never over-keen on losing you for international duty either, but he wasn't the only club manager to feel bitter about that.

It was a straightforward business back then – when the call came, you jumped and your club had to put up and shut up. At Preston, we often had up to four players missing at any one time, but there was no choice. Country came before club every time and a vital league match was rated a very poor second to an international fixture, even a relatively meaningless friendly. The situation was made worse for the clubs when their star players picked up long-term injuries while playing for their countries. All things considered, it surprised me that it took as long as it did for the authorities to allow clubs to postpone matches when a certain number of players were absent on international duty.

Cliff Britton and I had a further tasty encounter of the verbal kind when he suddenly decided he wanted to play me on the left wing instead of the right. We had signed Derek Mayers and Cliff fancied him on the right, which meant me having to switch. As a recognised right winger of some standing in the game, I felt aggrieved and told the manager so.

'What's the matter, you've played often enough as outside-left with England?' he countered.

'With all due respect, England is England and Preston is Preston,' I said. 'I will, of course, always play wherever I'm selected, but the fact remains that outside-left is my least favoured position and I simply feel of greater value to the team on the right.'

We rowed and he won, but not for long. I spent the last three years playing as an out-and-out centre-forward.

It is fair to say that Cliff Britton, great player and master tactician, but a cold man missing any sort of sense of humour, was the least popular of all the managers I played under at Preston. There were only four in total and one of them, James Scotland Symon, lasted just one season.

In a three-year period after the war, the club operated without a manager. Will Scott was the trainer, and Jim Taylor, the chairman, was just about everything else. We reckoned Jim picked the team. But Will was always destined for a place in North End's all-time Hall of Fame. He never played the game at professional level, arriving at Preston in 1923 from South Shields. He toiled manfully for most of the time under Taylor's considerable and often daunting influence, and his affection for the club was unquestionable. After 25 years with Preston North End, he left to manage Blackburn Rovers only for ill health to force his resignation. Once he had recovered, he returned to his first love, Preston (in retirement in his native Sunderland he called his house Deepdale). He was appointed manager and during four inspirational seasons he guided the club to the Second Division championship, to add to two Cup finals, a promotion and a wartime double.

In contrast to the chairman, Will was a quiet, unassuming fellow, a man who preferred the background and who shunned the limelight. He was a lovely guy who had the complete respect of his players in spite of his lack of personal playing knowledge. He was a shrewd judge and much better on tactics than many believed.

Frank Hill, manager from 1954 to 1956, was a decent chap, too, and another former Burnley boss. Without being a great player he had stayed around at Arsenal long enough to win three championship medals. Capped three times by Scotland he hung up his boots aged 41 and went into coaching. Burnley enjoyed top six finishes in three successive seasons under Frank, and he helped establish a youth policy at Turf Moor that became the envy of the land, producing the likes of Jimmy McIlroy and Jimmy Adamson. Frank also had spells in charge of Notts County and Charlton after his two-year sortie with North End.

We played some entertaining stuff under Frank, who had a young and modern approach for a man of close on 50. In his first season in charge, we opened up with a 5–0 win over Manchester City and 5–2 and 7–1 successes over Cardiff – we always did have a soft spot for the men from Ninian Park!

Although we skirted relegation during his tenure, Frank's departure came as a huge shock. I never really found out whether he jumped or was pushed. Recovering after an operation, I was sitting out in our back garden on Regent's Drive, chatting with Tommy Thompson, my North End team-mate and next-door neighbour, when Frank called round. He seemed right enough and asked how I was faring. Then he just blurted out that he was leaving. He reckoned his contract had been terminated, North End said he had resigned. Either way it was a bombshell. Tommy and I looked at one another in disbelief, unable to find the right words. Managers were rarely fired in those days and, if that was the case, we both felt genuinely sorry for Frank. North End allegedly paid him a settling-up sum of £500 on a salary of around £2,200 a year.

Perhaps the main reason for his downfall can be summed up in two words – Charlie Wayman. Frank was the manager who decided that Charlie, the Deepdale darling, had outstayed his welcome. He obviously thought that a bid of £8,000 from Middlesbrough represented good business for a player who, after all, was hardly in the flush of youth at 34. But he counted without the groundswell of support that Charlie enjoyed at Preston. Charlie actually came out and accused the manager and the directors of giving him short shrift and showing him little in the way of loyalty.

But Frank made good decisions, too, displaying excellent judgement in shelling out £27,000 to Aston Villa for Tommy Thompson and a quarter of that sum to Falkirk for Sammy Taylor.

The fact that Preston managed to hold on to Scott Symon for just one year, 1953–54, was a massive disappointment. He struck me as a top man from the moment I was first introduced to him and I felt we were destined for great things under his charge. No one I played under had a better football brain.

After a playing career with Dundee, Portsmouth and Glasgow Rangers, where he won a league championship medal in 1939, Scott took over as manager of East Fife and guided them to the First Division in his first season. Within days of arriving at Deepdale, aged a relatively young 42, he impressed me with his depth of knowledge of the game and of the players earning a living from it. He was not a tracksuit manager, but he supervised all the training sessions and was tactically brilliant. Eloquent and articulate, he hovered over his players like a mother hen, and nothing and nobody got in the way of him and his team.

He took us all the way to the FA Cup final and everything was going swimmingly until he was tempted back to Glasgow with Rangers. The once-in-a-lifetime opportunity proved irresistible and during his phenomenally successful career at Ibrox lasting some 14 seasons, they won six league championships, five Scottish Cups and four League Cups, not to mention making two appearances in the European Cup-Winners' Cup final.

Some say the eventual sad decline of Preston North End coincided with Symon leaving and I have often pondered on what might have happened had he stayed at Deepdale a little longer.

Over the years people have regularly asked me why I never moved into management. The easy answer is that after playing I had a ready-made job waiting for me in the plumbing and electrical business alongside my brother Joe; but that's only partly true.

The other reason is that I just didn't fancy the role. It was one of the few things that Cliff Britton and I agreed upon. Cliff said I wasn't cut out for the job and he was probably right. It wasn't that there were no offers or options to consider. Wrexham and Bristol City both wrote to me offering me a way in to management. Wrexham's interest made the papers and there was talk of a £2,000 a year offer being on the table. I gave it some thought, but decided on a 'thanks but no thanks' response. After spending most of my career at the very top level, how would I cope with dealing with players lower down the scale? Would I expect too much of them? Then there was my pride. Without wanting to sound smug or arrogant, I had always been used to success. The prospect of failing or getting the sack horrified me.

I did once have a short spell in management, however. In the spring of 1961, a year into my retirement, I accepted the invitation to go on an FA tour of the Far East, Australia and New Zealand. It was due to set out in mid May and to arrive home in the second week of June with eight or nine games listed on a busy but perfectly acceptable schedule. The FA officers made it clear that my actual role was 'player-manager' and all the decisions involving team affairs were exclusively mine. It seemed a dream trip with visits to exotic locations including Kuala Lumpur, Singapore, Hong Kong, Wellington and Auckland either side of a match or two in Australia. Well, there should have been matches in Australia.

While we were in Malaysia we got a communication from the FA in London to say that the Australian FA had been banned from competition after being found guilty of poaching players without paying proper fees for registrations. Under no circumstances, said the directive, must we play the scheduled matches there. We could visit, but not take part in any games.

Well, that was OK for the people in London to say – they didn't have to incur the wrath of a bunch of angry Aussies. The Australian football folk were not best pleased with the news. In fact, they went berserk and it led to me, as the figurehead of the FA squad, getting involved in a showdown in front of the media, television cameras and all.

As a former player, the ban didn't affect me personally, but as I politely tried to explain to our hosts, it would not be possible for me to play Australia's chosen team on my own. Something had to happen to defuse the situation so I took it upon myself to promise to stage some training sessions. It worked up to a point, but we were still pleased to head for the calm of New Zealand.

My former Preston North End team-mate Fred Else was our first-choice goalkeeper and we also had Colin Appleton (Leicester City), Ray Charnley (Blackpool), Alan A'Court (Liverpool), George Hannah (Manchester City), Johnny Fantham (Sheffield Wednesday) and Graham Shaw (Sheffield United) among the troops.

We opened up against Malaya in Kuala Lumpur and Ray Charnley bagged a hat-trick in a decisive win. George Hannah was the three-goal star when we put nine past a bewildered Singapore side, and we maintained our 100 per cent record with a 4–2 win over Hong Kong in the Government Stadium. More than 20,000 turned out for the final match against a Combined Chinese XI and we made it four wins out of four with a 3–0 success.

I was starting to believe that managing was a straightforward affair and not even the aggro in Australia could dampen my spirits. By the time we had chalked up back-to-back wins over New Zealand in Wellington and Auckland, scoring 14 goals in the process and conceding only one, I was ready to accept a full-time position if the FA felt so inclined.

Not everyone agreed with my ideas or team selection. Take the build-up to the second game of the tour in Singapore. There was a young boy in our squad who played half-back and had taken my eye during the early training sessions. But when I bit the bullet and pencilled him in the starting line-up, I was immediately taken to task by a couple of the senior players. 'What the bloody hell do you think you are playing at?' was the general essence of the question, and the tone was a little abrupt for my liking.

I explained that team selection was down to me and that I wanted to see the kid play in a match situation. Ever the diplomat, I also told them that they were worrying unnecessarily as there were more than enough games on the itinerary to ensure that everyone got a piece of the action. By the final whistle, even the most dissenting voice had been silenced by an outstanding display from the 19-year-old. Perfect of temperament, he always seemed to have so much time on the ball – the sign of a great player. He was strong in the challenge and was never hassled or harried out of his easy stride. He read the game brilliantly and had undisputed star quality.

His name? Bobby Moore. So can I lay claim to giving England's future World Cup winning captain his first proper taste of international football? Perhaps I could have made a go of management after all!

CHAPTER TWELVE

The pride of England

Saturday, 28 September 1946 stands as my proudest day as a footballer. Ask any player who has been chosen to represent the land of his birth and he will tell you that no feeling quite compares. To make your debut for your country is the ultimate honour. I had worn the famous white shirt in the wartime game with Switzerland, but that was considered unofficial and no one received a cap.

However, England's short trip to Belfast to tackle Northern Ireland was far more significant than simply providing me with my first full appearance. This was to be the first full international after the Second World War, coming just a month after the resumption of league football, and it generated hype on a massive scale.

In the weeks leading up to the Home Championship fixture, much of the media speculation centred around Stanley Matthews.

Nothing much new there – Matthews' future was always in debate, or so it seemed. But this time it was I who was being touted as a possible long-term replacement.

I read the papers – footballers might say they don't, but the vast majority do – and I knew full well what was being said and written. For all that, I certainly didn't expect a call-up. So imagine the frenzy in the small two-up two-down house in Brook Street that Elsie and I shared with her parents when a letter arrived from the Football Association. It informed me that I had been selected for a trial match and was to report to Nottingham Forest to take my place in a Combined XI that included other hopefuls, Chesterfield goalkeeper Ray Middleton, Derby defender Leon Leuty and Bolton wing-half Ernie Forrest.

It looked as though the game was going to be a bit unbalanced because listed among our opponents were Tommy Lawton, Stan Matthews and Raich Carter. Due to a late spate of injuries, the selectors were forced into some last-minute juggling and I ended up on the side of the International XI. We won by the odd goal and when the FA named the 14-strong party, it included me as Matthews' understudy. I had no problem with that, quite the contrary – just glad to be involved and thank you very much Mr Selectors was my view. However, the situation was to change long before we boarded the boat at Liverpool docks.

The last weekend of Football League matches ahead of the international resulted in Stan suffering a leg injury while on club duty with Stoke. He was immediately declared to be out of the reckoning and it soon became clear that I would step into his boots on the right wing.

A mixture of anticipation and excitement kept me awake on the Tuesday night prior to meeting up with the England party on

Merseyside for the overnight sailing. I was a new kid on the scene, but I was by no means alone in that; this was a first, too, for Frank Swift, Billy Wright, Neil Franklin, Wilf Mannion, Bobby Langton, Henry Cockburn, Laurie Scott and our captain George Hardwick. The seniors, Tommy Lawton and Raich Carter, went overboard – not literally! – to make us feel at home. They spent all their waking moments talking football and it became clear that goalkeeper Frank Swift was something of a comedian. Big Frank certainly had a laugh at my expense, or should that be expenses.

We were all handed expenses sheets prior to the match. I had never even seen one before let alone filled one in. Frank was something of an expert in such matters and he persuaded me to fill in my sheet by his rules – up the amounts in other words. Instead of the 2d bus fare from Preston to Liverpool, he recommended I put 5d and instead of 3s 8d for the train from Preston to Liverpool, he said five bob. He convinced me that a meal on the train (a meal I hadn't ordered, never mind eaten) would be another two bob; and I mustn't forget the return trip. I submitted the claim and forgot all about it until a letter arrived from the FA. It was signed by the treasurer and addressed, almost aggressively, to 'Dear Finney'. It was short and to the point. They didn't feel my expenses bore any relation to the actual cost, and questioned why on earth I should need to be fed and watered on such a short journey. The treasurer had gone to the lengths of finding out the real figures and he asked me to re-submit ahead of any payment being possible. It didn't so much make me angry, more concerned. What a way to start with England when I had so wanted to make the right impression. I could have swung for Frank Swift right there and then.

I have often been asked how I felt in the time leading up to kick-off. This was, after all, a giant stage on which to tread the international turf for the first time, in front of a record crowd of close on 60,000. Nerves were never an enemy for me. Of course, I was aware that I wasn't out for a walk in the park, but I still managed to eat the breakfast and the lunch without any worries. The odd butterfly fluttered around in my stomach, but nothing more.

I was fine, which is more than could be said for my father. My biggest problem was keeping him calm. We had received two complimentary tickets for the match. My father and brother immediately, and quite rightly, made it clear that they were the only contenders and they had sailed across on the overnight ferry. When we met up an hour or so before the game, he looked dreadful, shaking and sweating and a genuine bundle of nerves.

He need not have worried. We gave the Irish a right going over, winning 7–2 in a match that was delayed for several minutes after the crowd spilled out on to the pitch.

Raich Carter gave us the perfect start with a goal in the first minute, the maestro pouncing after the home defenders had failed to deal with a cross from George Hardwick. Inspired by Peter Doherty, Ireland tried to counter but were floored by a second England goal just six minutes later from Wilf Mannion. Tommy Lawton's thunderbolt nearly broke the crossbar in two before Mannion put us three up prior to half-time. I was seeing a lot of the ball and early in the second half managed to set up Mannion's hat-trick while easing my own name on to the scoresheet. It wasn't the greatest goal of my career but I can still see it now.

Apart from the euphoria of a winning start and the splendour of the huge occasion, I was struck by the stunning individual ability of my team-mates. These guys were good – very, very good – and no one impressed me more than Raich Carter. He seemed to be able to land the ball right at my feet from any distance irrespective of whether he was under the pressure of a challenge from a defender.

The following morning we left our lovely hotel (one of the genuine perks of playing for your country was the exceptional standard of accommodation presented to you by the FA) on the outskirts of Belfast and headed for home, but not before we had seen the papers. All the major sports pages proclaimed a fine English display and went so far as to suggest that the link between Raich and me had been more productive than the pre-war partnership of Raich and Stan Matthews. It made 'good copy' as they say in the newspaper business, but there was an element of mischief about it. I suddenly found myself in a head-to-head with Stan. It was not a confrontation of my making, or of his, but the papers loved to hint at a rift between us, and this was the start of the saga that was to go on season in and season out for the best part of a decade.

I had been very satisfied with my own performance, and Walter Winterbottom, the England manager, made a point of congratulating me. Good old Walter, a man who had the respect and loyalty of all his players, was still at the helm 12 years later when I trotted out for what was to be my final England appearance. Walter and I became good pals. We came on to the international arena at the same time and he showed great faith in me by selecting me 76 times, a faith I like to think I repaid by always giving of my best.

His own playing career with Manchester United had ended prematurely through injury but he remained a fitness fanatic. A sound Lancastrian – Oldham was the town of his birth – he attended the prestigious Carnegie College of Physical Education and reached the high rank of wing commander in the Royal Air Force during the war with special responsibilities for physical training and exercise.

Appointed England's first full-time manager in 1946, his forte was his coaching, and he played a part in activating a revolution. He had very defined ideas on how the game should be played but never tried to stifle individual skill, preferring instead to try to harness various abilities for the common good. His coaching manuals were bestsellers, both at home and abroad, his systems were copied by his fellow managers and he was known as a supreme judge of opposition teams. He was dedicated, articulate and a man you felt you could trust with your life, but he held office at a time when managers were kept in check and restricted in how far they could go. Throughout his 17 years, he was always answerable to those who sat in power and that must have brought all sorts of frustrations. Club managers didn't make life any easier for him, often complaining if their star players were selected when important league games were pending.

Walter stuck to his beliefs and, to me, it is no coincidence that during his tenure we saw the development of coaches who were to become leaders within the modern game – Ron Greenwood, Dave Sexton and Bill Nicholson, for example. I daresay Alf Ramsey picked up a few pointers by watching Walter in action. Like Ramsey the manager, Walter retained his dignity no matter what and treated victory and defeat the same, earnestly believing that there was always room for improvement.

People used to say he had a soft spot for me and I would not dispute it – I certainly had a high opinion of him, both as a man and a manager.

At 36, I knew my international days were numbered, but when I pulled on the number 11 shirt for the Wembley date with the Soviet Union on 22 October 1958, I didn't appreciate that the end was no more than 90 minutes away. This was England's first home game since the disappointing World Cup campaign in Sweden. It was listed as a friendly but provided us with an opportunity to regain some pride, and we did precisely that. Johnny Haynes scored a hat-trick, Bobby Charlton converted a penalty and Nat Lofthouse grabbed a fifth late on – a vintage performance it was called.

There was personal significance in Nat's goal. It took him to 30 for England and equalled the record I had set earlier that month in a 3–3 draw with Northern Ireland in Belfast. I was involved in the build-up but, contrary to popular belief over the years, it was Bobby Charlton and not me who supplied the pass for Nat to score.

There was a genuine Lancastrian feel about the England dressing room that afternoon. Nat, Bobby (an adopted Lancastrian) and I were joined by Burnley goalkeeper Colin McDonald and the Blackburn duo of winger Bryan Douglas and half-back Ronnie Clayton. Billy Wright was the only other survivor from my England debut against Northern Ireland. The supreme captain, Billy went on to play in seven more internationals before retiring the following May after winning his 105th cap (90 as skipper) against the USA in Los Angeles in what was his 70th consecutive appearance. Sheffield United defender Graham Shaw was making his first England start, and did extremely well, too.

As usual, Wembley was full to bursting with a crowd of 100,000 but the opening exchanges were fairly low key. Back in the side for the first time in two years, Nat Lofthouse got through an awful lot of hard work and running but found genuine scoring chances at a premium. However, on the stroke of half-time Bryan Douglas and I combined down the left and Johnny Haynes raced through to put us ahead. It was just the tonic we needed, not only to settle a restless crowd but to calm our own nerves, and we ran riot after the break. We left to an ovation as the home supporters shared the players' collective sense of relief for this was, after all, England's first victory in eight internationals.

Could I have played on for England? Probably. My fitness levels were high and I felt more than able to contribute. But age does not make allowances for anyone, particularly sportsmen, and I could understand the England management opting to freshen things up. They had the comfort of knowing that a batch of younger forwards were eagerly banging on the international door, Bryan Douglas and Peter Brabrook of Chelsea to name but two.

So the curtain fell on that autumn afternoon at Wembley. No one gave me the chance to retire from the international game; they took the decision on my behalf. But I didn't feel let down – how could I? After travelling the world representing my country for 12 years, I could only offer my grateful thanks to those who had made it all possible. The match fee went from £20 to £50 in my time and that was very useful income, especially in the early years, but the money was incidental – I would willingly have paid the FA to play.

Looking back, I can happily report that the good times far outweighed the bad. Those 12 years encompassed what I will always consider to be the golden age of the great game. England were involved in 101 internationals but injury kept me out of contention for 25 per cent of the time and I finished with 76 caps. I sampled victory on 51 occasions and played on the losing side just a dozen times. A further 12 games ended all square and one fixture, against Argentina in Buenos Aires, was abandoned after 23 minutes of goalless mediocrity.

I tried my hand against defenders in 23 different national sides and visited 21 countries. My tally of 30 goals included three penalties (I also missed one) and everyone reckoned I had a particular liking for the Portuguese. I scored six times against them, including five in two visits to the National Stadium in Lisbon.

I made 30 international appearances in England (only 16 at Wembley because we tended to tour around the country back then) and 46 on foreign soil. It wasn't until two-and-a-half years and 15 caps into my England career that I sampled a defeat – 1–3 at home to the Scots of all people! I played on the right wing 40 times, on the left wing 33 times, and the other three appearances were as a centre-forward.

For the most part it was five-star entertainment and those 76 games, which include three World Cups, actually yielded 329 goals. Put me on the spot and ask me to pick a few nuggets and I'd go for five games, all of which fell between 1947 and 1950: Portugal 0, England 10, Lisbon 1947; Scotland 0, England 2, Glasgow 1948; Italy 0, England 4, Turin 1948; England 9, Northern Ireland 2, Manchester 1949; Portugal 3, England 5, Lisbon 1950.

By the time of the trip to Portugal in 1947, the great debate revolving around the respective merits of Stanley Matthews and me was under way. We were both included in the 16-man squad for what was England's first-ever meeting with the Portuguese. Puzzled by the media obsession with the issue, Walter Winterbottom decided to take the bull by the horns. Instead of choosing between Stan and me, Walter picked us both. It was a masterstroke.

His decision was undoubtedly prompted by the fact that the regular left winger, Bobby Langton, failed a fitness test, but nonetheless it was a daring move. As I was naturally left-footed, I took the number 11 jersey, a position I had yet to play at top level, and the combination of two totally different styles on the flanks worked a treat.

The National Stadium in Lisbon was a delight to behold. What an arena it was! We changed in dressing rooms that would have done justice to a top hotel, the stands were carved from white marble and the grass was lush despite the searing heat.

The Portuguese love their football and they made a right old din as we waited to kick off. Within a minute their enthusiasm had taken its first knock, Tommy Lawton collecting a pass from Wilf Mannion to crash an unstoppable shot past Azevado, the Portugal goalkeeper many rated the best in the world. Lawton went on to get three more, Stanley Mortensen also got four and Stan and I chipped in with one apiece, just for good measure.

There had been much conversation beforehand about the ball. It was eventually agreed to use a British-style ball, but when Lawton got the show on the road within the first few seconds, the Portuguese officials kicked it into the stand and introduced a continental alternative. It made no difference and what later became known as 'The Lisbon Story' stands as one of England's finest footballing hours.

I had never experienced anything like that trip, but the short hop to play Scotland at Hampden in the April of 1948 was another memorable occasion. I loved the clashes with the old enemy and whomever else you faced and wherever it was staged, there was never anything to touch the fever of England versus Scotland. With all due respect to the Irish and the Welsh, the Scots were the only home nation really capable of giving us a run for our money. There was something extra special about going to Hampden Park – and winning! I was lucky enough to emerge victorious five times out of six at Hampden (the other was a draw), but at Wembley the opposite was the case, just one win and a draw from four clashes.

As with all home internationals we had to find our own way to the team hotel, usually three days before the match. I went by train, meeting up with the rest of the players at the hotel. We always used the same hotel in Troon as our headquarters.

Walter got everyone together for an informal chat on the first night and then it was down to the serious business of training and tactics on Thursday and Friday. On the Saturday, after a light meal, we boarded the team coach and headed for the ground – and what a ground! It matched anywhere in the world for atmosphere. The Scots love to see their team win, but they also appreciate the skills of the game and acknowledge when an opponent excels. We excelled that particular afternoon in front of a particularly vociferous and partisan crowd of over 135,000.

Putting modesty to one side for a moment, I count it among my better games, not least because of the great thrill I got from scoring a goal of stunning simplicity which left Hampden Park silenced, albeit temporarily.

Frank Swift punted a clearance downfield and Tommy Lawton flicked it to debutant Stan Pearson who, in turn, found me with the perfect through ball. I managed to keep my balance while under challenge and sent a shot beyond goalkeeper Ian Black. The ball had gone the length of the field and into the net without a blue shirt getting a touch. Magical! My greatest England goal? Quite possibly.

In truth, we had been under the cosh until that breakthrough, but Scotland found themselves thwarted by the blanket deter-mination of our defence; Neil Franklin had the game of his life. Scotland's fire was finally extinguished in the 64th minute when Lawton's power created an opening and Stan Mortensen nipped in to take full advantage.

Guest of honour at the game was none other than the great

Eighth Army chief, Field Marshal Lord Montgomery of Alamein, who, of course, had been my commander during the Middle East and Italian campaigns. Monty came up to me beforehand and wished me well, telling me not to let the Scots win. What I didn't appreciate was that he had just come from giving the same command in the Scotland dressing room.

During the half-time interval, a knock came on the England dressing-room door and in walked Monty. He made straight for me.

'Congratulations on that goal,' he said. 'It was a fine effort from a man who fought alongside me.'

A few days later a letter from the famous Field Marshal arrived at my home in Preston. This is what it said:

My Dear Finney, I was delighted to meet up with you once again in Glasgow and especially to see you score. May you score many more. I send you my programme from the game, which I have signed, and a photograph you may care to have.

The photograph showed Montgomery in his famous beret and was inscribed: 'To T. Finney, left wing for England at Hampden Park on April 10th 1948 and scorer of England's first goal.'

Monty never seemed to forget a face or an event and four years later when we were presented to him again, prior to a match against Austria, he said, 'Last time we met was at Hampden Park, wasn't it? Let's hope you get another goal today.' For the record, I didn't, but I am sure Monty enjoyed not only our win but the heroics of Nat Lofthouse whose performance earned him the Lion of Vienna tag.

The only display to stand comparison with the drubbing of Portugal came in Turin against an Italian side regarded as the undisputed world champions, a wonder team packed with talent. It was perhaps the finest all-round team performance of my England career.

A crowd of 58,000 packed into the Stadio Comunale for what was a friendly in name only. Our cause was not helped by the temperature soaring towards 90 degrees by kick-off time – I cannot recall playing too many matches at Wembley or Deepdale when the fans brought umbrellas to shield themselves from the sun.

Determined to put on a show, Italy opened up breathing fire and we looked set for a hammering. But the home pressure brought no tangible reward with Don Howe adjusting well to a difficult debut and Frank Swift at his brilliant best between the sticks in his first outing as skipper. When we eventually got out of our half, we did so with deadly purpose. Stan Mortensen picked up a pass from Stanley Matthews, cut inside the Italian defence from the left and hammered the ball home from the tightest of angles.

Italy poured forward in search of the equaliser, but our next attack of note brought goal number two and, once again, we were left to sing the praises of Morty – this time as a goal provider. Neil Franklin started the move from deep and Matthews and Mortensen cleverly worked an opening for Tommy Lawton to shoot past the bemused Italian keeper.

It was more than the Italians could stand, especially as they had seen two efforts disallowed and watched as Swiftie pulled off three great saves. We found that they allowed their tempers to get the better of them. At two down they were arguing among themselves and when I looked across at Morty he just nodded and gave me a knowing wink. When we heard the unrest we knew we had them, but not before we had soaked up quarter of an hour of non-stop pressure early in the second half. They hit us with everything, but still Swiftie and his co-defenders stood firm with Billy Wright truly magnificent. He wasn't alone, we had heroes all over the pitch and I certainly had my moments to relish, too – or should that be two? My name appeared on the scoresheet twice in as many minutes. The first was a volley courtesy of Wilf Mannion's cross and the second was from close range after good approach play by Morty and Henry Cockburn.

Only those who played for England in Turin, or the few supporters who were there, will ever properly appreciate the true merit of the performance. It was what today's pundits might call 'the ultimate professional display' and, aside from the 1966 World Cup victory, it had a very good claim to be the highpoint of the English game.

As a forward player, I was expected to be part creative and part clinical. Unlike Stanley Matthews, who was not expected to score, people wanted goals as well as tricky wing play designed to present chances for others. But football is a funny business; sometimes you score twice in a minute and sometimes you don't find the net at all – even when your team hits the back of the net nine times.

I experienced such a fate in November 1949 in a Home Championship clash with Northern Ireland at Maine Road. I had a hand in six of the goals but never looked like getting one myself – ah well, I always believed football was a team game.

Overcast skies and persistent drizzle could not dampen our style on that wonderful Wednesday in Manchester – the goals rained down. It was one of my best showings at international level, everything I attempted seemed to come off, and after Jack Rowley had given us the perfect start, I set up Jack Froggatt to head home on his England debut.

We were humming and the Irish were chasing shadows with Stan Pearson and Stanley Mortensen adding further strikes before half-time. Rowley made it five, Mortensen six and Rowley seven and eight with Ireland pulling one back before Pearson added number nine. Ireland had the final cheer, but this was England's afternoon and I had enjoyed every minute. There is pleasure in scoring and pleasure in providing – but most of all there is pleasure in playing well and winning.

Even though I am not a gambler, I might just have had a quid or two on me scoring one out of nine, but two internationals and six months later, the circle turned. I enjoyed my greatest scoring feat by grabbing four in a 5–3 victory back in the National Stadium in Lisbon. If Turin was team Utopia, this was my personal best.

It was the first game of a two-match European tour (we beat Belgium 4–1 four days later) arranged as part of our preparations for the forthcoming World Cup in Brazil. Portuguese football still carried the scars of the 10–0 whitewash of three years earlier, but this was by no means a canter. Portugal, although given no better than 40/1 to beat us, had made great strides as a football nation and they refused to buckle even after we had cantered into a three-goal lead.

I got into the game very quickly, hitting the crossbar from distance and converting a penalty after I had been tripped. Jackie Milburn also hit the woodwork before a headed goal from Stan Mortensen, following exquisite approach work from Wilf Mannion, established a comfortable position. Roy Bentley and Milburn gave me the chance to slot home my second and another rout looked on the cards. Portugal had other ideas. They got a goal back, the crowd responded and suddenly we looked a little rocky.

Thankfully, I was able to take the heat out of the situation by dribbling past a couple of defenders to curl a shot into the corner for my hat-trick. Portugal bit back again to reduce the arrears, not once but twice, and at 3–4 the crowd sensed a major upset.

We were pinned back, relying heavily on quick breaks out of defence, and it was from one such foray that I got the chance to put the game beyond doubt. Morty was unceremoniously chopped down and the Italian referee pointed to the spot. Given the circumstances, it was a brave decision, a very brave decision. My legs went a little to jelly as I walked back. To say the crowd howled derision as I stepped forward would be to understate the case. I tried to keep a clear head and shut out the racket, concentrating on hitting the ball low and hard. It worked and when I opened my eyes, the ball was nestling nicely in the net. It was enough to clinch the game for us.

The next morning I found myself lounging quite unashamedly upon the cloud known as nine. Let's have it right. What pleasanter flashback could a footballer have than to remember waking up in the millionaires' seaside playground of Estoril, the sun streaming through the bedroom window and the sports pages declaring 'Finney Dazzles – Scores Four!'

However, football is not just a catalogue of triumphs, more's the pity. There can be pain and I had the misfortune to experience three of the most shocking and depressing occasions experienced by our national side: USA 1, England 0, Rio 1950; Hungary 7, England 1, Budapest 1954; Yugoslavia 5, England 0, Belgrade 1958.

I would not like to say which one I enjoyed the least. For sheer humiliation it has to be the 1–0 defeat at the hands of a team of no-hopers from the United States, and in the World Cup no less. The dateline was Brazil 1950 and we had travelled 300 miles inland to Belo Horizonte to face the USA, a country where football was regarded as a very minor sport. The Pool Two game should have been a formality. It turned out to be a fiasco.

A far cry from the main Mineiro Stadium in Maracana, our venue was primitive in the extreme and the facilities basic. But the mountain air was much more to our liking than the sultry, oppressive climate of the capital city of Rio, and we were in a fairly privileged position as the official guests of the Morro Velho gold mine, an English-owned firm employing some 2,000 British workers.

The match was played in front of a crowd of just over 10,000. We started on the attack and stayed camped in American territory for the entire first half with opposing goalkeeper Borghi, of Simpkins FC St Louis, playing out of his skin. Stanley Mortensen, Wilf Mannion, Jimmy Mullen and I all missed good chances before the unthinkable happened and America scored. Eight minutes from the break, a shot came in from the left from Bahr, more in hope than expectation, and the ball seemed to hit Larry Gaetjens on the head, which deflected it past a disbelieving Bert Williams.

We hit the woodwork several times in the first half and we hit it twice more in the second. The American defenders made some incredible last-gasp tackles and saves and at least two clear-cut penalty claims were waved aside. Chances came and went at the rate of one every couple of minutes but no one was able to find a way through to goal.

At the final whistle, scoring hero Gaetjens was hoisted shoulder high by his colleagues and we trooped off with neither a plausible excuse nor a satisfactory reason for the débâcle. If we had blamed the pitch, the conditions or the referee – and none of those helped it must be said – we would have been slaughtered. The game was supposed to be as good as a walkover for us. After all, the Americans were part-timers and we were a highly rated world force. Most of our opponents would have struggled to get a game in the Third Division, but we failed to take any of umpteen chances while they had just two speculative attempts at goal in 90 minutes and one happened to go in.

As you might imagine, the English press had a field day. They slated the team and one account simply said: 'It was the worst performance ever by an English team; not a single player could be proud of his showing.' Those named and shamed were: B.F. Williams (Wolverhampton Wanderers), A.E. Ramsey (Tottenham Hotspur), J. Aston (Manchester United), W.A. Wright (Wolverhampton Wanderers, captain), L. Hughes Liverpool), J.W. Dickinson (Portsmouth), T. Finney (Preston North End), W.J. Mannion (Middlesbrough), R.T.F. Bentley (Chelsea), S.H. Mortensen (Blackpool), J. Mullen (Wolverhampton Wanderers).

The inquest ran and ran. England officials were dumbfounded by the defeat. Arthur Drewry, Football League President, declared it 'quite unbelievable'. Sir Stanley Rous, Secretary to the Football Association, reckoned that the Americans had been 'fitter, faster and better fighters', while Walter Winterbottom, sharing our embarrassment added that 'the team played badly, especially the forwards, who were far too eager'.

I still cringe when I look back on that game and I take absolutely no satisfaction whatsoever in being able to say that I took part in the soccer sensation of the century. One member of the ill-fated England team that afternoon, Alf Ramsey, guided England to World Cup triumph 16 years later. It defies belief that one man should experience such contrasting emotions in the same competition.

In all my years as a professional, at club and country level, only rarely can I recall leaving the field feeling that we had been totally outplayed. But I certainly had to stomach such an experience when England travelled to take on Hungary in Budapest's Nepstadion in May 1954.

Six months earlier, the Hungarians had handed out a football lesson to win 6–3 at Wembley and become the first continental team to beat us in our own backyard. I was spared that particular ordeal, through injury, although I was present after agreeing to cover the game for a national newspaper. My account centred squarely on the brilliance of the visitors and there were two reasons for that – one, the Hungarians were brilliant, and two, we were not allowed to make any critical comment on the team or any individuals in it to the media. That was an actual directive from the Football Association. That is why there were so few examples in those days of public rifts between players, or players and managers, or players and clubs etc. You couldn't sound off even if you felt like it. We were gagged, but that's how football was back then. The players didn't have the status they enjoy now. We had to put up and shut up and in many ways we were the game's poor relations – hard to imagine now perhaps, but true nonetheless.

In any case, it wasn't my style to sound off or be openly critical of my team-mates and I genuinely believed that our defeat that particular afternoon had more to do with Hungary being outstanding than us being poor.

The Hungarians were the reigning Olympic champions but that title carried little impact among England's hierarchy. How we were made to cough and splutter – on and off the pitch – as they totally overwhelmed us with a brand of football the like of which we had never seen. They had pace in all positions, people running off the ball in all directions and a quality about their passing that was utterly enchanting. Puskas, Kocsis and Hidegkuti were the ringleaders and we ran to their tune. It was a performance of breathtaking proportions; nothing I have witnessed since has got even close. I remember leaving Wembley thinking we were light years behind.

They had new ideas, not just on how the game should be played but on how players should prepare. For example, they came out well ahead of kick-off time for a warm-up – we all looked at one another wondering what was going on. But the Hungarians had discovered that it was unwise to expect their players to run out at 2.55 p.m. and play from a cold start. It was asking for injury trouble and their medical experts had advised the warm-up procedure. Everyone copied them; there was no disgrace in doing so. Teams even go out after the match nowadays to warm down. The Hungarians were pointing the way forward, even if to be cast in the role of student in the home of football was a bit hard to swallow for a few Englishmen.

In Budapest, we had the chance to exact some revenge and show how much we had learned from their lesson. What a laugh! It was even worse for us as we crashed 7–1, a result that still stands as the country's heaviest defeat. It was Thoroughbreds against carthorses.

The Honved pair of Puskas and Kocsis was in harness again, as was Hidegkuti of MTK Budapest. We had a strange sort of team on parade. Bedford Jezzard, the Fulham centre-forward, made his bow and the line-up also included Huddersfield full-back Ron Staniforth, Sheffield Wednesday inside-forward Jackie Sewell and Portsmouth winger Peter Harris. To be fair to those lads, they were hardly household names or international players of stature, and this didn't seem to be the right occasion for experimenting. But the selection committee deemed otherwise, although whether Walter Winterbottom shared that view I never found out. The manager didn't have the final say. The procedure was for Walter to submit his intended line-up and then for the committee to meet to decide in their expert opinion whether he had got it right or not.

They or he definitely had it wrong here. Hungary tore us apart. Their slick, quick-passing moves made our style look awkward and old-fashioned. We played like a team full of strangers, individuals going about their business oblivious of those around them, while Hungary played team football. Goals from Puskas, Kocsis and a thunderbolt shot from defender Lantos, put us three down by the break. We had mustered just a solitary shot from Ivor Broadis in the entire 45 minutes.

However, we almost got a break in the opening minutes of the second half when Peter Harris was unlucky to see a shot blocked on the line. If we thought a fightback was possible we were deluding ourselves and within the next 20 minutes Hungary had doubled their lead. Kocsis, Toth and the wonderful Hidegkuti were the marksmen and our goalkeeper, Gil Merrick, hardly knew what had hit him – he had no chance with any of them.

The Hungarians, nicknamed the 'Magical Magyars', relaxed and we did manage the occasional attack with yours truly guilty of missing an absolute sitter. We salvaged a little pride when Ivor Broadis connected with a Jimmy Dickinson free kick to score a consolation, but the Hungarians were not amused and had the final say through Puskas.

If Budapest in 1954 was bad, Belgrade in 1958 was not much better. It was a warm-up friendly for the World Cup in Sweden and we went there hoping to underline our credentials as a potential force. Unfortunately, it turned into a disaster.

We were thrashed, out-fought and out-thought, although I can vouch for the fact that some of the Yugoslavian tackling bordered on barbaric. They were an aggressive and physical unit. Once in front through a long-range shot from Milutinovic, they took complete control.

Our goalkeeper Eddie Hopkinson was not having the best of afternoons and we survived several scares before half-time with the home side hitting the crossbar and having three goals disallowed. It was left to captain Billy Wright to try to hold things together at the back in the face of wave after wave of home attacks. How we managed to stay only one down by the break was a mystery. The floodgates opened after Petakovic scored a sensational second. Winger Sekularac grabbed a brace and Veselinovic joined in the late fun as the delirious home supporters began to light fires of celebration on the terraces. I seemed to spend most of the time picking myself up off the turf after being the victim of foul after foul after foul, but we were unable to capitalise on any number of free kicks on an afternoon of bitter disappointment.

An honour one step down from playing for your country was selection for the representative games organised by the Football League three or four times a season against similar teams from the League of Ireland, the Scottish League and the Irish League. I was selected 17 times over the course of a decade between 1948 and 1958 and they were always great occasions, attracting some bumper attendances.

The beauty of it was twofold. Firstly, the League XI was a mixture of established internationals, fringe players and youngsters trying to make the step up to the top level. You didn't have to be English to feature either, or British for that matter – I recall my old Preston colleague Joe Marston, a true Australian, being involved at least once.

Secondly, the games in England were played on club grounds rather than at Wembley. It meant that fans in the regions could watch a top-class match without having to make the long trek down to London. Although I loved the Twin Towers and the prestige of Wembley, often the atmosphere was better out in the sticks.

Don't let anyone try to tell you that representative matches were two-bit friendlies. These were highly competitive fixtures and we knew for a fact that the England selectors took them very seriously. The players were either trying to hold on to an England place or trying to win one, so competitiveness was never an issue.

You got a medal, which I looked upon as a sort of unofficial cap, a small fee and your expenses. I recall the matches producing some vintage football. I have since heard some people who reckon they know best claiming that the matches were basically pointless and created little or no public interest. How ridiculous! Some of the best players in the land took part and as for no one being interested – well, I remember playing in front of a huge and partisan 90,000 crowd against Scotland at Ibrox.

There were 35,000 people present when I played in the Football League XI for the first time, in April 1948. Perhaps that had something to do with the game being played at Deepdale with a line-up including not only me but also my team-mate Joe Walton. Whatever the reasons, it still amounted to a gate double North End's previous First Division home fixture.

I think we can put the apathy claim to bed. In fact, the footballing authorities could do far worse than consider re-introducing the concept.

The League of Ireland provided the opposition on my debut and we won 4–0. I felt I did OK although the press observers reckoned I had been 'starved of proper service', and I could not mark the occasion with a goal. Joe Walton was an outstanding success and earned rave reviews. The media were unanimous in putting his name forward as the ultimate successor to George Hardwick in the England defence.

The Irish were of Second Division standard to be truthful, but every opponent has to be beaten and we should have done so by an even more convincing margin. We had the chances to have at least doubled our tally. Liverpool centre-forward Albert Stubbins is down in the record book not only for scoring two goals but also for missing two penalties, both of them for fouls on yours truly.

My next representative appearance, 11 months later and against the Scots at Ibrox, produced another win and my first goal at this level.

Over an entertaining ten-year period we played in front of appreciative crowds at Molineux, Bloomfield Road, Goodison Park, Hillsborough and St James Park as well as Ibrox, Windsor Park and Dalymount Park. I got to know players I would otherwise only have known as opponents, and my abiding memory is of a 9–1 victory, again at the expense of the League of Ireland, at Everton. I played on the right wing and Bobby Langton, who had just left North End to join Bolton, was flying down the left. Tommy Thompson benefited most from a stream of crosses to score four.

I got a couple when we also hit nine against the Irish League at Windsor Park and, all in all, I found myself on the losing side just three times. We scored 75 goals in those 17 matches – decent entertainment don't you think?

CHAPTER THIRTEEN

A global adventure

Playing for England was more than a privilege, it was an education in every sense. It taught me some important lessons, helped me to get a handle on life, gave me extra respect for my fellow man, and it did a fair bit for my geography, too.

At 24, I was basically handed a ticket to see the world – in luxury and for free – and I had the time of my life. I visited Moscow, Montevideo, Vienna, Florence, New York, Oslo, Zurich, Rio, Budapest, Copenhagen, Belgrade, Santiago to name but a few places; Alan Whicker would have been hard pushed to match up to that sort of globetrotting.

Outside the World Cup finals, I remember being particularly excited at winning selection on the England summer tour of 1953. We were bound for America, somewhere the vast majority of players in the party, myself included, had never set foot before.

We met up for a couple of days training at Hendon before taking off from London Airport for the long flight over the Atlantic. Not everyone was thrilled by that prospect and there was a degree of nervous apprehension, but flying never worried me over much. I was quite used to it by then and I rarely felt nervous.

However, I had been on a flight that was forced to make an emergency landing three years earlier. Something went awry with the aircraft as we made our way to Rio for the 1950 World Cup and we had to put down in Recife, a coastal port in Brazil some way short of our destination. We were delayed for some time while investigations took place and repairs were carried out. Eventually, permission was given for us all to re-board the aircraft, which some did more enthusiastically than others.

Talking of the fear of flying, I well recall feeling a mixture of concern and admiration for Bobby Charlton when we flew out to play Yugoslavia in Belgrade in 1958. The match came just 12 weeks after Bobby had survived the dreadful Munich air crash that had claimed the lives of so many of his Manchester United team-mates.

Bobby received his international baptism in the Home Championship game with Scotland at Hampden Park in the April while everyone was still trying to come to terms with the events at Munich. Although only 20, he was a level-headed lad and a player with a clear understanding of where he was going. Billy Wright and I had a quiet word with him before the game, but we need not have worried. Bobby was simply magnificent, capping his impressive debut with a stunning goal. He followed that up with two more gems as we beat Portugal at Wembley and it was no surprise when the travelling squad for Yugoslavia included one R. Charlton.

You didn't have to have a degree in human psychology to appreciate that Bobby may have felt a touch apprehensive as we prepared for the plane trip to Belgrade. Such feelings are natural for most people, let alone someone fresh from surviving a disaster.

But the media boys were not prepared to miss the moment and Bobby was going to have a 'shocking ordeal' whether he wanted one or not. The way they reported our flight to Belgrade via Zurich was quite unbelievable. According to the newspapers, a delay at Zurich was due to 'major engine failure'. Not true. Yes, there had been a slight problem, but nothing to cause undue alarm and the flights were really quite pleasant. Bobby was unperturbed and managed to get through his personal test with the composure that became his trademark.

The FA officials were far from happy with the media and there was a genuine feeling of unrest between the two parties. It was somewhat ironic that after being hammered 5–0 by the Yugoslavs the man asked to carry the can was Bobby Charlton. It was reported that he had not tried, he had fallen out with his colleagues and he had been hauled before the FA on grounds of misbehaviour – all of it absolute tripe, but you know what they say about the pen.

Seven days later we found ourselves in Russia. Organised to celebrate the 60th anniversary of the Soviet FA, it was the first fixture between the two countries and a game, the experts warned, that would be much more difficult than the confrontation with Yugoslavia. So, having got the straightforward matter of Yugoslavia out of the way, we were more than a touch wary of what the Russians may have in store for us.

We went into the match knowing next to nothing about their players or their style of play, although their results suggested a very accomplished unit. We also had to contend with a very partisan crowd. More than 102,000 squeezed into the magnificent Lenin Stadium in Moscow and the atmosphere leading up to kick-off was most intimidating. However, it didn't take long for the supporters to turn on their team and the Soviet Union were actually booed off the field at the final whistle.

Tommy Banks, that gutsy defender from Bolton with the broadest Lancashire accent in the world, was handed a debut, as was Burnley goalkeeper Colin McDonald and Wolves half-back Eddie Clamp. The new recruits performed to a high standard and had it not been for the heroic goalkeeping of Lev Yashin – West Brom forward Derek Kevan looked on in disbelief at three outstanding saves – we would have won with a bit to spare.

I felt I put on one of my best displays in an England shirt and was unfortunate to see an effort hit a post, Bobby Robson suffering a similar fate. Eventually our pressure told when Bryan Douglas broke free and crossed for Kevan to power a header beyond Yashin.

Russian winger Ivanhov grabbed an undeserved equaliser in the 78th minute when he managed to wriggle free of Banks' attentions and hook a shot past McDonald. Never one to stand on ceremony, Banks had given poor old Ivanhov a bit of a going over. After the match Bryan Douglas was quoted as saying, 'It made me laugh to see Ivanhov running for the safety of the tunnel at the final whistle with Tommy Banks in hot pursuit. The Russian thought his life was in danger when all Tommy wanted to do was shake hands.'

The way Tommy spoke and behaved always made me chuckle. Before the game, Walter Winterbottom took him to one side to explain that Ivanhov was a talented player who would need close attention.

'Reet, ah know what tha' means,' said Tommy in a dialect few of his colleagues could understand. 'So tha' won't mind if he ends up wi' a cinder rash on his ass then?'

I was in fits of laughter, but Walter looked like he needed help from an interpreter.

I was intrigued by the culture of the country and my newly purchased cine camera had plenty of use during our stay. No one spoke English – including Tommy Banks – and there was an eerie feeling about the place although the locals did try hard to make us feel welcome in their own way.

The scale of the place struck me immediately as did the acute shortage of shops. All the buildings looked the same, street after street of what looked like offices or Government property, and everywhere had a dark look about it, even though it was early summer. There was a distinct lack of colour and it was different, totally different, from anywhere else I had visited. Perhaps that was why I found it so fascinating.

We visited Red Square and the Kremlin and joined the long queue to witness Lenin lying in state. Moscow is renowned for its universities and we had a trip there, too, but there is only so much culture your average footballer can take.

'Looking around is great,' came the cry from one weary sightseer, 'but what about some entertainment?'

'Funny you should mention that,' came the response from an FA official. 'We have just managed to sort something out for you all.'

The high expectancy was lost in a chorus of moans and groans when we were eventually informed that the entertainment was a night at the ballet. But it wasn't just any ballet mind; it was none other than the world famous Bolshoi Ballet and how we all enjoyed it. The artistic prowess of performers at the peak of their physical powers was awesome, and simply enchanting.

Back in 1953, the FA had deemed that to make the long journey to the States worthwhile, the itinerary should include not two or three but four matches. We were there for nearly a month so it had to be made worthwhile. The fixtures were against Argentina, Chile, Uruguay and America. The big games were the first three. At least, they were the big games to everyone but Alf Ramsey, Billy Wright, Jimmy Dickinson and I. That particular quartet had more than a passing interest in the final game in New York. We had all suffered the misfortune of figuring in the World Cup disaster match against the USA back in 1950. We had lived with the stigma of that defeat for three years and there was a genuine feeling of revenge in the air.

Prior to that was the little matter of two tough tests against Argentina and Chile and a meeting with the reigning world champions, Uruguay, all in the space of 14 days. Fireworks were expected against the Argies as 80,000 packed into the Estadio Antonio Liberti Monumental in Buenos Aires but we ended up with a damp squib, a very damp squib.

We got caught up in a South American monsoon just before kick-off. The heavens opened and it bucketed down. Although the game was started it was farcical. After 25 minutes the officials decided to abandon proceedings at 0–0.

Incidentally, the man in the middle was Arthur Ellis, one of England's best-known referees, and he was under pressure to try to help get the match re-scheduled. The FA were quite happy to stay around for a day or so but the Argentine authorities were insistent that it would take the surface around five days to dry out and so we upped sticks and headed for Santiago.

There was another feverish atmosphere – the locals always seemed to come out in force when England were in town – and Chile made us work hard for our 2–1 win, courtesy of goals from Tommy Taylor and Nat Lofthouse.

Arthur Ellis was on duty again and he took charge once more for the clash with Uruguay. I had a lot of time for Arthur but he didn't offer me much in the way of protection that day. Rarely in my career did I sense that a team or a player had devised a plan to stop me at all costs with the use of unfair means, but that Sunday afternoon in Montevideo was the exception. We knew they were physical and powerful, their aggression had been a key factor in the World Cup triumph in Brazil, but we didn't appreciate the cynical side to their game.

I maintain that was the occasion when I confronted my toughest direct opponent on a football pitch. Uruguay's left-sided defender Cruz took great exception to the fact that I gave him the runaround early on. The team coach, obviously sensing danger, came over to the sideline to have a quiet word with Cruz who then set about stopping me any way he could. Brutal is the best description and I copped for a lot of the stick that was being dished out. It was ruthless and I wince now as I remember a whack I took to the shin courtesy of Mr Cruz long after the ball had left my possession.

The cut was deep and the swelling very sore. With a bit of help from Jimmy Trotter's magic sponge, I managed to hobble through, but over the next few days it turned septic. One newspaper carried graphic detail of the incident, exclaiming that I had every right to approach the Football Association for danger money. I was in a lot of discomfort, but the medical team worked a minor miracle to get me fit for the New York date with America although it took me the best part of a year to recover properly.

Along with my physical problem, I was also shocked to learn of the death of my boyhood hero, Alex James. How I had admired the little magician and how sad I was to hear of his passing – one of my few regrets is never having had the chance to play alongside Alex James for Preston. Now that really would have been something special.

Incredibly, that game against the USA came close to falling foul of freak weather conditions. It had to be delayed for 24 hours, which caused quite a lot of inconvenience, not least for a handful of English exiles who had travelled from various part of the country to watch.

The following night, England played under floodlights for the first time and America's obsession with their national sport of baseball took a back seat at the wonderful Yankee Stadium – the wonderful, but almost empty Yankee Stadium. The game failed to capture the imagination of the locals and the attendance figure of under 8,000 stood as an all-time low for an England international.

Those who did bother to turn out were treated to a nine-goal feast as we triumphed 6–3. The initial signs were very ominous. I don't know whether it was the false lighting, if the gods were against us or if we were simply trying too hard, but the USA threatened to cause another upset and it wasn't until two minutes from half-time that Ivor Broadis settled us down with the opening goal.

The second half was a different story and a couple of goals in quick succession from Nat Lofthouse and myself put us in the box seat. America got in on the act only for Nat to restore our three-goal advantage. The American referee awarded his countrymen a joke penalty for handball against Harry Johnstone and after that had been converted, the home side struck again to leave us with a slender

4–3 lead. I got in on the scoring act for the second time and Redfern Froggatt added a sixth late on to give us not only a welcome victory but the satisfaction of going someway towards erasing the memory of Belo Horizonte.

Although we did a good deal of travelling during the summer, the chances for sightseeing were limited. We did manage a trip to the top of the Empire State Building and carried out a few official engagements. Players were encouraged to go out in groups and you were rarely afforded free time as an individual.

All in all, it was a tour much enjoyed by those involved although we were a little careful on matters of eating and drinking after a few of the players suffered a bout of food poisoning. It was most unpleasant, believe me –– I know!

CHAPTER FOURTEEN

Game for a laugh

O n top of the great occasions we enjoyed, the marvellous
sights we witnessed and the various cultures we experienced as English international footballers, there was also
a tremendous sense of camaraderie and a feeling of belonging.

It would take more than the pages of this book – a few bound
volumes indeed – if I were to mention in detail each and every player
I encountered while on parade with England. But my story would
not be complete without relaying a tale or two about a handful of
those I counted among my closest footballing friends.

Inevitably there was friction from time to time and the odd clash
of personalities but, by and large, players got on well. We had a few
clowns in the circus, which helped keep spirits high – Frank Swift
and Stan Mortensen, for example. Perhaps it was something to do
with Blackpool, the entertainment capital of Britain, but when Swifty

(Blackpool born) and Stan (a Seasider with Blackpool FC) were in harness, the best advice was to watch out. I lost count of the number of times pairs of shoes would go walkabout in the middle of the night without any feet inside them. It was a well-used practical joke but irrespective of the number of times the prank was played, it always managed to succeed.

I was the victim prior to an international against Scotland at Hampden Park. We were told to put our shoes outside our bedroom doors last thing so they could be cleaned and returned by the morning. Mine went out as agreed but big Frank and little Stan, who actually looked like a comedy duo, nipped in before the official collection and hid them away. Breakfast time arrived and there was no sign of the missing footwear – my only pair, bear in mind. All the other players had hot-footed it downstairs for the official meeting and it wasn't until Walter Winterbottom intervened that my shoes magically re-appeared. No one owned up, but you sensed that Frank and Stan might have had an idea about who was to blame.

Such capers were commonplace and the two of them regularly had us all in fits of laughter. They did a mother-and-baby routine in which Frank would tie Morty up in a sheet, pop a dummy in his mouth and cradle him in his arms during a singsong. Frank had also perfected the art of mimicry and was particularly good at a spoof striptease act. He had all the mannerisms and a few more besides.

Frank was a wonderful character with a huge heart. He believed in getting fun out of life. He took the business of goalkeeping very seriously and was damned good at it, too, but he was also a great companion who was rarely without a smile on his face. With his laugh-a-minute personality, he was popular with colleagues and opponents and he had an unofficial fan club the world over. The continentals loved him. During one game in Switzerland, while we were attacking, he nipped behind the goal to accept a toffee from an admirer.

He was a seasoned international when I broke through after the Second World War and he stayed in the number one position until May 1949 when the curtain fell on his England career after our 4–1 friendly defeat against Oslo in Norway. Frank decided to make a farewell speech at the traditional after-match dinner but had hardly got into his stride when emotion took over and he ended up in floods of tears. It didn't deter him, though, and, showman to the end, he managed to finish on a high note and received an ovation. Frank lost his life in the Munich air crash.

Stan was a great foil for Swifty, not always quite so visually comical – Frank was a bit like Tommy Cooper in that his appearance alone could get you giggling – but very funny all the same. Someone once joked quite innocently that he had a screw loose, and there may well have been a grain of truth in that statement. During his wartime service in the RAF, a serious injury resulted in a metal plate being inserted in his head. You would never have guessed he had suffered in that way because he was fearless, going in where it really hurt in search of goals and, in spite of it, he was in the top drawer in terms of heading ability.

He averaged just short of a goal a game at international level (23 in 25), but will always be best remembered for his supporting role in the 1953 Matthews Final when Blackpool beat Bolton 4–3 to lift the FA Cup. Matthews' vintage performance secured the headlines but Morty didn't do too badly, either, his hat-trick standing as a Wembley record.

He also scored a goal I rate among the best of all time. It came for England against Sweden at Highbury in 1947. After racing into a three-goal lead, we were pegged back to 3–2, but Stan settled our nerves with a goal of pure quality. He had already bagged two when he won possession on the halfway line and scampered forward, swerving past a succession of challenges and unleashing a superb shot from outside the box. What a goal, what a way to complete an international hat-trick, what a player!

Off the field, he was generosity personified and was always around to help anyone who asked. If you couldn't hit it off with Stan, it was your fault because he made friendship easy. He liked company and his ideal was a room full of football buddies and a few jokes to tell.

Due to the rivalry between Blackpool and Preston and the close proximity of the two fine Lancashire towns, we saw a great deal of each other and I always took time out to call round to his shop near the main promenade whenever I was over at the coast.

While I find a smile coming to my face when I picture Swift and Mortensen, I cannot help but feel a sense of despair when recalling Neil Franklin, the best defender I ever played with or against – yes, that good. I know for a fact that Stanley Matthews, once his colleague at Stoke City, echoed the sentiment. There is no greater praise.

Neil and I were great pals, you could call him my best mate within the England set-up, but that didn't mean that I had advance warning of his decision to go to Colombia. The move rocked the football world, coming as it did just a matter of weeks before the 1950 World Cup. The newspapers had a field day. It was an astonishing decision and I believe he regretted it until his dying day.

Neil was a Potteries boy and proud of it. Born in the same year as I was, he joined Stoke City's youth team, rising through the ranks to become club captain and an England regular. Perhaps such parallels helped bond us as friends.

He once famously took on the Stoke directors after hearing suggestions from within that Stanley Matthews was 'unpopular' in the dressing room. Neil called a meeting of the players, sought their collective view, informed Stanley by letter of his intentions and strode off to see the board to quash the rumours and pay handsome tribute to his illustrious team-mate. That was Neil Franklin, a man with principles who liked to see right triumph.

I got to know him as well as anyone outside Stoke and I had detected his frustration over the limited financial rewards available within football. 'You know, Tom, we are at the top of the tree and clubs are taking fortunes off people who want to see us play. We should be getting more of that money. It's a scandal,' he once said on one of my many visits to his home.

He made his England bow on the same day as I did, against Northern Ireland in Belfast, and his ability was obvious from the first whistle. This was a player born to play at the highest level. He had the lot and a bit of style and swagger to go with it. He retained his place for the following 25 internationals over a three-and-a-half-year period. To field an England team without including him was basically unthinkable.

But a top-flight career that looked set to run and run ended in stunning fashion after we had played Scotland at Hampden Park on 15 April 1950. As we were lining up before the game, we had to wait until the marching bands cleared the pitch. Neil was standing alongside me, somewhat pre-occupied. 'See that lot, Tom,' he said, indicating the band. 'They're probably on more money than us.' I looked at him and laughed, but he wasn't laughing.

We were all concerned with turning over the old enemy and putting ourselves in line for World Cup selection. Neil gave his usual faultless performance and no one would have guessed he had other matters on his mind, but he clearly had.

Days later came the bombshell news that Neil and his Stoke colleague George Mountford had left the country with their wives and families to start afresh in Colombia, signing for the Independiente Santa Fe club. It was a sensation. Perhaps unwisely, the two had not informed their club or the FA and all hell broke loose. The FA felt they had been let down by Neil and claimed he had deceived the governing body when he declined invitations to play in the World Cup warm-up matches with Portugal and Belgium later in the spring.

It became clear that Colombian football was more lucrative than what was on offer here and Neil's head had been turned by the promise of greener pastures abroad. Other players followed – Charlie Mitten of Manchester United was another high-profile export. There was talk that Franklin and Mitten had been promised down payments of around £5,000 each and salaries that would treble their annual earnings.

It didn't turn out as they had hoped and much of the proposed income failed to materialise. Neil became disillusioned and homesick and made it known within a year or so that he intended to head home, but the damage had been done. He was an international outcast and the fact that he never played for England again, even though he was only 28 when he returned, underlines how seriously the FA felt about his move to a country that was not a member of FIFA.

Initially he was suspended from playing within the Football League but that ban was lifted in 1951 and I for one expected a host of top clubs to give chase for his signature. I made it my business to see the Preston manager Cliff Britton.

'I understand Neil Franklin is heading back and looking for a club. What an excellent signing he would be for us,' I said. The manager shrugged his shoulders in a gesture of 'thanks but no thanks' and I couldn't believe it.

I suffered the same fate when I tried to persuade Preston to recruit the great Jackie Milburn. I had heard that Wor Jackie was to leave his beloved Newcastle and checked the story with the man himself.

'I've had an offer to go over to Ireland and I'm seriously considering it,' Jackie told me.

I was incredulous. Here was a truly outstanding forward who had averaged a goal every other game over a decade at the top with Newcastle in danger of slipping out of our game – and he was only 32 into the bargain. The opportunity to play in the same forward line with Milburn at club level was very appealing, but Cliff Britton, who always knew best, was again unimpressed. Daft or what?

Managers should have been killed in the rush for the signatures of Franklin and Milburn. To see them as unwanted men was criminal. Milburn drifted off the scene and it wasn't until Hull City, then of the Second Division, came in that Neil was back playing at a competitive level. He stayed there for four years but struggled a bit with injuries and managed fewer than 100 games before moving on to Crewe and Stockport County, eventually retiring in 1957.

With all due respect to Hull, Crewe and Stockport, they were hardly clubs at which you would have expected to find a footballing star such as Neil Franklin. He was for the bigger stage but one ill-advised decision cost him his career. England's selectors consistently refused to re-consider his position even though they were for many years unable to find a suitable replacement alongside Billy Wright at the heart of the England defence.

We kept in touch – a beautiful pot figure of the great racehorse Red Rum that I have in my study was a gift from Neil – but he was never quite the same after his heartbreak in Colombia. In his later years he was troubled by mental health problems and cut a sad and lonely figure. I found his funeral particularly morose if only for the fact that his football life had not realised anything like its full potential.

Some people reckon that the Matthews-Mortensen-Lawton-Mannion-Finney combination was the best forward line fielded by England. How could I possibly comment apart from saying that the other four made it a joy for me to be involved.

Tommy Lawton was something of a father figure when I stepped up to the highest level in 1946. He was only three years my senior but he was already an England star with eight pre-war caps to his name. He scored 22 goals in 23 appearances for his country and averaged more than a goal every other game during his career with Chelsea, Notts County, Brentford and Arsenal. That's some record but there was more to Tommy's game than simply putting the ball in the back of the net. He was a powerhouse of a player with a lovely first touch for a man of his size. He was great in the air – as good as anyone before or since – and someone who took his business very seriously. If Frank Swift was the clown, Tommy Lawton was the prince. Serious and studious, you had conversations with Tommy, not banter sessions. He was a great player to have leading your front line and I will never forget the encouragement he gave me as a raw youngster trying to find his feet at international level.

Wilf Mannion was a class act, the inside-forward I rated as my perfect partner on the left flank. He could have taught telepathy and had the uncanny knack of getting the ball to you at just the right angle and with just the right pace. Small in stature but surprisingly strong, Wilf was a footballing artist and a great entertainer.

He got a reputation for being hard to handle, especially after an infamous fall-out with his club, Middlesbrough, but I always found him to be a nice chap, quiet and totally inoffensive. He may have crossed swords with the powers-that-be at 'Boro, but he was never considered to be anything other than a legend by the spectators at Ayresome Park. They loved him and rightly so.

He hit hard times after his playing days were over and eventually had to sell some of his prized England caps to pay his way. That's so sad.

Like thousands of Middlesbrough and England supporters, I will always remember Wilf for his supreme ability with a football at his feet. He was magical, gliding around the pitch riding tackles and then setting up a chance when no one else could spot an opening. He reminded me of the great Brazilians.

I missed the opportunity to play against the greatest Brazilian of them all, perhaps the greatest footballer of them all, Pele. In the 1958 World Cup we were drawn in the same group and Pele was the talk of the tournament. I was ruled out of the game in Gothenburg with injury and Pele, just 17, was rested. People thought he was tired but we found out the real reason – the Brazilian authorities were reluctant to pitch their boy wonder against the 'ruthless and physical' English. We were taken aback by the very suggestion. I would never argue against the fact that our football was competitive and full of tackles and challenges, but in no way did we take competitiveness beyond what was considered acceptable. Pele went on to prove that his guardian angels were acting without reason in wrapping him up in cotton wool, proving that he could hack it in a man's world with a superb goalscoring performance in the final itself.

So I never shared a field with Pele but I did meet him many years later, and he took the points. He was the guest of honour at a glorious football gathering held in London to celebrate a milestone for the

FA. More than 500 people attended what was a showpiece occasion and I was honoured to be introduced to the great man.

'Ah,' he said. 'Tom Finney – I remember my father once taking me to watch you play.'

Intrigued, I asked, 'Oh yes, and when was that?'

'The World Cup in 1950. You were playing for England in a group game in Belo Horizonte against . . .'

'Enough!' I said. 'Thanks, but if it's all the same to you that game is not up for discussion.'

Pele saw the funny side and we shared a laugh. It was a lovely moment.

CHAPTER FIFTEEN

All the luck in the world

I was lucky enough to figure in three World Cup tournaments, although whether the word 'lucky' gives an accurate reflection is highly debatable.

In Brazil in 1950 I played in the three Pool Two games against Chile (win), USA (defeat) and Spain (defeat). In Switzerland in 1954 I appeared in the Pool Four fixtures against Belgium (draw) and Switzerland (win) and the quarter-final versus Uruguay (defeat). Sweden in 1958 was the biggest personal disappointment. After featuring in the opening Pool Four match with the Soviet Union (draw) and scoring a crucial penalty, a knee injury left me a frustrated spectator for the remaining matches with Brazil (draw) and Austria (draw) and the play-off with the Soviet Union (defeat).

My World Cup record, therefore, lists just two victories, with England managing to get past the pool stage once in three attempts.

Considering England's status and the expectation levels, this was hardly the stuff of dreams. Why we fared so poorly so consistently remains a mystery.

But playing in the World Cup is about far more than just results. Well, I would say that wouldn't I? It's about the thrill of the glamour stage, the opportunity to rub shoulders with the greatest players on the planet, the chance to experience different cultures and witness first hand how others play the game. What a wonderful education for a one-time plumber's apprentice from Preston, to be chosen to travel to South America, Europe and Scandinavia as a football ambassador for his country. That's how I always looked upon it. When I played at international level, it was the honour of honours. I felt an affinity with the soldier on the battlefield, representing not only myself and my family but the entire nation, with a duty to uphold the great name of England.

I was just 16 when Italy beat Hungary in Paris to lift the World Cup in 1938 and it didn't mean a right lot to me. The tournament was hardly big news over here, mainly due to England not being one of the participating countries. As an avid football fan, I obviously knew bits about the background and the format, aware that a Frenchman called Jules Rimet had conceived the idea and that Uruguay had been the first winners. But foreign football and foreign footballers were not part of our lives. The English game was unashamedly parochial – to sign a southern player was unusual – and if you had asked any of the Preston teenagers of the day to name the Italian goalscorers against Hungary they would have looked at you in bewildered silence.

Most people were too entrenched in what was going on here to worry over much about foreign footballing affairs. The World Cup was a faraway competition in every sense although much of that changed in 1950 when, at long last, England competed.

I might not have known much about the previous tournament 12 years earlier, but this time I found myself on the official aeroplane as part of the national squad. If that wasn't exciting enough, the fact that our destination was the fanatical football nation of Brazil simply added to the attraction, the mystique and the charm.

We qualified by winning the Home Championships, ultimately accounting for Scotland at Hampden Park thanks to a fairly streaky goal from Roy Bentley. The World Cup committee had deemed that two countries from Britain should attend the finals and the second place was offered to Scotland. For some crazy reason the Scottish football authorities let pride get the better of them and declined the invitation on the grounds that they had not won the Home Championships. The Scottish players were incensed. I remember our captain Billy Wright encouraging his Scottish counterpart George Young to appeal against the decision. George took up the mantle but got absolutely nowhere.

It was a great pity because in spite of our fierce opposition out on the pitch, there was great camaraderie between the England and Scotland camps. In fact, the intense Anglo-Scottish rivalry probably applied more to the supporters than the players. That said, the last thing you ever wanted was defeat against the Jocks. England versus Scotland, be it at Wembley or Hampden Park, was the biggest international fixture of them all during the fifties. I played in some fairly hefty matches both at home and overseas, but for atmosphere to the point of frenzy, this was number one.

The Scots were – still are – incredibly passionate about their football and I got to know many of their top players well, both as opponents and team-mates. At club level, there was a time when we could have been re-named McPreston, such was the depth of the

Scottish contingent. At one stage, more than half our team hailed from north of the border, players of the calibre of Willie Cunningham, Willie Forbes, Tommy Docherty, Jimmy Baxter, Bobby Beattie and Angus Morrison.

The connection started way back before the Second World War when the famous 1938 FA Cup final squad included Bill Shankly, Jimmy Dougal, Andy Beattie, Jimmy Milne, Bud Maxwell, Hughie O'Donnell and Tom Smith. They were all of a type – strong characters with fire in their bellies who didn't need a manager or a crowd to get them motivated. To a man, they were always up for a game and they liked nothing better than to put one over England.

The two exceptional Scotland full-backs of my time were the captain George Young and Sammy Cox, both of Glasgow Rangers. They were classy defenders who liked to try to out-wit rather than out-muscle you, and I had some real tussles with them both.

Our road to Rio started in Europe. The FA put together a short tour, which included matches against Portugal and Belgium, neither of whom was among the 13 nations due to go head-to-head in Brazil. After winning 5–3 in Lisbon, we carried on our rich vein of goalscoring form by putting four past the Belgians at a venue that was to achieve tragic notoriety a few decades later, the Heysel Stadium.

Belgium were ahead at the turnaround, but then came a watershed moment that was to change the course of the match. Jackie Milburn was injured and unable to continue, and Wolves winger Jimmy Mullen became the first substitute ever to appear for England. Jimmy was not content with that and promptly underlined his entry into the celebrated pages of football history with the equalising goal.

I had swapped to the right flank to accommodate Jimmy and the positional manoeuvring gave us a renewed head of steam. Stan Mortensen headed us in front from a cross before a brilliant interchange of passes between Morty and Roy Bentley put Wilf Mannion in for number three. The Belgians had gone by this point and Roy popped up with number four on the whistle.

Preparations for the main event had gone like clockwork and our 21-man squad looked well balanced with plenty of flair. Without getting carried away, we felt we had a fighting chance of doing well in England's first taste of World Cup fare. Under the leadership of Walter Winterbottom we had Billy Wright, Stanley Mortensen, Wilf Mannion and myself, while Wolverhampton Wanderers' goalkeeper Bert Williams had finally edged out the legendary Frank Swift. It was no surprise that England were among the fancied four, along with Italy, Sweden and the hosts.

Our send-off from London was surpassed only by our reception in Rio, but behind the carnival atmosphere we soon sensed that everyone was out to get us. Our reputation had gone before us and we were considered the team to beat.

Although we were very well looked after, we found that coping with the climatic conditions was far from easy. It was hot and humid and most of us needed extra oxygen to get by. The people were something else. They never seemed to stop singing and dancing for a second, with outdoor parties going on all day and all night. It was an amazing way of life, a far cry from the sedate environment back home, and when we went along to watch the opening game of the competition, Brazil versus Mexico, it blew my mind.

There were 200,000 people in the immense three-tiered Maracana Stadium, the biggest football ground in the world, and the noise – well, it made you shudder just to sit there. A moat surrounded the pitch to keep the supporters from getting too close to the action for comfort, and the players ran out through a steel trapdoor on the touchline. The Brazilian players just didn't look like footballers, with their low-slung boots and no shinguards, but when the action started, I was mesmerised by their speed and agility and the way they seemed to caress the ball.

Brazil won – any other result would probably have been declared null and void – and the tournament was off to a flying start, which gave the people even more reason to party.

England's first task was to win Pool Two, which as well as ourselves included Chile, Spain and the USA, the latter viewed very much as a team making up the numbers. The Maracana Stadium was less than a quarter full when we crossed swords with Chile. Their line-up included the Newcastle forward George Robledo, and we had a debutant in our ranks, Laurie Hughes of Liverpool.

Stan Mortensen became the first Englishman to score in the World Cup when he headed in a cross from Jimmy Mullen. Robledo, the most potent weapon in the Chilean armoury, was unlucky not to equalise when his shot crashed against a post, but that served as an alarm call and Wilf Mannion got on the end of one of my crosses to secure our win. We were on our way and the dressing-room atmosphere was very upbeat. Walter Winterbottom told us to be encouraged but stay focused.

'It was a good win, fellows, but we have played better, we can play better and we must strive to play better,' he told us.

Everything in the camp was rosy. We trained hard and found plenty of opportunities for sightseeing and relaxation although at night it was hard to shut out the incessant beat of the drums and get some sleep. But, so what? We could live with that, and with two points on the board we were sitting pretty. We were totally unprepared for the shock that lay in store four days later. To lose to America was a catastrophe. The World Cup has never produced an upset of such proportions. Instead of riding high with one foot in the final stages, we went into the final pool game against Spain in Rio in genuine need of both a good performance and a positive result.

We managed the performance. Stanley Matthews was recalled on the right (he was actually flown in from an FA tour of Canada as the result of an SOS call), I was on the left and Jackie Milburn operated down the centre. We looked a formidable unit going forward and played some decent stuff despite having to endure some dreadful tackling. Spain were obsessed with underhand tactics and I was one of several Englishmen who felt aggrieved at being denied straightforward claims on a penalty. The only ingredients missing were goals although with a hint of good fortune we could have had three or four. Spanish keeper Ramammets had one of those 'thou shalt not pass' matches, making several superb saves and riding his luck as we tried but failed to find a way through.

The neutrals in a 74,000 crowd at the Maracana Stadium definitely sided with England, mainly due to Spain's blatant abuse of the rules, but we simply couldn't conjure the goal our display deserved. Jackie Milburn did get the ball in the net only for what seemed a perfectly legitimate goal to be disallowed. Spain, who eventually finished top of the group table, made us pay in full with a goal from centre-forward Zarraonandia.

Our World Cup adventure was over almost before it had begun. Two defeats, two goals and two points were nothing approaching the sort of return people had predicted. We held an inquest among ourselves, talking things over as a unit and listening to the views of the management, but there were more questions than answers. No matter how we tried to look elsewhere for reasons, the events in Belo Horizonte kept rearing up to haunt us. On returning home, we faced a new backlash over the defeat by the Americans. The media would not let go and I maintain that it took English football close on two years to win back some pride and prestige.

Switzerland was considered something of an odd choice for the staging of a World Cup. This was no leading football nation by any means and, in 1954, they found both the organisation and the administration something of a struggle. However, for us the tournament proved a little more rewarding than the previous one. As one of the seeded teams, we qualified for the quarter-finals from a pool that included Belgium, Italy and the hosts, and were unfortunate to go out to the reigning champions, Uruguay. The firm favourites, Hungary – we could vouch for their credentials – were grouped with Germany, their eventual conquerors in the final.

England were going through a transitional period on the international front. The biggest problem still was finding a suitable replacement for Neil Franklin, and the selectors had plenty of hard decisions to make with other positions up for grabs, too. No settled line-up jumped out of the names on the list.

Our warm-up programme did little to offer reason for optimism. We did record a morale-boosting 4–2 win over Scotland at Hampden Park, but from then on it was downhill fast, a short tour resulting in defeats by both Yugoslavia (0–1), on the occasion of my 50th cap, and Hungary (1–7). Ivor Broadis, of Newcastle, was the dressing-room comedian, not in a loud or flamboyant way but he had a sharp wit and dry sense of humour. When we lost to the Hungarians, he warned the other players not to go near his boots as they were 'bloody red hot'. Ivor was a very gifted player, and he and I had developed a promising partnership. We were close friends off the field, too.

With a pre-tournament record reading played two, lost two, goals for one, goals against eight, it came as no surprise to me that the bemused selectors once again turned, if somewhat grudgingly, to Mr Magic. Stanley Matthews, by now within months of his 40th birthday, was called back into the fray, having been among the scapegoats in the wake of the infamous Wembley defeat by Hungary. Nat Lofthouse was to lead the front line and there were places, too, for seasoned campaigners Billy Wright, Ivor Broadis and me.

We looked on in awe as the Hungarians rattled in 17 goals in their opening two group matches, thrashing Korea 9–0 and Germany 8–3. How the Germans, re-admitted to the competition for the first time since the war, must have relished their final day revenge!

There were goals galore in our first outing, against Belgium in Basle, eight in fact, equally shared. It made for entertaining viewing, not just for the 14,000 in the St Jakob Stadium, but also for a worldwide audience. Televised football had arrived and the game would never be quite the same again although viewing figures in 1954 were relatively modest.

Stanley Matthews took it upon himself to turn in a vintage display, beating the full-back time and time again to set up opportunities after we had fallen behind early on. Inspired by my fellow flanker, we struck three times, Ivor Broadis scoring twice and Nat Lofthouse once with a spectacular diving header. But we dug ourselves a hole with indifferent defending and the Belgians drew level to force extra time. Almost immediately, Ivor presented Nat with the chance to restore our lead, but the match ended in disappointment, especially for one of our most consistent performers, Jimmy

Dickinson, who had the misfortune to deflect a free kick into his own net.

Walter Winterbottom had good reason to question a suspect defence and his answer was to switch Billy Wright from half-back to centre-half. Experimenting is not advised at World Cup level but the move worked a treat.

Next up we confronted the hosts on a boiling hot afternoon in Berne. Stanley Matthews and Nat Lofthouse were missing through injury but one of the replacements, Wolves' veteran winger Jimmy Mullen, more than justified his inclusion by netting our first goal. His Molineux team-mate Dennis Wilshaw put his name to the second. The game was played in a cauldron-like atmosphere at the Wankdorf Stadium and it was very difficult to play at a high tempo.

So we were through to the quarter-finals as winners of the group. We played Uruguay in Basle and although we lost 2–4, it was considered one of the tournament's finest matches. Once again, Stanley Matthews was England's shining light, making a nonsense of his advancing years with a performance full of craft and guile. By contrast, Gil Merrick had what can only be described as a nightmare in goal. The Birmingham custodian should have saved two, possibly three, of the Uruguayans' hits.

Nat Lofthouse and I got our goals, Nat levelling things up early on and me pulling us back into it at 2–3 with 20 minutes to go. My effort set up a grandstand finish and Stan Matthews was within the thickness of a post of producing an equaliser. However, the Uruguayans put the game beyond reach when Merrick was beaten by a weak shot from Ambrois.

Merrick became the scapegoat for our elimination from the tournament and I felt desperately sorry for him. He was criticised unmercifully in the media, England's public enemy number one according to them. They slaughtered him for days and seemed to have ganged up to ensure that he was banished from the international arena forever. If that was the aim, it worked; Gil never again pulled on the England jersey. All players make mistakes and no one individual should ever carry all the responsibility for a result, irrespective of how poorly he might have played. Goalkeepers always suffer for a bad game because their mistakes are vital. If I get a second life, remind me not to come back as one!

Switzerland 1954 did not see Tom Finney at his best. The tournament rather passed me by and my form was so unpredictable that I actually feared for my place against Uruguay.

One of my biggest regrets is never having had the chance to take the international field against Brazil. When they played England for the first time, in May 1956 at Wembley, I was absent through injury and the same fate befell me during the 1958 World Cup in Sweden when a young man called Pele took the football world by storm.

I thought Sweden, like Switzerland, an odd choice of venue. It's a beautiful country but hardly one of football's hotbeds. I fully appreciate the merits of taking the tournament around the world but I believe preference should be given to nations with a passion for the game. However, the hosts did overachieve on a massive scale by having the audacity to reach the final itself before being blown away by the brilliant Brazilians.

The grounds were small – except for Gothenburg and Stockholm – and the crowds even smaller. Fewer than 6,000 spectators watched some of the matches. Northern Ireland, Scotland and Wales were in Pools One, Two and Three respectively; we were pitched into Pool Four with the Soviet Union, Austria and Brazil. Those who knew best – the media and the pundits – estimated at least a quarter-final place for us, but it was not to be.

We opened up in Gothenburg against the USSR and forced a 2–2 draw. Now, I experienced many nerve-tingling moments during my career but few to match the feeling I had in the pit of my stomach just minutes from the end of this thriller. It was early evening – Sweden had beaten Mexico in the afternoon opener – and we were trailing 1–2 when a chance to grab a priceless point was presented to me in the form of a penalty.

The Russians had established a two-goal lead before we responded with a great attacking show to pull one back through West Bromwich forward Derek Kevan. Our opponents, so confident and sure-footed early on, began to get the jitters. Bobby Robson had a goal disallowed for an infringement before Johnny Haynes was unceremoniously chopped down from behind to win the spot kick.

There was an astonishing reaction, not least from the giant Russian goalkeeper Lev Yashin who lost the plot completely. He raced from his area to contest the decision and actually manhandled the Hungarian referee Istvan Zsolt. When the referee opted against a change of heart, Yashin threw his famous cap to the ground in disgust. It was an extraordinary scene, a right old commotion, and all I could do was stand there and ponder my penalty kick. All sorts of thoughts and theories passed through my mind as Don Howe came running upfield with the ball. I thought Don was about to take the responsibility off my shoulders and had he offered I would have said 'yes, please!' But he had only come to hand me the ball.

'Thanks, Don,' I said, or at least that's what I think I said.

I was also struggling with a sore right knee, sustained in a first-half challenge, but the pain was nothing compared to the sense of apprehension as I finally stepped forward to put the ball on the spot.

Yashin was an imposing figure at the best of times but his angry outburst had made him even more of an intimidating opponent. At the very last minute, almost at the point of turning back to face the goal, I opted to take the kick with my right foot, my weaker foot. 'That'll fox him,' I thought and, thank the Almighty, it did. My low shot was well out of reach of his lunge.

Without wishing to overdramatise the situation, skipper Billy Wright was not the only England player to turn and face the other away as the kick was taken. Hero status was mine. My back was sore with the congratulations of my colleagues, but it wasn't my back I was worried about.

That night during dinner my leg began to ache. I had suffered delayed injury reaction many times, but nothing like this. By morning, stiffness had set in and I could hardly walk. My room-mate, Tommy Banks, the Bolton full-back, had to help me to dress. I shuffled down for breakfast, had a chat with Walter Winterbottom and England trainer Harold Shepherdson and was packed off back to bed for a complete rest.

Unbeknown to me, Harold arranged a hospital appointment and for the next 24 hours things went well. I awoke the following morning – a day before the eagerly awaited clash with Brazil – fairly confident that I was getting close to a full recovery. As you would expect, Walter and Harold wanted to know exactly how I was as quickly as possible, so they scheduled a fitness test, but the knee was not ready for running or kicking and I had to concede defeat.

Taking bad news on the chin is something I have prided myself on down the years. Rarely have I let events, no matter how disappointing, get the better of me. This, though, was one time when I felt almost cheated. The opportunity to put my skills to the ultimate test was being whisked from my grasp faster than you could say Pele.

Liverpool's Alan A'Court took my place in Gothenburg's Nya Ullevi Stadium and I was among the 40,895 spectators.

Watching was a pleasure. Brazil's silky smooth style contrasted with England's competitiveness and effectiveness on the counter-attack, and how the game stayed goalless I will never know. Pele, the precocious 17-year-old, and Garrincha, the 'Little Bird', were both missing from the Brazilian front line, while Billy Wright proved a tower of strength at the heart of our defence, but a 0–0 draw still represented an excellent result for us.

The brilliant Didi caught my eye – supremely gifted players who seemed able to make the ball talk were always my favourites. I will never forget seeing him at close quarters. He was known as the 'Black Magician' in his homeland and it was easy to see why.

He was the man who devised the banana kick. No one had bent the ball until Didi did it, but he wasn't even sure of a place in the Brazil squad until the last minute. Some of his countrymen felt that, at 30, he was too old, and the fact that he had married a white woman and didn't always appear to be trying were other factors that counted against him. But play he did and what a joy it was to see his amazing control of the ball.

That said, Wolves defender Bill Slater did a damn good job as a man-marker – for evidence look again at the scoreline. To record a clean sheet against Brazil in those days was an achievement in itself and the England lads deserved all the plaudits that came their way. They battled like tigers and with an ounce of luck might have won.

The stage was perfectly set for the final pool game against Austria – a win would take us through. The Austrians were sitting ducks, having not managed so much as a goal in back-to-back 3–0 and 2–0 defeats against Brazil and the USSR. My injury was no better and my personal hard-luck story meant another chance for Alan A'Court at the Ryavallen Stadium in Boras. I sat on the bench fully expecting a relatively straightforward afternoon but, in spite of vocal support from 300 British sailors, we floundered. Austria got their first goal of the tournament to take the lead before Johnny Haynes forced an equaliser. Hardly renowned for their goalscoring exploits, the Austrians surged ahead again but Derek Kevan rescued England with a second equaliser late on.

We had messed up big style. Qualification now rested on a play-off with the USSR and, once again, I was unable to play an active part.

Brazil had qualified after bringing in the wonderful Pele and Garrincha (something of a Stanley Matthews lookalike). Pele was exceptional. He was some way short of 6 ft tall and must have weighed in at little over 10 stone, but he could jump like Tommy Lawton and twist and turn like no one I had ever seen before, or have seen since. It mattered not how the ball was delivered, Pele was able to get it under control and play. On top of his phenomenal ability, he also had the perfect temperament. Much to the annoyance of his opponents, he played with a smile on his face.

Our game against the Russians was the biggest match of the tournament so far. The winners went through, the losers boarded a flight home.

It was the third time we had confronted the USSR in just five weeks and Peter Brabrook, of Chelsea, and Peter Broadbent, of Wolves, were both handed baptisms of fire. I was feeling a little better, the knee had settled somewhat, and I felt I could re-join the squad in an active capacity if we won through.

No such luck. The Russian players stormed forward like men possessed from the word go and we looked destined to be on the wrong end of a thrashing. Peter Broadbent had other ideas and set up a stream of attacks only to see his colleagues squander chance after chance. Peter Brabrook twice hit the post and it became abundantly clear that this was not going to be England's day, a fear confirmed when Russian winger Ilyin scored the game's only goal with shot that beat Colin McDonald via an upright.

By the time the final came around, I was back home in Preston some 1,000 miles away, watching events unfold via the television set. Brazil were bound to win in my book; they had the better players and the better system. Other people felt they were vulnerable, mere exhibitionists with little backbone, and that someday soon, perhaps against Sweden, they would get found out. It was as though the English and Europeans were united in wishing Brazil to falter. But inspired by the astonishing Pele – was this boy really only 17? – the men from South America won with plenty to spare. They had won five out of six matches during the tournament, scoring 16 goals and conceding just four. Brazil were world champions for the first time and I was delighted for them and for football.

I recalled an incident I had witnessed during the World Cup in Brazil eight years before. A small boy, no more than six or seven, bare-footed and only partially dressed, approached us outside our hotel. Just imagine our reaction when he placed an orange on one instep, flicked it into the air and caught it on the other. He must have repeated the trick 20 times and we felt obliged to reward his brilliance with a few coins. It wasn't long before we became used to such stunning displays of ball control in match situations.

From humble beginnings Brazil has gone on to become a world force and I believe they are every football supporter's second team. They are certainly mine – if Brazil are playing, book me a ticket.

England could not be faulted for effort or commitment during the '58 World Cup – I am starting to sound like a modern-day manager – but our technical ability left much to be desired. We were determined to play in a certain way no matter what and there lay the root of our problem. Somewhere along the line, someone had to call a halt, re-assess our tactics and take a close look at what was happening elsewhere. Alf Ramsey was the man to do it but it took a further eight years before the penny dropped.

Wembley '66 was Alf's finest hour – lifting the World Cup still stands as England's greatest sporting achievement. Ask anyone to select English football's most memorable moment and it is a fair bet that the overwhelming majority will come back with Wembley '66.

I was lucky enough not only to be present to witness the triumph over West Germany, but also to attend the celebration party and present Geoff Hurst with his man-of-the-match award. As correspondent for the *News of the World*, I watched the final from the Wembley press box and one of my duties was to select England's star player. It had been arranged in advance that, win or lose, I should go along to the Royal Garden Hotel in Kensington High Street, the official team hotel, for the after-match function and present the chosen player with his award.

What a fantastic experience that turned out to be! The tournament may not have smiled kindly on me during my playing days, but here I was personally congratulating Bobby Moore and co. just a couple of hours after their finest achievement. But let me let you into a little secret. Up until the moment when Geoff Hurst slammed home his hat-trick goal, I wasn't for making him man of the match. I felt that accolade belonged to Alan Ball for a wonderful display of skill, stamina and strength, but how can a fellow score three goals in football's showpiece match and not take top prize?

The atmosphere at Wembley that July afternoon was like no other. In the hours leading up to kick-off, long before the dramatic events unfolded, the crowd seemed to sense that something special was about to take place. How right they were, and I will never forget the scenes at the end. It was all so moving, especially to see those around you, including some hard-headed and experienced hacks, unable to hold back tears of joy.

With a photographer in tow, I scurried from Wembley to meet up with the England party at the hotel. Once we had secured a picture of Geoff receiving his award from me, I was free to mingle and share in the sheer pleasure of the happiest group of players of all time. Even Alf Ramsey was overjoyed – in his own way.

Alf and I played together many times for England, but he was not someone I could say I knew well. Very few people got close to Alf; the man was a loner. He was very serious, even as a young man, and obviously thought hard about the tactical side of the game. To win the league championship for an unfashionable club such as Ipswich and be the only England manager to lift the World Cup speaks volumes for his record, but he always seemed to be on his guard.

He was a classic full-back, lacking great pace, but he made up for that with a quick brain and the ability to smell danger and take up good positions. A quietly efficient defender, more functional than outstanding, he preferred to let his football do the talking – apart from once, when I couldn't really determine his motive. In the FA Cup of 1952–53, we drew Spurs at Deepdale and Alf and I came into direct opposition. It was a cracking game and I converted a penalty in a 2–2 draw. I often made a point of popping my head around the opposition's dressing-room door just to say well done or hard luck or shake hands with players of my close acquaintance,

England colleagues and such like. It was a quick in-and-out sort of arrangement, but on this particular occasion it went on for a few minutes longer than usual. Alf, who was standing close to the door, seemed quite animated.

'Not much point you lot coming all the way to London for the replay,' he barked. 'There will be nothing for you at Spurs.'

I was taken aback, not so much by what had been said but more by who had said it. I looked Alf in the eyes for a moment but it was impossible to tell whether he was being aggressive, jocular or simply mischievous. He was dead right though – four days later we lost by a single goal at White Hart Lane.

The other, starkly contrasting, event that most people remember in football's history is the dreadful air crash in Munich in 1958 when eight Manchester United players, four club officials and nine football journalists, many of them my personal friends, were killed.

I was working on a plumbing job just outside Manchester on the day of the disaster. One of my colleagues came running over to relay the terrible news. It was so terrible that I found it hard to accept. It was beyond comprehension, so many lives wiped out at a stroke, the team that experts tipped to dominate English football for years to come gone forever.

That evening, along with millions of football followers the world over, I watched and listened to the grim bulletins and newsflashes on television and radio. What it must have been like for the wives and mothers, sons and daughters of those involved doesn't bear thinking about.

Three of my England international colleagues, the magnificent Duncan Edwards, the impressive Tommy Taylor and the underrated Roger Byrne, perished in that crash along with Bert Whalley, the

United coach who was a particularly close friend. I had known Bert since my schoolboy days at Preston and respected him as someone with an astute football brain and an exceptionally generous man who worked tirelessly for charity causes. But for me, the biggest loss of all was Frank Swift. Big Frank's death hit me like a thunderbolt and it took me quite some time to face the fact that I wouldn't see him again.

In spite of the anguish, the grief and the tears, the fact that their squad had been decimated and their manager, Matt Busby, lay in hospital on the critical list, United officials declared their intent. 'We will carry on' was the defiant and emotional message from Old Trafford, but it wasn't seen as disrespectful, quite the opposite. Just 13 days after the crash, United took on Sheffield Wednesday in the FA Cup fifth round, a personal triumph for assistant manager Jimmy Murphy.

Jimmy worked a miracle in getting a team together at all. It included survivors Harry Gregg and Bill Foulkes, who had emerged from the plane shocked but unhurt, raw youngsters Freddie Goodwin, Shay Brennan and Ron Cope, and the odd new recruit such as the dazzling Ernie Taylor from Blackpool.

As you might imagine, the publicity and exposure focused around the Cup tie reached an unprecedented level and there was great demand for tickets. I rang Jimmy Murphy to see if I could secure a couple of seats for a friend of mine – a prior engagement in Preston that night meant I was unable to attend myself but I told Jimmy my thoughts would be with him. Jimmy thanked me and said, 'Tom, can you do me a huge favour?'

'Of course,' I replied. 'How can I help?'

'Cancel your appointment for a start and get along to the game. I'm trying to sign a defender and would like you to help me sell United to him.'

I was dumbstruck – how could I, a registered player with Preston North End, help a rival club secure a transfer? I told Jimmy my concerns but he convinced me that the situation was exceptional and that no one would think any the worse of me. Tommy Docherty agreed to stand in for me at a Preston sporting presentation and three hours before United took the field against Wednesday, I was sitting alongside Jimmy in a Manchester hotel.

I thought it was to be a secret rendezvous so the fact that the hotel reception was alive with newspaper reporters and photographers was a little unfortunate. However, my presence was missed by the media as I was whisked to a private suite to meet the mystery United target, Aston Villa star Stan Crowther.

Accompanied by his manager, Eric Houghton, Stan didn't have a lot to say. He had known no football home other than Villa and was clearly nervous about the prospect of signing for United and stepping into the huge gap left by Duncan Edwards. On behalf of Jimmy Murphy, Manchester United Football Club and all its supporters, I donned my salesman's cap and got to work on Stan. My persuasion must have helped do the trick. Stan clearly warmed to the idea, signing on the dotted line before we all shot off to watch United win 3–0. What a night!

CHAPTER SIXTEEN

Benefit . . .

I
t cost eight bob (40p) to buy the best seat in the house at my testimonial match on 26 September 1960 and I remember thinking it sounded a bit pricey. I was keen that it should be a showpiece occasion for the town and didn't like the idea of putting off would-be spectators by the cost of admission.

'Should it not be priced cheaper than a league fixture?' I queried, but those assisting me with the arrangements said I was worrying without due cause. It wasn't as though we were expecting everyone to pay that much, they argued. That was the top-priced, South Pavilion Stand seat. You could pay 7s (35p) in the West Stand, 3s (15p) in the Paddock, and the general ground terrace price was just 2s 6d (13p). I held my hands up in acceptance but I still had reservations.

However, those on my committee were proved absolutely right.

The crowd figure on the big night reached 33,157 – between 6,000 and 8,000 up on the average during the previous four seasons at Deepdale – and we had a party. While my farewell match against Luton five months earlier had played out to an overwhelming feeling of sadness, this was totally different. A galaxy of stars turned out on a night of nostalgia, laughter, back-slapping and great entertainment. Rarely, if ever, has so much soccer talent gathered within the confines of one stadium.

I skippered a Preston North End Select XI against an Invited All Stars XI and, believe me, these were all stars in the true sense of the word. Stanley Matthews was the big draw in the opposition team, marginally accepting top-of-the-bill rating ahead of Billy Wright, Stan Mortensen, Wilf Mannion, Neil Franklin, Bert Trautmann, Jimmy Armfield, Nat Lofthouse . . . it was a footballing who's who of the 1950s.

And there was Bill Shankly. When I got in touch with Shanks to tell him the plan he reacted like an excited schoolboy. The telephone conversation went a bit like this:

'Bill, Tom here – how are you doing?'

'All the better for hearing from you, Tommy my son.'

'North End have granted me a testimonial and I would very much like you to be there on the night – would that present any problem?'

'No problem, son – if I have anything else on, I'll just have to cancel. Nothing could keep me away.'

At that point I should have quit, thanked him, said how much I was looking forward to seeing him again and replaced the receiver. I didn't and it was a huge mistake. I had already decided that my old North End pal Andy Beattie would run the line and had it in mind that Shanks, also by now well into his forties, should run the other. I put my plan forward and it was greeted with a second or two of total silence. Then Bill let rip and it was a wonder the telephone line connecting Preston and Liverpool didn't catch fire.

'Run the so-and-so line, you must be bloody joking. Listen up, Tommy, I'm coming as a player and that's the bloody end of it,' or words to that effect.

'Very well,' was my meek response, 'that would be wonderful. I just didn't think . . .'

'No, that's the problem, Tommy – you just didn't bloody think.'

I put the telephone down and laughed aloud. The one truth about Bill Shankly was that he never ever changed. Before my first full game for North End I remember him wandering across the dressing room in my direction.

'Now look, lad, during the course of the game, and most likely every game we play together from now on for that matter, I'll shout and bawl at you. I'll call you all the names under the sun when we're out there. It isn't personal, it's football – understand?' That was Bill all over. He did it his way or not at all.

My problem concerning the benefit match was that by including Bill, someone would have to make way. This was very much last-minute stuff – the match-night programmes had been printed and Shanks was down in black and white as the linesman with the red flag. Funnily enough, we had more trouble recruiting linesmen than players. Andy Beattie had to withdraw at the last minute after being appointed manager of Nottingham Forest the previous weekend.

Somewhat fortuitously, Ronnie Clayton got in touch to say he was suffering from laryngitis, had been unable to play for Blackburn on the Saturday and wouldn't be fit for the benefit game either. That meant Shanks could play, which he did right through the 90 minutes. His style was just how I remembered as a young boy – short steps, hands flicking backwards, always playing with his head raised, his passing as crisp and accurate as ever.

The mood of expectancy increased every time a star player confirmed he would be taking part. One night the newspapers proclaimed 'Matthews' "yes" to Finney'; a couple of days later it was 'Wright to line up for Finney's big night' and so on. From memory, no one declined. The biggest doubt was me – injury threatened my appearance at my own testimonial. But how, I can hear you asking, could I have picked up an injury when I hadn't played since the previous spring?

The previous week, Billy Liddell invited me over to play in his benefit game at Liverpool and I lined up alongside Jimmy McIlroy. I remember a challenge coming in as I stretched for the ball and felt my knee click. Ligament damage was diagnosed and my fitness for the forthcoming match at Deepdale was on the line. It was a desperate few days. The thought of missing a game organised in my honour and for my benefit was as unthinkable as it was absurd. It was to be my first appearance at Deepdale since my retirement and I was determined to be there, injury or no injury. I had intense treatment and got to the stage where I knew I could perform to at least a satisfactory level. I wasn't 100 per cent by any means, but I got through and loved every minute.

I asked to be allocated some space in the programme and wrote the following:

Tonight is an occasion I will always treasure, even though my heart is heavy with the thought of saying au revoir to football.

Through the generosity of the Directors of PNE FC I am provided with this opportunity of saying a big 'thank you' to you, the public, for all your encouragement, sportsmanship and tolerance towards me over the years. Every footballer needs support and I ask that you give the same to my successors.

It has been my pleasure to play before you and I hope you have enjoyed watching my efforts. I find it difficult to express in words my feelings, but I can simply say that my career here has been extremely happy.

The banter between the players, in the dressing room beforehand and at the after-match reception, positively crackled as everyone tried to out-do the other with a favourite funny story.

While Bill Shankly was the oldest man on view, 45-year-old Stanley Matthews wasn't far behind. The difference was, of course, that Stan was still playing regular league football and his fitness level was amazing. Deepdale football watchers over the previous decade or so had become well used to seeing Stan and me go head-to-head in many rousing tussles between North End and both Stoke City and Blackpool. They were left in no doubt on this particular night that the master magician still possessed a trick or two with which to tease defenders and charm spectators.

Billy Wright strolled through the game, watched from the main stand by his wife Joy and her twin sisters. Together they formed the hugely successful singing trio, the Beverley Sisters. Billy and Joy were the Becks and Posh of their day I suppose. She was a high-profile singing star and he was England's football captain.

I liked Billy very much. He was a shy and rather unassuming guy, not 100 per cent comfortable when the showbusiness spotlight was turned full on, I always felt. Much like me, he preferred to play his football and go home. And what a player, too! There were few better defenders to my mind, and I remember having some real tussles whenever North End met Wolves. He was quick and agile and surprisingly strong in the air for someone who finished a few inches short of 6 ft. But his biggest quality was his anticipation. He could see what was going to happen well in advance and usually stepped in to stop it.

When I am asked to name my most difficult opponents, Billy Wright always gets a mention, and if you are after a couple more, look no further than Newcastle's Alf McMichael and Bolton's Tommy Banks.

Born in Belfast and a full-back who clocked up 400 appearances for Newcastle and won 40 caps for Northern Ireland, Alf never gave you an inch, a shadow defender who liked you to feel his breath on the back of your neck.

Tommy was a no-nonsense defender with a 'thou shalt not pass' philosophy. We were great mates, England room-mates no less, but in the cut and thrust of Preston-Bolton derbies, we might as well have never met before. Tommy was more a tackler than an interceptor; he didn't mind clattering in and letting you know he was around. I quite enjoyed the physical side. I relished the man-against-man combat that was around in those days, enjoyed tackling and felt that defending from the front was part of my job.

Not everyone saw it that way. Stanley Matthews was hardly renowned for chasing back or getting stuck in, and Bill Shankly once gave me a real rocket midway through a game at Preston. 'Tom!' he screamed from the other side of the pitch. 'Don't keep coming back into our half – defending is my job. Get up the other end and do some bloody damage.'

For the record, the North End Select won 9–4 and I managed to nip in for a couple of goals, a hat-trick eluding me to the bitter end. Tommy Thompson did manage the three-goal feat for us as did Nat Lofthouse for the opposition. There were goals, too, for Bryan

In action for England against Northern Ireland in 1947, when they equalised in the last minute in a 2-2 draw. (*Popperfoto*)

Training with England at Highbury prior to an international with Scotland at Wembley in April 1951. L-r: Henry Cockburn, Billy Wright, Wilf Mannion, Alf Ramsey, Stan Mortensen, me, Stanley Matthews, Harry Johnston, Harold Hassall and Bert Williams.

Relaxing on the beach ahead of that famous 10-0 victory over Portugal in May 1947. I am second from the right in a line-up of (l-r): John Robinson, Eddie Lowe, Phil Taylor, Billy Wright and Neil Franklin.

Stanley Matthews, Johnny Haynes and I discuss tactics at Highbury ahead of an England international. Those who didn't know often claimed there was a feud between me and Stan, but that was never the case. (*Empics*)

Taking it easy in Italy with my good pal Neil Franklin prior to us handing the Italians a football lesson in Turin in 1948. I scored twice in a 4-0 win.

Scoring England's fourth goal to complete a magnificent victory over Italy in May 1948 – it was one of the greatest performances by England during my time. (*Getty Images*)

The decisive moment in what was surely England's worst-ever defeat, against the USA in the 1950 World Cup. Alf Ramsey looks on as Bert Williams concedes the only goal of the game. (*Popperfoto*)

Off to the World Cup in Switzerland in 1954. L-r: Laurie Scott, Eddie Lowe, me, Stan Mortensen, Jimmy Hagan, Frank Swift, Tommy Lawton, George Hardwick, Neil Franklin, Raich Carter, Billy Wright, Phil Taylor, John Robinson, Bobby Langton and Wilf Mannion.

Scoring against the USSR's Lev Yashin in the 1958 World Cup – I took it with my 'wrong' right foot and foxed the great goalkeeper. (*Lancashire Evening Post*)

A couple of years after hanging up my boots here I am, aged 40, signing for Distillery before playing for the Irish champions against mighty Benfica in the European Cup. Distillery manager George Eastham, watching me put pen to paper, just would not take no for an answer. (*Lancashire Evening Post*)

In Hong Kong in 1961 when, as player-manager, I took an FA XI on a tour – giving Bobby Moore his first taste of international football.

I could never manage to eat three! But, along with our Brian, I was the first sportsman to advertise Shredded Wheat back in the early 1950s.

I got my share of sponsorship deals – even without the assistance of an agent. They often proved lucrative, too, like this one with the football boot manufacturer Raundes of Kettering.

Cheers! Bobby Charlton came along in the 1970s to help me do the honours when a new public house in Preston was named in my honour. (*Lancashire Evening Post*)

Being appointed Chairman of Preston Health Authority in 1984 provided me with four most interesting years – the service employed more than 5,000 people and I certainly learned a fair bit about politics. (*Lancashire Evening Post*)

Playing bar football against Prince Charles at Deepdale during a Royal Visit to Preston when HRH officially opened the Tom Finney Stand. We both seemed to be enjoying the action although I really cannot remember the final score! (*Lancashire Evening Post*)

I spent 15 years working for the Football Grounds Improvement Trust, the body which assisted clubs to improve their grounds. Bolton's impressive Reebok Stadium was one such venture and here I am with my former England colleague Nat Lofthouse (the Bolton President), Prime Minister John Major and Wanderers manager Colin Todd.

Douglas, Jimmy McIlroy and Bobby Langton for us, and Stan Mortensen for them. Bill Shankly had the misfortune of scoring for us, putting the ball past his own goalkeeper under pressure from Jimmy McIlroy. And, I'll tell you what, Shanks didn't thank anyone for reminding him of it later in the evening; nor, I suspect, was anyone brave enough to send him a copy of the following evening's paper. The main sports headline proclaimed: 'All in a night to remember . . . hat-tricks, 13 goals – and Shankly scored too!'

But the scoreline and the details were hardly significant. The testimonial – proceeds hitting £4,966 – was always intended to be an event more than a football match. The players had a ball, the spectators wallowed in the occasion and the media waxed lyrical. The following extract from the *Lancashire Evening Post* is typical of the reports:

Football's international supremacy that once belonged to our hardy race of islanders came flooding back to this country, to Preston, last night. It was seen in only fleeting glances, disguised by greying hairs, or lack of them, or middle-aged corpulence, but here were the men of England, particularly, and Scotland, who made in their day this very greatness.

Perhaps the younger men will forgive little mention for they are having their day. This was the night for the men of yesteryear, a night of sentiment and old-world charm. No fouls, no pressure for two points. It was an evening of memories of past achievements of personalities who will live on in the game.

The two teams lined up like this:

Preston North End Select XI: Fred Else, Willie Cunningham, Joe Walton, Tommy Docherty, Joe Dunn, Jimmy Baxter, Bryan Douglas, Tommy Thompson, myself, Jimmy McIlroy and Bobby Langton.

Invited All Stars XI: Bert Trautmann, Alex Parker, Jimmy Armfield, Bill Shankly, Neil Franklin, Billy Wright, Stanley Matthews, Stanley Mortensen, Nat Lofthouse, Wilf Mannion and Billy Liddell.

Not bad, eh? What about a collective value on that little lot. Would £200 million cover it? Possibly, but what about the North End team as well!

At the final whistle, I remember being quite overwhelmed by the reaction of the crowd. The cheering and applause were deafening and I was deeply moved. It left me in no doubt that my services to Preston North End had been appreciated and, even more than in the last league match, I found myself saddened by the finality of it all.

The fact that more than 33,000 had turned out to say goodbye spoke volumes, especially as Preston's attendances for their two home league fixtures either side of the benefit match, against the attractive opposition of Sheffield Wednesday and Blackpool, had been 17,499 and 17,455 respectively. In fact, we had been a little concerned that North End's poor start (they lost the first three matches in a season that ultimately ended in relegation) would harm the testimonial gate. Thankfully, problematic matters of the present seemed to count for little on my big night and the attendance was actually 8,000 bigger than North End's best of that campaign.

Match proceeds were topped up by staggering programme sales. A souvenir issue, priced at 6d (3p), sold well over 20,000 copies while the *Lancashire Evening Post* produced a special edition the previous Saturday night selling at 2d (1p) to boost the Tom Finney Testimonial Fund.

The *Post* also reported the latest news on a variety of individuals and organisations who had contributed to the fund or were planning fund-raising events – Preston Cricket Club had sent the proceeds of their weekend match; the Bridge Inn at Penwortham was arranging a dinner dance at the Masonic Hall; St Ignatius Men's Club was to stage a snooker and darts tournament; all local football leagues and licensed victuallers had been issued with contribution sheets; and letters had gone out to the other 91 professional clubs inviting participation. On top of that little lot, one of the Preston town-centre outlets displayed a range of my football treasures while inviting onlookers to make a cash contribution.

Whether I was right or wrong to participate in all of this I don't know. I was certainly grateful for the money because it enabled us to buy a house, but I felt very uncomfortable about it all. There had to be a way of calming my conscience and after much deliberation I decided that it would be a nice gesture to give a percentage to a charity or a worthy cause. So I duly wrote out a cheque to Preston Royal Infirmary.

Apart from doing the rounds of benefit games and coaching the North End youth team from time to time, plus playing in the occasional game of six-a-side, football became very much a part of my old life as I concentrated my efforts on building up the business with Joe. But there was a major surprise in store for me shortly after I had turned 41 – the opportunity to play in the European Cup.

CHAPTER SEVENTEEN

. . . and Benfica

N o, I kid you not. I was invited to play in the world's biggest club competition against the then biggest club side in the world, Benfica – and I accepted with some relish, once the initial shock had worn off.

The opportunity came out of the blue. I was relaxing at home one evening when the telephone rang. It was George Eastham, pre-war international with England and the father of the superb inside-forward of the same name who played for Stoke City and Arsenal. George senior had taken over as manager of the Irish club Distillery and, after asking about my well-being, he said, 'The purpose of the call is quite simple, Tom. We have a European Cup tie coming up against Benfica and I wondered if you would fancy playing.'

I laughed. Well, I think I laughed. If I didn't, I should have because it was all too daft for words.

'George, are you serious?' I said. 'I'm very flattered, but I haven't played a proper match in two years and my fitness level is hardly at a peak. I'm not match fit and too old. Sorry.' But George was not to be easily put off.

'Tom, I know what you're saying, but I've heard such fantastic reports of your displays in challenge matches around the country. We have a young side and I'm looking for someone, preferably a famous face with experience, who can bond the team together. Not only that, but to have a big name on our teamsheet would lift the tie to a new level in terms of public and media interest.' George should have been a salesman, and he hadn't finished yet. 'You're my first choice, Tom. This is a very special game for Distillery and to have you in the side would be such a boost. Please don't dismiss the idea out of hand. Give it a bit of thought and I'll ring you back.'

While I was thinking it over, George journeyed across to Preston to come to see me face to face. His ploy worked – how can you say no to someone who will go to such lengths and obviously has such faith in you as a player?

George was also a man I respected. He would surely have gone on to add to his only cap, against Holland in 1935 when he played with Bolton, had his career not been interrupted by the war. An inside-forward of considerable ability, he broke through to the Bolton first team at just 17 and later spent time with Brentford and Blackpool before his career closed at Lincoln City in 1949.

I knew him vaguely from his days with Blackpool, the town of his birth, and he always struck me as a real student of the game. When he moved across the water to Ireland, he began to make his mark in management. In 1958, he led Ards to the Irish League championship for the first time and a European Cup tie with Reims, and then took the reins at Distillery. When George moved in, he inherited a club living in the shadow of Linfield and Glentoran. He soon changed all of that. Distillery earned their right to participate in the biggest club tournament on the planet in 1963 by winning their domestic title for the first time in 57 years. Little wonder that George was hailed as a genius.

Very knowledgeable about the game, he liked his teams to play with style and to entertain. He was an advocate of simplicity. I was always a disciple of that particular gospel so he was kicking against an open door when he spoke with me. He explained that I could play a key role both before and during the game, reiterated that my presence would lift the profile of the tie and confirmed that it was not too late to register me to play.

'And, quite frankly, Tom,' he added, 'I daresay that apart from this, your chances of playing in the European Cup are fairly slim.'

Then he waxed lyrical about Benfica, not that he needed to – their record spoke for itself. Real Madrid had won the competition for the first five years in succession, but in the early sixties Benfica replaced them as the giants of European football. They won the European Cup in 1961 (3–2 against Barcelona) and in 1962 (5–3 against Real Madrid) and had missed out on a glorious hat-trick by losing to AC Milan in the spring of 1963. Their players were coveted. Eusebio, the inside-right from Mozambique with the rocket shot, was to become a household name worldwide. Humberto, a no-nonsense defender with a deft touch would have walked into any team. Mario Coluna, the inspirational captain and left-half from Angola, scored magnificent goals in the 1961 and 1962 triumphs.

George was very persuasive and I think he could sense my excitement.

'So, Tom, all things considered, what do you say?'

'Oh go on then, George. If you think it will help, count me in.'

But there was a proviso. I told my new manager that my business commitments were such that I couldn't possibly take off the best part of a week for the away leg of the tie in Lisbon. He accepted that and I spent the next week or so stepping up the training. I have always tried to follow a fairly strict personal exercise routine and it wasn't long before I felt that I was getting in decent shape.

The media loved the story – comebacks are always warmly welcomed, but this was a comeback with a difference. Not everyone approved. The *Daily Mail* sent one of their writers to see me.

'Don't you think you're taking an enormous risk?' he inquired.

'How do you mean?' I countered.

'Well, you have had a great career. Wouldn't it be a shame if you flopped and that became the way people remembered you, as little more than a has-been? Won't the pace of the game just be too much for you now?'

Talk about a red rag to a bull. Indirectly, the journalist had spurred me on even more.

'Look here,' I said. 'I'm very confident in my ability and I feel sure I'll do myself justice. If there was any doubt about any of that, I wouldn't be going. Anyway, you'll all get your chance to judge me on the night, so let's wait and see what happens.'

Distillery sent over the relevant forms for me to sign, and agreed to pay me a one-off fee in the region of £100. They organised the travel and the hotel accommodation and I flew out from Speke Airport accompanied by my uncle, Joe Grimshaw. Joe's brother had married my mother's sister and his son, Derek, worked for many years as assistant secretary at North End before holding top administrative positions with both Blackburn Rovers and the

Central League. He also spent some time on the payroll at Tom Finney Limited.

Joe was a keen North Ender, who spent many years at Deepdale working as a matchday steward, and when he heard about my decision to play for Distillery he could hardly contain his excitement.

'Would there be any chance of me coming over, Tom,' he pleaded. 'It would be one of the highlights of my life to see you play in the European Cup.'

I could find no reason why not, so Joe was my travelling companion on the short flight.

We went on the day of the game and the excitement and anticipation hit us as soon as we touched down in Ireland. George met up with us and agreed that I would best serve the team plan by playing centre-forward. That seemed like the best idea and if, just if, the *Daily Mail* chap had been right in questioning my ability to match the pace, I would have a better chance of disguising it from the middle rather than the flanks.

Wednesday, 25 September was a big night for European football in the UK. While Benfica were over in Northern Ireland, Real Madrid were preparing to face Glasgow Rangers at Ibrox. Media attention was massive.

The night is vivid in my memory, not least because of the weather. It was atrocious with rain lashing down almost from first whistle to last. I met up with the other players just an hour or so before kick-off and they seemed genuinely pleased to see me.

I admit to being nervous; nothing wrong with that. This was a first – I have never checked whether anyone older has debuted in the European Cup – I was playing in a team of strangers and we were facing a top Continental side at the peak of its power. Just a few years later, Eusebio and co. played Manchester United in that wonderful Wembley final in the very same competition.

I am not particularly superstitious but I was quite encouraged to hear that Distillery officials had sensibly decided to switch the tie from their own Grosvenor Park ground in Lisburn to the country's main stadium, Windsor Park. I won my first England cap there in 1946 and scored my 30th and final England goal there in 1958. I had played there four times in full internationals and twice for the Football League XI in representative fixtures and never once finished up on the losing side. Could I maintain that record? Well, very few people thought so. It is fair to report that Distillery were not expected to win. What an understatement!

An Irish team had never progressed beyond the first round and a creditable defeat would have proved more than acceptable to the officials and followers of Distillery. But players are nothing if not optimistic and our dressing room was very upbeat in the minutes leading up to kick-off as we heard the pipes, drums and bugles of the 6th Battalion Royal Ulster Rifles Regimental Band striking up outside.

And did we give it a go! Irish eyes weren't just smiling they were disbelieving as we raced into the lead in under a minute. I got up high to head the ball across the Benfica defence for wing-half John Kennedy (his brother, Jack, was in our goal) to shoot past Costa Pereira. Nothing much usually flustered the veteran goalkeeper but he certainly looked a bit shaken at conceding that one.

Benfica responded quickly for Serafim to equalise but we continued to attack with real menace and got back ahead before half-time through a well-taken goal from winger Ken Hamilton. The second half was fairly even; both teams created chances but defences held firm. The Distillery fans afforded us magnificent support and as the clock ticked down they, like us, began to believe in miracles. Unfortunately, Eusebio had other ideas and two minutes after he had grabbed an equaliser, a second goal for Serafim put Benfica in the driving seat.

Even that cruel double setback couldn't dent our resolve and we grabbed a richly deserved equaliser ten minutes from time. The scorer was a real gutsy player called Freddie Ellison – and what a story that was. Once on Aston Villa's books as a kid, Freddie, now in his mid twenties, should not even have been playing. He had broken his nose in a league game the previous Saturday and had been discharged from hospital on the Tuesday to get married! With all due respect to his wife, Freddie's main goal seemed to centre around convincing George Eastham that he was fit enough to face Benfica. How glad we all were that George agreed and the goal was fair reward for a truly courageous effort from Freddie.

He wasn't alone on that score. Distillery may have been rank outsiders – the bookies had them at 16/1 – but the team played with a passion to delight a capacity crowd, and the 3–3 result was heralded as a moral victory.

I felt I had played a part useful enough to justify George's faith and to silence any doubters. In an interview in the *Belfast Telegraph* beforehand, I had been keen to say how I took the invitation to play not only as a great opportunity but as a real compliment and that I had trained hard to do justice to myself, the club and the spectators. My performance was well received – and I didn't once call for oxygen or an iron lung!

There was a sense of over-achievement within our camp and the players and officials of Distillery certainly seemed to enjoy the after-match dinner more than their Portuguese guests. The pressure was on for me to play in the return, but I refused to change my original decision. It was tempting, especially given that Lisbon contained so many happy football memories for me, but I have always believed that once you make a decision you should stick to it.

To be fair to George Eastham, he didn't join in with the clamour for me to change my mind and I appreciated it. Unfortunately, the Distillery dream ended in tears when they were walloped 5–0 in the second leg.

So, a career that started with an England appearance in Switzerland in 1945 ended with a European Cup tie against Benfica in 1963 – with a fair bit squeezed in between.

CHAPTER EIGHTEEN

Finney business

The media love to hand out tags and nicknames. From the moment I first stepped forward on the professional football stage I became known as the 'Preston Plumber'. Some sportsmen and women take exception to being labelled with such monikers but not me. I have never found it the slightest bit offensive or derogatory and why should I? I am most definitely from Preston and most certainly a plumber.

People have often joked that it was a good job I didn't serve my apprenticeship as an electrician as the 'Preston Electrician' would not have had quite the same ring. Fair point and, anyway, I didn't need to be good on the electrical side; my brother Joe was an expert in that field.

Joe and I took immense pride and satisfaction in establishing our business as one of the most prominent plumbing and electrical firms in Lancashire, but the story behind it, how we started, who got involved and where the finance came from has not been told until now.

You need to backtrack all of 60 years to the middle of the Second World War. Joe was stationed in Burma with the Royal Engineers and I was in Egypt with the Royal Lancers. We didn't see each other in years and relied on writing letters as a means of keeping in touch. I looked forward to receiving mail from Joe; he always wrote in positive tones and helped to keep my spirits up during some difficult days.

There was one letter I will always remember. In it, Joe hinted for the first time about the possibility of the two of us getting together some day to set up in business. It made great sense, he wrote, what with my plumbing apprenticeship at Pilkington's and him being a time-served electrician with the local electricity board. I was immediately excited by the prospect and wrote back to tell him so. The next few letters that went winging to and fro always contained some reference to the idea.

Joe and I had confidence in each other, not to mention mutual love and respect, and the thought of working in partnership was never considered a risk. When peace was declared and we met up again back in Preston, it wasn't so much a case of 'if' we would start but 'when'. He could get cracking straightaway, but I had to complete a short stint back with Pilkington's to satisfy the terms of my B Release.

However, it wasn't long before Finney Bros was born. We took some premises on the first floor of a Preston warehouse owned by a local milkman. Both capable tradesmen, we soon discovered that being in business required a bit more than a practical understanding of the job. Neither of us had any money to talk of. We had left the

Army skint, aside that is from £75 gratuity pay and a demob suit apiece. You can have all the ability in the world and match it with desire and determination, but you still need help from others and a break or two along the way.

Preston North End director Ewart Bradshaw, a local car dealer, provided the first helping hand by supplying us with a small van, but it was crystal clear that we needed some professional financial help – an accountant. We plumped for Clifford Thornton, the Army officer who brought the news of my first England call-up back in 1945. At the time of my call-up against Switzerland, Clifford had said he worked as an accountant in the Preston area and the information just stuck in my mind. So when we needed financial advice, I told Joe about Clifford and he agreed that we should seek him out. It was somehow satisfying to have a link between my football, my plumbing and my days as a soldier.

Clifford was a sole trader in those days, working from an office in Cross Street, but he later helped to establish one of Preston's premier accountancy firms, Thornton, Harper and Relph. It did not surprise me that Clifford went from strength to strength for he was simply brilliant at his job and absolutely fundamental in Finney Bros getting off the ground. He worked tirelessly with us to ensure that we made the right moves at the right time. He was a charming man with real foresight, and he never minded us calling round for guidance. Looking back, I think he realised that while we were sitting on a winner, we were also very vulnerable and mistakes could have cost us dearly.

Clifford handled our business affairs for years and stayed a close friend of the family until he retired to the south of England. Regrettably, he fell foul of a dreadful wasting disease and died some years ago. I well remember going to see him after he had suffered a major stroke. It was so sad to see him frail and drawn and hardly able to communicate. Apart from Joe and I, no one played a bigger part in the rise of our business than Clifford Thornton.

Joe and I never talked of failing; for one thing, we hadn't got the time. Business was good from day one with Joe left to carry on for long spells due to my dual role as a footballer-plumber. But we both knew that the football element was absolutely vital to our chances of success. The officials at Preston North End went out of their way to make our early years in business as comfortable and problem-free as possible, not only in their capacity as understanding employers but also by giving us any plumbing and electrical work that needed doing at Deepdale. Chairman Jim Taylor and two directors, Bill Cross and Bert Ingham, also saw to it that we got extra jobs through their own firms and families.

Additionally, and far more significantly, the war had taken a toll on the region, especially in places such as Manchester and Liverpool where the German bombs had hit the hardest. Plumbers and electricians were in great demand. Central heating was making an impact, too, as people began to look for a few home comforts after years of rations and restrictions.

The work flooded in. It almost got to the stage where we had more work than we could handle and we seemed to be recruiting extra help every week. A move to bigger premises in Aqueduct Street helped, but not for long. Clifford Thornton suggested a meeting.

'The business is moving at a phenomenal pace,' he said, as if we needed telling. 'It's my considered view that to control future development and ensure maximum return, you need to become a limited company.'

How could we disagree? After all, everything Clifford had told us thus far had worked out fine. But we needed to raise some capital, not least to buy a bigger base and invest in new vehicles, and all our money was already accounted for on a day-by-day basis.

We found the answer at Deepdale, but not at the football club. Messrs Taylor, Ingham and Cross decided to club together the necessary £4,000 personally and lend it to us on a pay-us-back-when-you-can basis. Even faster than we had dared to hope, Tom Finney Ltd was born.

The loan had nothing – repeat nothing – to do with the football club. It was simply made possible through the generosity of those three directors acting in a personal capacity. It is important that there is no misunderstanding.

They said that there was 'no panic' about the repayment and emphasised that they 'weren't seeking a return', but we were keen to pay off the loan as quickly as possible. In fact, it took us about three years. We weren't keen to involve anyone in the long term. While it was a fantastic gesture, one we could hardly believe, this business was our idea, our dream and our company. Some might consider it selfish, but Joe and I didn't want outsiders involved.

We bought a former foundry on Moor Lane and spent a lot of the capital on renovation work. We bought extra vans and a couple of cars and took the workforce to about 20, with electricians out-numbering plumbers by about three to one. We limited ourselves to a geographic area of about a 30 to 40 miles radius and took on all sorts of contracts.

Most of the business came through commercial customers, but we also undertook what we called jobbing work, that is domestic repairs and re-fits. Along with the business of management, that was where I played an active role, getting out and about to fit an immersion heater, cut and solder some replacement piping or fix a leaking tap. Many myths sprung up about this, stories that belonged in story books but were recounted as fact simply because people wanted to believe them to be true. Sorry to disappoint, but I can never remember being up a ladder clearing someone's blocked drain in Fulwood just minutes before shooting Preston into the lead at home to Manchester United!

Joe was the first to acknowledge the way my name as a footballer had kicked open our door of opportunity and there was never a hint of bitterness from him about often being referred to as 'Tom Finney's brother' or 'Joe, that electrician chap from Tom Finney's'. The fact that I was a footballer, and a well-known England international at that, was a genuine plus even if it did delay the job from time to time. Many a time I would go out on pricing, inspecting or plumbing duties only to spend the first hour deep in conversation with the customer on how North End were faring or whether England stood any chance against so-and-so. On one occasion, I remember defending Stanley Matthews' corner while I changed the ballcock on a WC!

Of course, not everyone was prepared to give Tom Finney the easy route to a contract. We had an inquiry from the Lion Brewery in Blackburn about tendering for their plumbing and electrical contract and I drove the ten miles or so to meet with the managing director. He explained the nature of the brewery business, then looked me squarely in the eyes and said, 'I just want to say this, Mr Finney. You may be a great footballer, but it's as a plumber that you'll be judged here and we expect the highest standards of work-manship.' I assured him that would be the case to which he replied, 'Just as well because you being a great footballer is no good to us when a plumbing problem occurs.'

While I concede that we had the breaks, we worked exceptionally hard. People laugh when I tell them that I spent six to eight hours a day at the business even during my playing days. I would get in for about 7.30, check the work for the day, see the lads and solve any problems that had cropped up overnight. At around 9.30, I would hurry down to Deepdale for training, do three hours there, nip home for a sandwich at lunchtime and be back at work for 2 p.m. More often than not it would be 6 o'clock when I got back home for tea and we were always on call at night so you could never be sure that work would allow you a free evening with the family.

Joe, a fair but indomitable character, was equally committed to the cause, determined never to let anyone down and hell bent on doing the best possible job at all times. Nothing was considered too small. We got a lot of lucrative jobs through John Turner and Sons and Thomas Croft and Sons, two well-known Preston building contractors.

Our business went from good to very good to better, busy to busier to busier still. The workforce rose steadily, the order book bulged and we became one of the first firms to install a full showroom facility within our premises. Then, as often happens when life looks perfect, there came a devastating double blow. Joe's health was poor and starting to affect him quite badly, and at about the same juncture the local authority decided to issue us with a compulsory purchase order on the premises. The letter informing us wasn't even particularly polite – in rough speak we had 12 months to find a new home and get out.

I had been retired from football for a few years and, through changing circumstances involving Joe, I was starting to play the more senior role. I began the search for new premises and found an ex-laundry building that seemed to fit the bill, on Lytham Road in the Plungington area of town. In order to acquire it, I had to negotiate a better deal on our existing site with Preston council. It was a struggle but we got there eventually, and I found sufficient funding to buy both the laundry and the house next door.

Tragically, Joe never set foot in Lytham Road. The wretched events of the winter of 1964 are ingrained in my memory. I lost not only my brother but my father, too, all in the short space of seven shocking weeks. Dad, who was 73, died after a long illness in late October. Joe, struck down by cancer, followed him, aged 47. It was Christmas week to be precise, and it was almost too much for me to take.

My father was always reasonably healthy, but he did puff away on a pipe and had a smoker's cough. We were forever pestering him to give up, but he didn't – or couldn't - and a chronic chest condition proved his downfall in the end.

I was working as a reporter on the *News of the World* on the Saturday of his death and had gone to cover a game at Anfield. Dad had been admitted to Deepdale Hospital during the week and on the Friday night I had popped in to see him. He had just finished his tea, eating quite a large dish of ice cream, and although he was rambling a little he certainly didn't seem to be worsening. When I got the message at Anfield to get down to the hospital as quickly as possible, I hurried back but it was too late. To be told he had just passed away minutes earlier was a terrible shock.

Joe had been diagnosed with cancer earlier in the year, just at the time when we were getting our business on its feet. It spread to his lung and he started to deteriorate rapidly after Dad died. He was so ill by the time the funeral came around he was unable to attend. It hurt him deeply not to be present. It hurt me, too, because he would have found it very moving to have witnessed the huge turnout at St Jude's and heard the wonderful things people said about Dad.

Those two months were the saddest of my life. My father was such a strong man, high in principles, and I always looked to him and Joe for guidance. My sisters were always there and equally supportive but all the encouragement for my football came from Dad and Joe. I have endeavoured to live my life by their standards. Many times when faced with a problem or a big decision, I have sat back and thought about what Dad would have done. In some respects I suppose I felt I was left to carry on the good fight; that's what both of them would have wanted, but I still miss them so.

Mary, my stepmother, died just a few years later after having a heart attack on a coach trip to Blackpool.

Joe's passing served to further increase my responsibilities to the business. Luckily, I had some good people around me. My old North End colleague Ken Horton had joined us in our fledgling years, initially as a secretary but later on the accounts side, and there was also Fred Hackett, a former apprentice with Joe who had forgotten more about electrics than most electricians know. Ken helped make sure the financial affairs stayed tightly in order while Fred took over as manager of the electrical side. They were both part of the extended Finney family and I owe them both a huge debt.

Ken was not the only former North End player to find employment with us. Dave Seddon, an inside-forward who had arrived from Dundee in the late fifties, joined as an electrician. There was a link, too, with my old team-mate and next-door neighbour Tommy Thompson. Tommy was a joiner by trade and when his playing career finished he was keen to get back to work. We found him a unit within the Troy Buildings on Lytham Road and as well as acting as his landlord, we also managed to find him a steady supply of joinery work, although he always retained his independence as a self-employed tradesman.

Things continued to blossom and we took the decision to diversify, establishing two new companies under the group banner, Tom

Finney Acoustics and Tom Finney Autos. Ken Horton took a directorship at Autos while Roy Pinder filled a similar role within the Acoustics division. My son Brian (plumbing) and our Joe's two boys, Robbie and David (electrics) also jumped aboard to increase the family connections. Robbie and David inherited shares following the death of their mother, Beatrice, also of cancer, and all three of the Finney boys later became directors.

I retired from the business in 1984 to take on what was a full-time role with the Health Authority, and although it may sound big-headed and arrogant, I believe my departure signalled the beginning of the end for the firm. I would be lying if I said everyone lived happily ever after at Tom Finney Ltd after I had gone – anything but.

The firm ran into financial difficulties. There were some bad debts but there were some bad decisions, too. It all got a bit messy, which was particularly distressing for me – not at all how I intended, or expected, things to turn out.

During the good years we employed more than 100 people and the future always seemed assured. Of course, we felt the pinch from time to time – what business doesn't? – but we were never in debt. When I left, everything was in good shape. We had a strong plumbing and electrical base and a growing division in acoustics, there was money in the bank, we owned our properties and the order book was expanding.

Somehow, though, things began to go awry until a major part of the group of companies went into liquidation. The operation was saved from closure in 1998 when it was taken over by St Helen's-based Cross Services Ltd. The surviving section – acoustics – eventually changed hands, too. The new owners, Carlton Contractors Ltd, asked if I would be a patron and whether they could keep my name in the title. I said yes to both requests.

I suppose I consider myself fortunate in not having had to face many disappointments, but the decline of the business certainly upset me. A lot of it was down to the inexperience of those left in charge. I always prided myself on the way I kept watch on the books. The building trade has always been riddled with bad debt and empty promises, so this was a vital aspect of the job.

If you were doing a commercial job under contract over say six, twelve or eighteen months, I believed that you should set up a monthly payment scheme. On the domestic scene, customers paid on invoice unless, of course, it was going to be a lengthy job with a lot of outlay on our part. Then I arranged stage payments so we were never at risk. That philosophy went out of the window after I had gone. They kept telling me it was 'different in my day' and that they were moving forward at a rapid rate and 'turning over millions'.

I said, 'That's as may be, but have you looked at your bottom line?' It has always been my belief that while turnover is OK, profit is critical.

CHAPTER NINETEEN

A political football

Few people are fortunate enough to meet the Queen; I have enjoyed that privilege three times. The first occasion was in 1961 when I received the OBE, the second in 1992 when it was the CBE, both for services to football, and finally in 1998 I received the country's highest honour, a knighthood.

Plain old Tom Finney became Sir Tom on publication of the New Year's Day honours list, more than three decades after my great contemporary Sir Stanley Matthews had become the first football knight. I was fifth with Alf Ramsey (1967), Matt Busby (1968) and Bobby Charlton (1994) sandwiched in between. Geoff Hurst, Alex Ferguson and Bobby Robson have followed.

People had talked for years about my turn coming around soon, but it was always a topic that interested others more than me. I never gave it any thought, even in 1989 when there was wholesale speculation that Cecil Parkinson, the Tory Minister and former Preston North End fan, had put my name forward and received a more than favourable response. What did come as a surprise was the decision by the local newspaper, the *Evening Post*, to put their weight behind a campaign initially started by two girls young enough to be my grandchildren, even great grandchildren. Heather Oatridge and Kate Clarke, both 15, had never seen me play, but they had made it their personal goal to see me knighted. Don't ask me why, perhaps they felt I had been left out! Bobby Charlton and Alex Ferguson were among those who signed up and it was all a little overwhelming, quite a bit embarrassing to be truthful.

Whether it was purely coincidental I will never know, but the campaign certainly helped to produce a result. One morning, we had just finished breakfast when the post arrived and among the usual crop of bills and junk was a letter that stood out. It looked different and carried the royal stamp. It was one of those letters that got you thinking, even a touch anxious. I turned over the top section and soon realised what it was – I had been proposed for the Insignia of a Knight Bachelor. I wanted to shout aloud, but the final paragraph was a strict instruction prohibiting me from sharing the news with a third party.

For the next few weeks I kept the news back from Elsie and the family for it isn't until the honours list is made public that you know for definite you have been included. When the news hit the streets, Elsie was overjoyed, the telephone was red hot and calls and letters came from well-wishers around the world. Everyone seemed to know within minutes let alone days and even some of the lads from my Army days of 50-odd years ago got in touch. One letter was simply addressed to 'Tom Finney, Preston' – the Post Office made sure it found its destination.

North End invited me to be guest of honour three days later for an FA Cup third-round tie with Stockport County at Deepdale. To walk out on the pitch that day with the crowd cheering and the players applauding counts among my greatest moments. It was so moving and it was hard to hold back the tears. Even the fact that County pulled off an upset by winning the tie couldn't spoil my afternoon.

The big day arrived on 18 February 1998 when I attended Buckingham Palace for the royal investiture. It was a procedure I knew well. I had first experienced the thrill back in 1961 shortly after my retirement from the game.

I was a long way from home when news of my OBE was announced. I could not have been further away in fact – down in the depths of New Zealand where I was player-manager on the Football Association trip that included representative games in Australia and Malaysia. I knew I was in the frame, having received the standard letter of intent, but it was still a surprise and a thrill. The lads threw an impromptu party by way of celebration.

The CBE followed the exact same route 31 years later and six years after that I was back to receive a knighthood. The ceremony involved 140 people from all walks of life and Mark Hughes, the former Manchester United and Wales striker was among the number to receive his MBE.

I remember the day in detail. Determined to make the most of this once-in-a-lifetime opportunity, Elsie and I, our Brian and his wife Marlene and our Barbara and her husband Jim booked a hotel in London for an overnight stay in advance. After a relatively relaxed morning, it was hard to ascertain who was the most nervous as we were driven to Buckingham Palace in a sparkling chauffeur-driven limousine.

I recall getting kitted out in formal dress, complete with top hat, and thinking back to my early days. Could I ever have believed that one day that skinny working-class kid from the cotton town of Preston would be preparing to meet the Queen to receive my country's greatest accolade? It was a defining moment.

On arrival at the Palace, I was separated from the family. They went straight into the room where the ceremony takes place while I was taken into a waiting room. Then it is a matter of waiting for your name to be called out. When you hear it – 'Thomas Finney' – you walk forward and kneel on your right knee before the Queen who touches you on both shoulders with the sword once owned by her father, King George VI.

The Queen didn't mention that I had been a couple of times before but she did remark that I must have seen great changes in the game. I replied, 'Yes, Ma'am.' What my father would have given to witness that scene.

I never saw red as a footballer, or even yellow. I went through my entire playing career without so much as a booking. But in 1989 I did see red – the famous red book presented to many a surprised subject on the popular television show 'This Is Your Life'.

Up until it was my turn to stand back in open-mouthed astonishment, I must concede that I wondered if some were put-up jobs. Did the people really know and were they just pretending otherwise? Would the programme risk another Danny Blanchflower moment? That great Spurs star had declined the opportunity to take part, in full view of the nation. But I can confirm here and now that I was totally in the dark right up to the moment when Michael Aspel confronted me with that celebrated line, 'Tom Finney, this is your life.' Don't ask me how but Elsie and our Brian and Barbara managed to keep quiet.

In fact, it very nearly didn't happen at all. When the ITV researchers first approached Elsie about it, she refused, believing that it would cause me more embarrassment than pleasure. It was only after the television people persuaded her to chat the matter over with the family that the kids convinced her it was a good idea.

The lengths to which the programme makers went in order to get me to the right place at the right time without suspecting anything were amazing. I received what turned out to be a spoof letter from a footballing organisation, inviting me to be a guest at a special sporting function in London linked to the making of a soccer documentary. My immediate reaction was to say thanks but no thanks. 'It's a long way to go for a dinner,' I said, delivering just the sort of reaction Elsie didn't want to hear. She didn't panic, though, cajoling me into accepting by saying that it would be rather rude to say no when the organisers were banking on my attendance.

I decided to travel by train and was informed by Elsie that the organisers had been on to say there would be a courtesy car and driver at Euston station to meet me. I asked Elsie if she fancied coming along and spending a little time in the capital doing a bit of shopping and sightseeing but she declined saying she had arranged to meet up with a friend, Lucy Lee, in Lytham St Annes for a day out. There was nothing suspicious in that although I was a bit bemused by the fact that Elsie seemed very keen to get off at the crack of dawn.

'Why do you need to go so early?' I asked.

'Well, we're hoping to get to the shops for opening time and Lucy has asked me to pop to her house first for a coffee.'

Well done, Elsie – still no reason for doubt. Off I went to Preston station, totally oblivious of the fact that my wife, children, sisters and friends were following right behind on a coach.

As promised, the car was waiting as I stepped off the train three hours later, but as I got in I noticed a coach parked close by. 'That's funny,' I thought to myself. 'I could swear that was Ronnie Clayton getting on the coach, followed by Bryan Douglas. Yes it is . . . and there's Nat Lofthouse, too!' I opened the door and called to them. They shouted hello and waved back.

'Where are you off to?' I inquired.

Someone, I can't remember who, was quick enough to answer, 'We're going to the same place as you.' That made sense; they must have been invited, too.

'See you there, then,' I said and got back into the car. The driver said we would be moving off any moment. Suddenly, though, the door was opened and there was Michael Aspel – you could have knocked me down with the proverbial feather.

We were whisked off to the studio and I was guided into the make-up room where the producer ran through the overall plan of the show without giving any secrets away. Then the title music started and on to the set I walked with Michael close at hand. Elsie and co., grinning from ear to ear, were the first to be introduced followed by all the footballers I had just been chatting with so innocently. Billy Wright was there along with George Hardwick, Neil Franklin, Laurie Scott, Johnny Haynes, Wilf Mannion, Ivor Broadis, Ronnie, Bryan and Nat.

Stanley Matthews made an appearance on film from South Africa where he was on a coaching mission, and the other guests included Omar Sharif and Cecil Parkinson. Cecil relayed stories of his days as a schoolboy in Lancaster when he made the weekly pilgrimage to

Preston to watch me play, while Omar Sharif revealed how he nearly faced me as an opponent. Apparently, he was a substitute in a game between our Eighth Army team and an Egyptian side during the war. As a full-back he said he was very concerned that the first choice player kept fit so that he didn't need to come on and mark me.

Among all the famous faces was a chap by the name of Tommy Johnson and was I pleased to see him again. Tommy was a time-served fully fledged plumber when I was a wary 14-year-old apprentice at Pilkington's back in the mid thirties. He was good to me, kind and considerate and always ready to show me the ropes. You don't forget that sort of help and although we went our separate ways it was great to see him again. A smashing chap, Tommy is dead and buried now, God bless him.

After the show, we were invited to a buffet reception and then, courtesy of the television company, the family was treated to over-night accommodation in a smart London hotel.

As well as meeting the Queen, you could also say that I spent time at Her Majesty's pleasure. In fact, I visited prisons on more than one occasion as part and parcel of my role as a magistrate. I sat on the Preston bench (something I never did as a footballer!) for two decades and it was some experience.

Someone once told me that to see a bit of real life all you needed to do was to pop along to the magistrates' court any weekday morning and, I'll tell you what, they weren't far wrong! Petty thieves, armed robbers, drunks, brawlers, fraudsters – every sort of criminal imaginable came before us, and the main difficulty I found, especially early on, was staying detached. You heard some real sob-sob stories, some of them not without merit, and it was hard not to get sentimentally involved.

I remember one young woman standing in the dock charged with stealing food from a local shop. It was a straightforward case in that she pleaded guilty, but her circumstances were far from clear cut. We heard how she had been left alone with a couple of kids after her husband had done a runner, how she had been unable to find work to pay her bills and how the kids were 'going hungry'. She was a pitiful figure, with no previous record. In desperation, she had resorted to theft, but all she was trying to do was find food for her children. I daresay the three people sitting on the bench that morning might have done the same thing in her situation.

I first got involved with the justice system in 1962 when a neighbour of ours on Regent's Drive approached me with the idea. I agreed that he should put my name forward and I was sworn in. I did half a day a week for the next 20 years (you have to retire as a magistrate at 70) and I spent the later years as chairman of the bench. It was both interesting and enlightening. We dealt with minor offences and were restricted to a maximum penalty of six months' imprisonment. For more serious matters, including murder or sex offences, we heard the preliminaries before referring the cases to the County Court.

I did get a few opportunities to sit in the County Court alongside a judge, and I also went on prison inspection visits. It was considered appropriate that magistrates should see prisons at first hand to give them an idea of the life of an inmate. I was always pleased to get out.

Although sitting in judgement is a position of great authority and not something to be taken lightly, it can have its lighter moments. One morning a Scottish chap stood before us, guilty of a crime that necessitated a prison sentence. We gave him a month but as he left the courtroom he turned back for a moment and smiled at me.

'Thanks,' he said – not a word we were used to hearing from those heading for jail. 'When I get free, I'll be able to tell my mates that I was sent down by Tom Finney!'

I smiled and nodded – what do you say to that?

It is hard to imagine that any honour could be comparable to a knighthood but receiving the freedom of Preston ran it very close. To be made a freeman of my own town back in 1979 was marvellous. I think I am right in saying that I am the only surviving freeman in the borough and I know it is accurate to say I was the first to get such recognition for sporting reasons. Traditionally, the distinction belonged to guild mayors, philanthropists and belted earls, and I remember being rather overawed by the pomp and circumstance that surrounded the ceremony.

Preston council chamber was packed to capacity as I was handed a beautiful silver casket containing an illuminated scroll. When council leader Joe Hood paid a tribute in which he called me 'Preston's greatest son and the town's number one ambassador' it was truly overwhelming.

Someone asked – I got the impression that the question was staged – why it had taken so long, and Councillor Hood replied that the local authority had wanted to pick a moment in history that would be worthy of the occasion. Therefore they had waited until 1979 because it was the 800th anniversary of Preston's royal charter, granted by Henry II.

'What better time could there be than our octo-centenary for the town of Preston to honour its most famous citizen?' he said.

It was a sumptuous night, unashamedly nostalgic. Many a story was recounted, suitably embellished with a fair sprinkling of exaggeration, of my playing days at Deepdale. I might have been good but I was never quite as good as the speakers made out although it was jolly kind of them to try. A wonderful banquet was laid on with Elsie and me as guests of honour and the banner at the back of the hall read: Congratulations 'Sir' Tom! Elsie leaned across at one point to squeeze my hand and say, 'Wow, this really is something quite special, Tom. I feel so proud of you and so happy for you.'

Elsie accompanied me on many a gala occasion, happy to be my support but always a step away from the limelight. After she became ill, we attended fewer and fewer events although we did turn out in force as a family unit when the Preston North End Former Players' Association threw a bash to celebrate my 80th birthday in April 2002. They took over Garstang Golf Club and the list of footballing guests included surviving North Enders of my era. Tommy Thompson was there, and Tommy Docherty, Sammy Taylor, Les Dagger, Ken Waterhouse and Peter Higham, not forgetting Harold Iddon, an inside-right who was in the same youth team as me before the Second World War. Charlie Wayman, laid up in hospital, sent a message as did Joe Marston all the way from Australia. Messages also arrived from Bobby Beattie in Scotland and Fred Else in Cyprus.

Other north west clubs were represented by Ronnie Clayton and Bryan Douglas of Blackburn Rovers, Jimmy McIlroy and Brian Pilkington of Burnley, Tommy Banks of Bolton Wanderers, Ivor Broadis of Carlisle and Bill Perry of Blackpool. Another ex-Seasider who turned up to help me blow out the candles was Allan Brown, who captained Luton Town in my final game for Preston North End 42 years earlier.

I played at some wonderful grounds over the years, and the more I travelled the more I came to realise that England was in no way a world leader in stadium facilities and comfort. Spectators overseas, particularly those lucky enough to watch their football on the Continent and in Scandinavia, would have been appalled by many of the facilities our own people had got used to and considered the norm. We can all recall the quite shocking sanitary conditions, queuing outside in the rain behind the stand (sometimes next to the refreshment kiosk) to stand shoulder to shoulder and 'perform' against a brick wall.

We asked people to stand on crumbling terracing, in rotting wooden enclosures or to pay a premium and sit on a bench in the grandstands where pillars obstructed the view. The catering facilities were dreadful – a cup of Bovril and a Wagon Wheel was about as far as the menu stretched.

I was quite outspoken on the subject, saying it was high time the football authorities, who had the audacity to say that they would like more women and young children to attend matches, invested money in ground development. In one article, I told of discovering grounds abroad without girders where everyone got the perfect view. I described the first-class toilet facilities, the good-quality refreshments and seats with cushions in stands fit to be prefixed with the word 'grand'. The powers that be responded with the usual 'not enough money' argument and for many years not a lot happened.

Then came the Football Grounds Improvements Trust, a body established to drag old, dilapidated stadia into the new era. It was the start of a revolution and the main reason why there are now so many wonderful grounds across the country. It was big business, funded in the main by money from the football pools, and I was one of those responsible for the distribution of this new-found wealth. I was invited to get involved by David Dent, the former Football League secretary, and I spent the best part of 15 years calling in at grounds across the north of England to listen to proposals, carry out inspections and make recommendations.

We existed purely to make significant improvements and we made them all over the place – trust me, even the big boys such as Manchester United and Liverpool had reason to raise a glass to the FGIT. So did my own club Preston, and Blackburn and Bolton and a host of clubs right through the league. It was very satisfying to call back at the clubs sometime later and see what had been done.

Unfortunately, with the arrival of the National Lottery fewer and fewer people filled in weekly pools coupons and so the money dried up.

Politics have never interested me, so it was rather ironic that I should be the central figure in a major political row, which blew up in 1984.

The Conservative government of the day was keen to appoint business people from within private industry to positions of authority on various public bodies. I must have fitted the bill because I was approached to become chairman of the Preston Health Authority.

I had just taken my first step into retirement by announcing a reduced role in the running of the business. I wasn't going to be involved on a day-to-day basis any longer. Word filtered through to Westminster – I still don't know how – that I had some free time on my hands and may be worth considering for a regional post.

The invitation to head up the local health authority came from the junior health minister and I went along to London on a fact-finding mission. It was explained to me that the government firmly believed that an increased input from the private business community could be of significant benefit across all sorts of services.

They said a vacancy as chairman existed within the Preston Health Authority and asked if I would consider filling the post.

It was very flattering and the concept certainly appealed, but it was very much a surprise and I bought a bit of time. But the more I thought about it, the more I was attracted and intrigued although the scale of the operation was a little daunting. The PHA employed 5,500 staff and worked to an annual budget of £60 million. Not only that, the National Health Service was in a degree of turmoil, consistently criticised for a whole host of reasons.

I also realised it would be totally different from running my own business where I could see a member of the workforce face to face within minutes of a problem arising and get things sorted out.

But, in spite of all the obvious negatives, I decided to give it a go, having first been assured from the top that it would be no more than a two-day-a-week commitment. Wrong! The role proved to be full time and for the next four years I saw even less of Elsie than I had during my footballing days touring the country and the world with Preston and England. Indeed, the pressure on my time was the reason why I opted out of a second term of office when it was offered in 1988.

When Sir John Page, chairman of the North West Regional Health Authority, made news of my appointment public, it received what can only be described as a mixed response. I had not broadcast the fact in advance and the news came as a surprise to many of my business acquaintances and friends. Some thought I had lost the plot. They didn't say so in as many words but I could sense their concern. They had a point, too. I was 62 years of age with some time to call my own at last and a few bob in the bank – I certainly didn't need the £8,300 a year salary. Yet here I was, putting myself forward for what some reckoned to be a no-win role in public office.

My predecessor, a barrister called Robert Hodd, had left nine months earlier, allegedly because he wasn't prepared to bang the drum for privatisation. Within hours of my appointment the trade union leaders were up in arms. All sorts of claims were bandied about. They said the appointment was politically motivated, that I had Tory sympathies and would prove little more than a figurehead at best and, at worst, a government yes man. The Public Employees Union (NUPE) said I had previous connections with the Tory party and that while I may have done a lot for the town, I was 'just a plumber' with little knowledge of the health service. Most of those asked – and isn't it always the dissenting voices who shout the loudest at times like this? – were clearly of the opinion that I just wasn't up to the job.

Now it is fair to say that I have faced a few kickings in my time, with many a defender keen to bring me down to earth with a bump, but to be used as a political football was a whole new experience. I have never sought confrontation but I felt I could not let these people get away with talking baloney. I decided to talk to the media and make my feelings known. I said how honoured I was as a proud Prestonian born and bred to be invited to chair such an important service and that I was looking forward to the challenge of the role. I refuted in the strongest possible terms that I was politically motivated and revealed that I had never had any associations with any party.

It seemed to work and it should have worked because it was the gospel truth. Those trying to score political points by attacking me were put in their place and I set about the task of finding out just what was expected of me.

What an eye-opener! The PHA was a massive concern incorporating two major hospitals, Preston Royal Infirmary and Sharoe Green, and it relied on sound management, shrewd spending and the sterling efforts of both the nursing and administrative staffs, many of them working tirelessly for little reward.

While £60 million seemed a lot at the outset, it was never going to be enough to solve all the problems. The NHS is a hungry beast with an insatiable appetite. We were often faced with delicate decisions on who and what should benefit from the cash.

You couldn't really win, but I knew that from day one and my philosophy was to listen to as many voices as possible before opting for a course of action. We had meetings and seminars galore to attend, but we also found time to bring in the public and listen to what they had to say. They were, after all, the ones who used the service. I believe in the voice of the people, always have and always will.

The four years were demanding, very demanding, and quite pressurised, too, but although we experienced difficulties, we also achieved a fair bit – the opening of a new combined maternity unit and a new orthopaedic unit, advanced renal services and improvements in the treatment of the mentally ill.

My salary rose each year until, finally, it was £12,000. I was not overpaid – goodness knows what hourly rate that would have worked out at – but money was never the motivation. I was curious to see what I could do to improve the most critical of public services in my hometown.

Every Christmas I did a tour of all the hospital wards to visit patients and listen to their views, good and bad. They were invariably pleased to see me and this is where I think my being well known proved an advantage, especially with the men, who temporarily forgot their aches and pains to talk about the great days at Deepdale.

Six months ahead of my tenure coming to a close, I was asked to consider a second term. It was a hard decision, but I opted out. I cited personal reasons, for I genuinely felt that Elsie had been neglected and it was now right to spend more time with her.

My view of the NHS is the same today as it has always been – it is right and proper that everyone should have access to high standards of care and attention in times of illness or accident. As with all public services, it could always do better, would benefit from extra funding, doesn't pay enough to the key workers and stands wide open for those who wish to find fault and criticise.

Our family still has close links with the health service. Our Barbara works as a secretary at the Preston Royal Infirmary and our granddaughter Donna (Brian's daughter) is a ward sister at a new cancer unit at Blackpool Victoria. As PHA chairman, I saw at first hand the absolute dedication of the people on the ground, the doctors, nurses and carers who make the service work. They are angels in uniform.

I left saying that in my opinion the Preston Health Authority was a first-class service and in 1999 I had the opportunity to find out for myself – on the receiving end. After 77 years of good health with only occasional visits to the doctor, aside from a few football-related problems, I suffered a heart attack. It is not public knowledge and will come as a surprise to many people reading this book. It came as a huge shock to me.

It all happened early one evening when I took a stroll down to the local post office at Withy Trees, no more than 500 yards from home. After posting some letters I made my way home and started to feel a little breathless. By the time I reached the front door the discomfort had increased quite noticeably. Elsie could see something was the matter straightaway and I admitted to feeling below par.

'I don't know what it is but I feel lousy,' I said. 'Coming back, I got breathless but I'm sure it'll pass if I sit down for a while.'

Fortunately, Barbara was there and she took control.

'Dad, I don't like the sound of that – I'm going to ring the doctor.'

'Don't be daft,' I said. 'Just give me a few minutes and I'll be fine.'

Barbara was unimpressed and promptly rang our GP, Dr Max Smith. Within minutes I was sitting in the surgery being examined. Max has been my GP for many years; he enjoys a laugh and a joke but he talks a straight game.

'Have you got an overnight bag with you?' he asked.

'Well, no,' I said. 'Why would I need one?'

'Because I'm going to admit you to hospital. There are checks that need to be made and the sooner we make them the better.'

With that he picked up the telephone and arranged for me to go to Preston Royal Infirmary. That was shock enough in itself but worse was to follow the next morning, after the tests had been carried out. The consultant paid me a visit.

'So tell me, Tom, when did you have your heart attack?' he asked.

Heart attack? I was flabbergasted.

'I'm sorry, doctor,' I recovered my composure enough to say, 'but I wasn't aware I had ever had a heart attack.'

'Well, I'm afraid you have. It shows up clearly on the chart. We're going to put you on some tablets and send you to Blackpool Victoria Hospital for further tests.'

It later transpired that I must have suffered a mild attack when walking back from the post office. The tests showed conclusively that there was a partial blockage to one of my main valves. The specialists explained that the condition could well require a bypass operation but they had decided to wait to see whether the tablets worked well enough to defer the need for surgery.

It was all quite alarming – you are never ready for these things – but I am happy to report that the pills are working well and I am continuing to get favourable reports when I call around for my six-monthly check up.

That episode apart, I have been fortunate, but I have always worked hard on my fitness. Long after I retired from the professional game in 1960, I carried on doing a whole host of exercises in a daily 20-minute routine. These were exercises I had learned at Deepdale including step-ups and sit-ups, stretches and deep breathing. I feel sure it paid handsome dividends in my general well-being.

I also continued to play competitive football until I was 50 – maybe not quite to the level of Stanley Matthews, who reached his half-century milestone while still operating in the professional arena, but I was able to hold my own in testimonial matches. I always found it hard to say no when the chance of a game came along and I doubt whether anyone took part in more one-off games than I did. I nearly made a second career out of it.

I was lucky enough to be invited to take part in some cracking occasions, including benefit games for Jackie Milburn up at Newcastle, Billy Liddell at Liverpool and Nat Lofthouse at Bolton. The pick of the bunch has to be Stan Matthews' farewell night at Stoke. It was so big, with so many great players anxious to take part, that the organisers decided to have two matches running back to back to satisfy the demand. Every great star from the era seemed to be in the Potteries that night and not just the greats of the English game – Puskas and Di Stefano pulled their boots on, too.

I also did the round of fund-raisers for players from the lower divisions who had either spent their careers at one club or who had been forced into retirement through injury. It was good for them to be able to put some well-known names down on the teamsheet. It helped to heighten interest levels and attract more spectators. Very rarely did I pass over such an invitation unless it clashed with a prior booking or took me away from the business for too long. There was never any fee involved although sometimes you might get basic out-of-pocket expenses, or 'petrol money' as Nat Lofthouse used to call it. It was a gesture for a fellow player and a way of putting something back into the game.

Nat was another regular on the testimonial circuit and we often travelled together, sometimes journeying as far as London or Portsmouth. I once remember us going across to play in a benefit match at Grimsby. We had played similar games at Blundell Park in the past and knew the ropes – they gave you some fish for your trouble. True to form, the fish was stacked up in boxes for the presentations; I received plaice and Nat was given cod.

'Hang on a minute,' said Nat, tongue in cheek, as per usual. 'We have both made the effort to come here tonight but while I get cod as a thank-you that fellow Finney ends up with plaice. How come?'

'Oh that's quite easy to explain,' said the organiser. 'Mr Finney is a better player than you are.'

Nat has earned himself a few quid relaying that story on the after-dinner circuit.

Playing charity football obviously assisted me in my efforts to stay trim and I also popped in to Deepdale twice a week for evening training sessions with the kids. The youngsters used to train on Tuesdays and Thursdays and it was not uncommon for me to be involved. I might have been well into my forties and some of my team-mates and opponents might have been too young to order a drink, but I always felt I could compete. The day I felt I could no longer make a telling contribution, I decided to pack in.

CHAPTER TWENTY

Laughing stock

Retiring is not an easy thing to do and, having done it twice, I know the pitfalls.

When I packed in playing, I feared that spectating would be a poor substitute. Luckily, a long spell working in the media helped me cope although it meant I lost touch with playing matters at Preston. On leaving the *News of the World*, I found consolation in being able to re-introduce Preston North End into my life – not that I had missed an awful lot, and a lot of what I had missed had been truly awful!

Reaching the 1964 FA Cup final and eventually losing to West Ham stood out like a beacon. Otherwise the period was hardly awash with glory unless you call a Third Division championship something worth shouting about. But if I thought the lean years were consigned to the history books, I was in for a shock. It was to get worse, much worse. In fact, it got so bad that I nearly packed in altogether and could you blame me? When Preston plunged to the depths of the Fourth Division and had to apply for re-election to the Football League, it was almost too much to take.

Bobby Charlton arrived as player-manager in 1973 (it meant I lost my record as Preston's most-capped Englishman!) and invited me, by now installed as club president, to take a more active role on the playing side. I obliged by going out on several scouting missions and helping wherever I could, but Bobby simply wasn't able to deliver success and never really found comfort in the manager's chair. He was eventually sacked, a fate that also befell his successor, Harry Catterick.

It wasn't until the arrival of another ex-United World Cup winner that fortunes took a temporary up-turn. Nobby Stiles, bursting with the bubbly and infectious enthusiasm that had typified his playing career, was an instant hero as he guided North End from the wilderness of the Third Division in 1978. But even Nobby ran out of steam and the club once again drifted backwards.

My old mucker Tommy Docherty quit a coaching post in Australia to try his luck, but the North End sickness was terminal and way beyond any cure the Doc could prescribe. I was there on the day the Doc returned, full of hope and belief that his sheer love of, and enthusiasm for, the club and the game could prompt a revival. But Tommy was in and out in a matter of weeks, shocked by just how low the club's fortunes had sunk and unable to stimulate players who fell well below his standards.

Gordon Lee, who had fared well during an earlier spell down the road at Blackburn, moved in only for his name to be added to the list of those who tried and failed to stop the rot.

The club was in turmoil. Results went from bad to worse and the financial picture became so grim that the famous old ground was sold to the local authority to raise capital. What a massive mistake that was! North End suddenly found itself stripped of asset value with the bank refusing to let the overdraft rise above £200,000.

My beloved North End sank almost to the point of no return in 1985–86 when the club had to seek re-election after finishing second to bottom of the Fourth Division during the worst season on record. The previous campaign had been bad enough – 26 games lost, 100 goals conceded and relegation to the basement. Now Preston North End Football Club, founder members and first champions, had to go cap in hand to the Football League, hoping to gain sufficient votes to stay in.

A win over Doncaster Rovers on the opening day of that dreadful re-election season served only to mislead the public. A series of crushing defeats was followed by the horror of an FA Cup exit at the hands of Telford. It wasn't the fact that Telford had won, or the 4–1 margin, that was so bad although both of those things were bad enough; it was the pitiful way Preston's players performed, the lack of heart, fight and pride. I have stomached a lot watching North End but this was too much and midway through the second half I got up from my seat in the directors' box and walked away in sheer disgust. It was not done for show or to generate newspaper headlines and neither was it preconceived. It was a spontaneous gesture, not so much against the club, more against the players.

At that time, Preston's playing personnel were poor in the extreme. The squad included players with few aspirations who had done the rounds of lower division clubs, consistently underachieving. These were players with little in the way of skill or determination, who did not understand that to pull on a Preston North End shirt was special. They were patently not fit to represent the club.

As I walked down the main staircase of the Pavilion Stand and made my way to the car park, I remember thinking back to the players of my era, Willie Cunningham, Tommy Docherty and the others. We didn't always win, but by God we always gave it a go. Never ever did we fall short in the effort stakes. Willie and Tommy took defeat personally; to lose a match would ruin their weekends. These were tough guys who not only struggled to understand the meaning of the word defeat, but didn't care much for injury, either. They played with knocks and strains they didn't know they had and, to some extent, I was as guilty as anyone of that. On occasions I played for Preston when short of full fitness – sometimes I had the pain-killing injections and wasn't much better than 50 per cent. Although a player always had the final say, that doesn't mean he was never kidded or pressurised. Like Willie and the Doc and many more of their ilk, I was always part way to agreeing because I desperately wanted to play in every game. Players were reluctant to miss a match in case their replacement did well and kept the place. I know now that it was foolish. It was just the way it was.

Thankfully, I cannot recall being on the wrong end of many upsets although we did suffer the indignity of an FA Cup defeat by Watford, then of the Third Division, in the 1949–50 campaign. We had drawn 2–2 at their ground – I scored from a penalty – and were hot favourites to brush the Hornets aside in the replay four days later. But Watford had other ideas, stunning a Deepdale crowd of more than 27,000 by recording a single-goal win. I wasn't playing, having picked up the flu, and I remember sitting at home listening in disbelief to news of our exit. But I don't recall anyone faulting us for commitment the way I faulted North End for the manner of defeat against Telford. Supporters will always forgive a trier; they don't expect world-beating displays from every player in every game but they do, quite rightly, demand 101 per cent effort.

Manager Alan Kelly, such a great servant during his time as a goalkeeping fixture and the holder of the record number of league appearances, resigned shortly after that. Poor Alan Kelly, someone who understood what it meant to wear the Preston colours and who appreciated in full the glorious history of the club, had had a torrid time. A member of his faltering team, Tommy Booth, took charge with Brian Kidd drafted in as number two. Booth and Kidd seemed to me out of their depth and, to be blunt, the task was quite clearly beyond them.

If season 1985–86 hadn't been so sad, it would have been laughable. There were moments of acute embarrassment – even the floodlights packed in. The pylons, first erected in 1953, were condemned as unsafe and consequently there were no night-time home fixtures for five months. North End secretary Derek Allan blushed when he told me he had to seek permission from the Football League in order for a November game with Scunthorpe United to go ahead on a midweek afternoon.

'What's happening, Mr Finney?' Derek groaned. 'The club's dying and no one seems able to stop it. It's tragic.'

I felt so sorry for Derek, who was a hard-working chap, often left to face the wrath of a disgruntled public and this was the final straw. The few supporters left who still cared enough to get angry were astounded, ringing me at home and stopping me in the street to vent their feelings. But the story had more twists, with North End later announcing that they might not be able to fulfil the fixture due to injury and illness.

Mel Tottoh, a striker who played local parks football, had to ask for time off from his job at British Aerospace in order to be included in the North End squad. I am reliably informed that the afternoon itself was a bit like attending a wake, eerily silent aside from the occasional derisory chant. I cannot confirm that as fact because I wasn't there; like thousands of others, I had chosen to go to work instead.

No one will be surprised to hear that Preston lost, but the biggest talking point was the attendance of 2,007, which remains the lowest on record. People voted with their feet and the average gate for the season was not much better, a paltry 3,502. No longer was Deepdale the place to be on a matchday, no longer did every schoolboy aspire to pull on the white shirt, no longer did the very name of Preston North End send a shiver down the spine. I could have wept. Here was this once proud club – my club – little more than a laughing stock.

North End was not alone in tumbling towards oblivion. You only had to look across Lancashire at what was happening elsewhere. Blackburn Rovers endured a hand-to-mouth existence for many seasons, dropping into the Third Division and struggling to pay their way. Jack Walker changed all that with a few bumper cheques. Blackburn rose again to take the Premiership title in 1995, and good luck to 'em.

If Preston was bad, it was even worse for Burnley and Blackpool who both fell headlong into the Fourth Division. In 1987, the Clarets retained Football League status only by winning their final game against Leyton Orient. The Seasiders had an equally bad time with their dilapidated stadium sometimes housing short of 3,000 spectators for games in the lower reaches of the bottom division. I think I know how Jimmy McIlroy and Stanley Mortensen felt – totally disillusioned and completely embarrassed.

The man holding the poisoned chalice at Deepdale throughout this roughest of rides was Keith Leeming, a local farmer and landowner with an impressive business pedigree, and boy did I feel for him. I got to know Keith well; he and his wife Margaret remain among our dearest friends, and he is a genuine and honourable man for whom I have the utmost respect.

I actually knew of Margaret long before I met Keith. Whereas Keith was primarily a rugby union man, playing with some success for Preston Grasshoppers, Margaret was always an avid North Ender. During my playing days I remember seeing her and her friends at games up and down the country. It was through Margaret that Keith first got involved with the club — I daresay he cursed her for that more than once!

Keith succeeded me as chairman of the North End supporters' club and when I was made president he was on the board of directors. Not many people know the lengths Keith went to in an attempt to revive North End. I know for a fact that he consistently dipped his hand in his pocket to bail the club out and one summer he funded the entire wage bill. On another occasion, supported by vice-chairman Malcolm Woodhouse, who later took over as majority shareholder, he funded the £60,000 signing of Mike Flynn, a centre-half from Norwich. Keith did not court publicity, preferring instead to do his good deeds in private, and consequently the facts rarely surfaced. No one knew just how close, or how often, Preston came to closing down for good.

So what was Keith's motivation and how was he rewarded? Well, Margaret is the short answer to the first part and as for reward — what a joke! Week after week, game after game, Keith and Margaret would turn up on Saturday afternoons and Tuesday nights, more in blind hope than genuine expectation, to face the most appalling abuse from supporters ignorant of what was going on behind the scenes. Sometimes it got so bad, with groups of angry demonstrators crowded outside after games, that Keith would walk across the pitch and pick up his car on the opposite side of the ground. He was made the scapegoat and it was all so totally unfair. I don't know how he put up with it all.

He was badly let down, not just by indifferent managers, uninterested players and misguided supporters, but by his predecessors. Most football clubs go through sticky spells – Liverpool were once a mid-table Second Division outfit and Manchester United suffered relegation – but few experienced a fall from grace as ugly or as prolonged as Preston. Keith Leeming inherited problems because those in power during the golden years had failed to plan ahead.

There is no argument about the fact that in my day the overwhelming majority of clubs were solvent. Income from giant weekly attendances easily accounted for expenditure in the era of the maximum wage. So how come Deepdale stayed largely unchanged? Where did the money go? It certainly didn't go on transfer fees or players' wages, as would be the case today.

To be chairman when things are running sweet as a nut on the pitch is Utopia; to be at the helm when times are tougher than tough is a living hell. Whatever could go wrong did go wrong. Even the bold decision to try to increase the commercial use of Deepdale by laying a plastic pitch brought howls of derision. I stood with the minority on that particular issue, dismissing suggestions that the standard of football would suffer. Well, that was a joke for a start – the standard could hardly have got any worse – and I had experienced non-grass pitches during my time in the Army and found that, if anything, my skill level improved. The problem wasn't that the plastic pitch prevented good football, it was that poor players were found wanting when asked to play on a surface on which they had to be able to pass and control the ball.

The shame of applying for re-election did prove a turning point, albeit a temporary one, due to the arrival of an unlikely Messiah. John McGrath, a one-time rough-and-tumble centre-back with Southampton and Newcastle, had cut his managerial teeth with some success at Port Vale and Chester. Known as a disciplinarian and someone well used to working to a shoestring budget, he appeared to have the necessary credentials for tackling a club in crisis.

I remember meeting him for the first time and being very impressed. An imposing character with a laugh you could hear from the car park, he seemed to tune in straightaway to the absurdity of North End's plight.

'Tom, how the bloody hell has the club ended up here?' he boomed. 'It's like a Sunday pub team.'

John liked a joke but didn't like the thought of working for one; the gospel according to John was straightforward. He attacked the job like a man possessed and immediately hit it off with Keith Leeming. At last the chairman had a manager to whom he could relate, someone to share the burden, share the dream and share a glass or two of the hard stuff.

The playing staff was decimated and during the course of his first season – a campaign that ended in promotion as runners-up – no fewer than 18 newcomers made their debuts. That number was a mix of free-transfer signings, kids from the youth set-up and a sprinkling of those to whom football folk refer as warhorses. Sam Allardyce returned from America to stiffen the backline, Les Chapman combined coaching and playing and actually got the goal that secured promotion, and Frank Worthington jumped aboard in the closing stages to add some stardust and grab some vital goals.

Sam was a key signing, a centre-half of the old school for whom pain was conceding a goal, and it did not surprise me that he later made such a success of management. I know that Sam was a big fan of John McGrath and regularly rang him for advice right up until his untimely death from a heart attack a few years ago.

The cynics attributed the success to the plastic pitch, but the fact that McGrath's men managed double figures in the away wins column tended to destroy that argument. McGrath was the all-conquering hero, Keith Leeming was no longer the subject of cheap jibes, the club announced a profit of £80,000 and a disbelieving public was back onside.

Consolidation was achieved with some comfort the following season, the team finishing just below halfway in the Third Division, and it got better and better in 1988–89 with a sixth-place finish. Unfortunately, that was McGrath's nirvana. By February 1990 he had departed on the back of four straight defeats, much unrest on the terraces and the team staring relegation in the face – and there was the little matter of Whitley Bay.

That unforgettable – for all the wrong reasons – trip to the north-east coast marked the beginning of the end for McGrath. Well down the football ladder in the Unibond League, Whitley Bay's part-timers should not have had a prayer, but the Preston manager made the fatal mistake of dismissing the non-league club's chances in advance and in print. How that came back to haunt him!

I travelled to the match with Keith Leeming and as soon as we got to the tiny ground you could detect a strong sense of 'so you think it'll be easy, well, we'll show you' among the home fans. The Whitley Bay players clearly felt the same way and we sat and squirmed as North End lost 2–0 in front of the watching 'Match of the Day' cameras. The manager, usually such a cooperative figure for the media, didn't surface from the dressing room until the opportunity for interview had long gone. Was he hiding? Yes he was, and I must admit we made a fairly sharp exit, too.

Les Chapman took over as manager and the team stagnated, hovering in the bottom half for a year or so before finally succumbing to relegation back to the basement in 1992.

Sam Allardyce was handed the chance to show what he could do as caretaker manager and, in my opinion, he did enough to warrant being given the job on a full-time basis. The board felt otherwise and turned to long-ball exponent John Beck.

Beck had built quite a reputation with Cambridge and although he was unable to stop the rot initially, he did take the club to a promotion play-off at Wembley in his first full season. I never properly understood the man or his management style or, for that matter, his method of play. The big boot, hit-and-hope game has never appealed to me and to watch it played badly on a plastic pitch with the wind swirling and the ball bouncing over the crossbar was no fun at all.

Right-hand man Gary Peters took over when Beck got the big boot, and he stopped me in the corridor one particular Saturday.

'Mr Finney, have you got a moment?' he asked. 'I wonder if you would help me out by coming in for a chat after home games to give me your opinion? I would really appreciate it.'

I was made up. In all the 34 years since I had finished playing, no one had requested my input on such a regular basis. I said it would be a pleasure.

By this juncture, the club was owned by heating giants Baxi, who brought with them considerable financial clout and a sound business strategy. New chairman Bryan Gray promised to rebuild Deepdale, by now one of the most dilapidated grounds in the country, and the first phase was a new main stand to replace the famous West Stand, the oldest wooden structure still in use in the whole of the Football League. Better still from a personal perspective, it was to be a new main stand named in my honour. Bryan Gray first broached the subject in the boardroom after a first-team game.

'We are currently looking at completely redeveloping the ground and hope to create a unique design structure based on the Italian stadium in Genoa. It's a very ambitious and exciting project and the first phase is a new main stand, which we would like to name after you, if that's agreeable.' I took less than a second to say that it was, and Bryan added, 'We also intend to use your portrait in the seating plan so that you'll always be there looking down on future generations of Preston footballers.' It knocked me sideways.

Baxi clearly meant business. After the Tom Finney Stand, they built two more superb structures, named in honour of Bill Shankly and Alan Kelly.

In Bryan Gray they had a businessman who enjoyed the business of football. I wouldn't call him a football man, or for that matter a Preston North End fan, but in many respects I reckon that worked in his favour. Unlike so many club chairmen, he wasn't left to fight a constant battle between head and heart; he ran the club on strict business lines, spending when there was money to spend and keeping a tight hold on the finances, especially the wage structure of the playing staff.

Many good things happened during his tenure, not least a couple of promotions back through to the First Division, the redevelopment of the ground, the shrewd appointment of David Moyes to the manager's chair and the achieving of some sound balance sheets. He was wise enough to retain Malcolm Woodhouse and Keith Leeming as executive directors and I know they both appreciated that gesture.

They also got some of their money back, and why not? It was the least they deserved after supporting the charity that was Preston North End so generously and so faithfully for so long. I can put the record straight on those stories that linked me and the club in a financial sense. I never ever rejected the opportunity to put money into the club – truth is, I was never asked.

I was particularly sorry when Bryan Gray eventually decided to sever his connection with the club due to the time demands of his other business interests, and equally upset when David upped sticks and took up the challenge of managing Everton. The two of them made an excellent team and both played key roles in breathing new life and hope into North End.

Whether Preston, Burnley or Blackpool can ever emulate Blackburn and become a leading force again is debatable, but Bolton have managed a few seasons back in the top division in recent years. Along with all non-Premiership clubs, they suffered from the unexpected loss of television revenue, money they were counting on and could ill afford to lose. It cast doubt on the survival of many clubs, but might it just prove to be for the long-term good of the game? A shift in policy might signal a return to sanity.

Some clubs, and North End is certainly one, are having to re-examine the crippling issue of players' wages. Without the handouts from rich television sponsors, there is a real need for sound financial management and good business practice. Players, ordinary players at any rate, will lose out and might even find themselves having to take dramatic pay cuts to retain a professional career. Fair enough. Clubs should pay what they can afford and no more.

In my day, we were well paid compared with the average working man but we were very much aware of the pitfalls, particularly the length of our contracts. Every player in my time had to be satisfied with a one-year deal. It didn't matter if you were Stanley Matthews, Billy Wright or Tom Finney, as far as Stoke City, Wolverhampton Wanderers or Preston North End were concerned, you were employed on a 12-month basis from 1 July to 30 June. At the end of the season, you went along to see whether your name appeared on the retained list. If it did, you got the offer of a further year – usually at the same terms – and if it didn't, you were paid up the remaining month and told you were free to leave.

I saw the latter happen to a great many players and it was a distressing state of affairs. Players didn't just lose their jobs, they often lost their houses as well. Back then, a club would own a selection of properties in and around the vicinity of the stadium and players would be actively encouraged to rent these club houses at a knock-down rent of around £1 a week.

That was fine and dandy while you were a wanted man but as soon as the club decided to dispense with your services, it could be a very painful experience. Just think about it. A player might move to the club from the south of England or Scotland; he might be married with a young family with all the problems of relocating. It made no difference to the terms on offer. A year was the deal and a year is what you got, take it or leave it.

It was typical of the power the clubs held over the players and those entrusted with running the clubs were far from foolish. They didn't offer long contracts because it wasn't in their interest to do so. What if a top player got injured in the first month of a new agreement and was out for a year or more, or even worse, didn't play again? The dictatorial chairmen of my day always erred on the side of financial caution. You couldn't imagine it happening now, could you? These days the boot is on the other foot with star players being protected as well as, if not better than, their employers.

Fifty years ago I was paid roughly four times the wage of the average working man. If the same mathematics applied today, David Beckham and co. should be earning somewhere between £1,600 and £2,000 a week. Instead, they are handling ten, 20 and 30 times that amount, which means my contemporaries missed out in a big way – but what on earth would I have done with £360 a week in 1950? I might have considered buying a football club, but I doubt it.

CHAPTER TWENTY-ONE

Caring for my Elsie

For the past few years I have watched my wife Elsie fight a brave battle with the dreadful illness that is Alzheimer's. The bright, fit, alert and healthy woman with whom I have shared my happiest moments is now lost in a world of her own, unable to look after herself and oblivious to much of what goes on around her. She is totally reliant on my support – support which, I hasten to add, comes with a cast-iron guarantee for the rest of my days.

Elsie cared for me for close on 60 years and was largely responsible for the upbringing of our two children, Brian and Barbara, while I travelled around the world on football business. She was always there for us, a true family woman who didn't see why being married to a famous footballer should alter her way of life. Honest and straightforward, yet witty and comical, she has never really understood the fuss over football, but always did her best to make things easy for me.

I cannot begin to explain the role she has played in my life. Whenever important decisions had to be made she would shrug her shoulders and say, 'Look, Tom, you know best about this, you decide – if it suits you, it suits me.'

When I look at Elsie now, I still see the young girl I first set eyes upon way back in 1938. We went through so much in those early years together as teenagers. Within a matter of months of meeting, the country had gone to war. There were long spells – one for three full years – when we didn't see one another in the flesh, but the bond remained and, if anything, our love for each other flourished.

After the war, we moved in with Elsie's parents and stayed there for about 18 months. The reason was purely financial. We had no money – I came out of the Army with £75 and a suit, which hardly amounted to much for a couple of young lovebirds wanting to set up a life together. Jim and Ruth went out of their way to make us welcome and comfortable, but it was never going to be an easy situation. How could it be?

It wouldn't have been so bad if they had known a bit about football. One day when I was due to play for North End at Deepdale, I got up from the dinner table and went upstairs to change for the match. After a wash and brush-up, I came back down only for Elsie's mother to look round in a state of shock.

'Tom?' she said, a puzzled tone in her voice. 'Please tell me you don't intend to go and play football in your best suit, do you?'

As I said, they knew precious little about football.

The arrangement couldn't go on indefinitely and I might have known that Jim Taylor would pop up with an answer. Jim was always keen to keep me happy. The fact that I told him I felt unsettled after Preston's relegation seemed to make him all the more determined to ensure that my garden was as rosy as possible. I told him of our predicament and he put me in the way of a few club properties. We viewed a couple near Deepdale and didn't care for either, even though Bill Shankly and Andy McLaren both lived in the vicinity. Club houses were convenient for the ground and, with their low rent, a bargain, but they were basic.

'Not for us, I'm afraid,' I told the chairman, who looked disappointed but not despondent. Jim always had an alternative.

'Tell you what, Tom. How about I build you a nice little bungalow in the grounds of my house on Victoria Road? We have a tennis court there that's overgrown and underused and the plot would be perfect.'

'Well, if you don't mind, that would be – well, it would be wonderful,' I enthused, knowing full well that Elsie would be made up with the idea.

'That's it then, let's do it,' said Jim. 'You can rent it at a nominal rate and, better still, when the time's right, I'll sell it to you for the exact sum it costs me to build it.'

I was finding this generosity a little too much to take, but I took the chairman up on his offer just the same and he proved true to his word. After the war, due to the shortage of good housing, developers were not permitted to build properties to sell; they could only build them to rent. So we had to wait some time but when the laws of the land were relaxed, we paid Jim Taylor £1,500 for our first home. A nice little place it was, too, very modern with two bedrooms, a lounge, kitchen, bathroom and toilet and a lovely garden. We loved it there and would have stayed but for two reasons – the arrivals of son Brian and daughter Barbara on 15 December 1947 and 29 December 1949 respectively.

Our next house was a semi-deatched property on Regent's

Drive. Sammy Baird, an inside-forward North End had signed from Glasgow Rangers, was our next-door neighbour.

At about the same time, I also purchased my first car, thanks to the efforts of North End director Ewart Bradshaw. Ewart was in the motor business and although cars were hard to come by, he managed to fix me up with a Ford. It wasn't a gift – or a sponsorship deal – I had to buy it, cash up front, but at least I didn't have to pass a test of any sort. I had gone into the Army not knowing which pedal was for braking and which for accelerating, but I came out an accomplished driver, having sat behind the wheel of a lorry, a jeep, a van and, most frequently, a tank.

Sammy didn't stay long, but the house stayed in club hands with the arrival of Tommy Thompson and his wife Mary. We enjoyed the extra space and forged a great relationship with Tommy and Mary. It wasn't until my retirement in 1960 that we considered upping sticks. The proceeds from my benefit game allowed us to climb a little higher up the property ladder and we splashed out £12,500 for a handsome detached house on Black Bull Lane. It was a lovely house to begin with, but we spent a lot of time and money on it and installed the latest central heating system and a deluxe bathroom suite.

Then at the turn of the seventies, we spotted a plot of land just off the main road in a little oasis in the Fulwood district. Elsie fell head over heels for the location so we bought it and built the bungalow that has remained our base for the past 30 years.

Elsie adapted to motherhood as though she had known nothing else. I left her to it. Being away such a lot, I cannot pretend that I was an always around sort of husband or father. Without the unswerving support of Elsie, my career could have turned out so differently. Some players I knew were governed by the instructions of their better halves. You would be amazed at some of the high-profile soccer stars who declined the chance to play for their countries because the missus put her foot down.

I never faced that particular predicament. Elsie knew what was expected of me as an international player and accepted that there would be periods when she would be at home alone with the kids. She has always been 100 per cent of my private life and 1 per cent of my public life, but it is only in the last few years that I have really begun to appreciate the sacrifices she made for me and my football.

Elsie didn't watch me a great deal. One of the first times I wasn't playing for Preston but for Newcastle as a guest in a wartime match. We had not been engaged for very long and it was quite an adventure for Elsie to travel up to Tyneside on the train. Stan Seymour, then heavily involved with Newcastle, was kind enough to make sure that Elsie was well looked after and even arranged for us both to stay over in a city hotel. Elsie rang home to explain, but her mother went up the wall. She was definitely not having her daughter do such a thing and ordered her to return home after the game. Elsie accepted her mother's view, even though it meant she didn't get back to Lancashire until 3 o'clock in the morning. We thanked Stan Seymour for his thoughtfulness.

Football in general did not make it easy for wives and girlfriends to get involved, quite the opposite. In common with many clubs in the 1950s, North End offered sparse comfort and few privileges for the players' wives. There was no special room, no social suite, no executive club, barely a cup of tea and a biscuit. They were provided with a seat in the stand and not much else. After the games, they were expected to walk down to the main door and hang around until we appeared. If it rained, they got wet. It was hardly surprising that so few showed any desire to attend. Elsie often said the wives were treated like second-class citizens and claimed that people from within the game ignored her when talking with me.

North End did organise socials and day trips for the players, up to the Lake District or over to the seaside, and wives were sometimes given the chance to go along. I remember those trips being a lot of fun.

In spite of her lack of passion for the game, Elsie has always been quick to acknowledge her debt of gratitude to football. We have enjoyed a very comfortable standard of living and travelled the world, but it was far from a bed of roses in the early days when cash was tight and we kept special tins in which to collect coins to pay off the weekly gas and electricity charges.

Elsie never got much involved in the business, either. She was always happy to know things were going well and to listen to my problems with contracts and staff. She would chip in with words of wisdom as and when she saw fit but the business was essentially my business – her business was the family.

We have never disagreed about much, but we certainly didn't see eye to eye on the subject of our Brian and the prospect of him attending a boarding school. Brian was a bit of a rebel in a mild sort of way and it was recommended to me that he might benefit from attending the Friends School in Lancaster. He left Fulwood and Cadley County Primary School and went up there as a boarder for five years before completing his education at Preston Polytechnic.

The idea did not please Elsie at all initially, and we had a few heated conversations before finally agreeing to give it a go. I felt it would help Brian if he got away from Preston and the obvious difficulties attached to being Tom Finney's son. He was teased and tormented quite a lot at junior school and I think it troubled him, so I feared what might happen if he went into secondary education in Preston.

Full credit to him for the way he didn't just cope but flourished at Lancaster – even though it was a rugby union school. Football had dropped off the bottom of the agenda there, not that Brian worried over much as he always fared better with the oval ball. He never showed many signs of following in my footsteps at football. He played for fun in the amateur leagues for a few years but that was about it. On many a Sunday morning during my career, I would go down to Deepdale for a gentle jog and Brian would come with me, constantly pestering for the chance to get out on the pitch with a ball. Would I have liked it had he made the grade as a footballer? I don't know, but what I do know is that I never put him under any pressure to try.

He has always shared my love for Preston North End, though, which reminds me of a funny incident just after the ill-fated FA Cup final of 1954. Brian was in floods of tears when we lost and was still carrying the upset a few weeks later when we were on holiday in Blackpool. By complete coincidence, staying at the same guesthouse was Ray Barlow, a member of the West Bromwich Albion Cup-winning side. Brian made us laugh when he made it quite clear to Elsie and me that he was more than a little perturbed by the fact that Ray had the nerve to stay in the same place as us.

As you might expect, Brian enjoyed a few privileges in and around Deepdale. On one occasion, he and Tommy Docherty's son Michael were allowed to watch a game from the dug-out. That was when we beat Birmingham 8–0 and Brian's eyes still light up if you mention it.

Brian didn't like it when people criticised North End and he once got into a right old scrap when a group of kids taunted him mercilessly over Stanley Matthews being better than me.

Our Barbara was always more interested in horses than football and rarely came to watch me play. Even on the night of my benefit match at Deepdale, I remember Barbara not being overjoyed at the prospect of tagging along. I rarely got hot under the collar but on this occasion I left Barbara in no doubt about how I felt. 'There is no choice,' I said. 'You're coming and that's that.' So she came and enjoyed it.

Had it been a showjumping display, she would have been there like a shot. I lost count of the number of times I came home from work for Elsie to pull me to one side and say, 'Tom, we really are going to have to look into the possibilities of buying our Barbara a horse. It's her entire life.' When she was 22, we finally gave in although Barbara was responsible for the general upkeep.

Barbara knew how to play me – thank goodness she wasn't an opposing full-back – but don't all daughters have the ear of their fathers? I was strict, but I always argued that it was strictness born out of care. Brian was given quite a lot of rope in terms of going out with his friends, but I was only happy to let Barbara do the same if I could drop her off and pick her up.

Elsie wasn't so much of a worrier as I was. She was prepared to let life run its course but she was never prepared to take any risks. Now that self-same woman who stood by me for more than half a century is dependent upon me.

The problems started five years ago. One evening, around 7 o'clock, the telephone rang and I went from the lounge to the kitchen to answer. Elsie was sitting in a reclining chair, watching television. When I came back into the room, I was horrified to find Elsie lying prostrate on the floor. She had fallen awkwardly while getting up from the chair and had caught herself against the coffee table. There were scratches all along her arm. I tried to help her up but it was obvious that she was in considerable pain. She was holding herself rigid and screamed if I touched her or if she tried to move.

The ambulancemen arrived within minutes and managed to get her on to a stretcher, reckoning that she may well have broken a bone in her leg. However, a series of X-rays and tests up at Preston Royal Infirmary clearly showed the damage was much worse than first feared.

'I'm afraid Mrs Finney has a badly broken hip and will need to have an operation tomorrow morning,' said the duty doctor.

The following day, I rose early and rang to see what time Elsie was due in theatre. They said the operation might have to be delayed but could not offer any real explanation why. I hit the roof.

'Just what is going on?' I demanded. 'This just isn't good enough. My wife is in her seventies and clearly in distress and we are both very concerned.'

The outburst was rather out of character. I think the worry had got the better of me. I even went to the lengths of ringing the higher authorities to vent my anger. It certainly did the trick. Just after lunchtime, Elsie was taken down for the operation.

She stayed in hospital for a further three weeks, but a couple of days after the op one of the ward sisters stopped me in my tracks.

'Mr Finney, have you noticed any other problems with your wife?' she asked.

'No,' I replied, somewhat taken aback. What exactly did she mean?

'Mental problems,' she said, looking me straight in the eye. 'It's just that we have noticed her talking in a strange and rather incoherent way from time to time, a sort of rambling, if you will.'

I expressed surprise. It certainly hadn't struck me and after 50 years of marriage there was surely a decent chance that I would spot any change.

Elsie was finally allowed home and although she found movement difficult to start with, she appeared to be making a full recovery. The health visitors turned up daily to help with bathing and dressing and the consultant seemed very pleased with her physical progress.

But I was slowly beginning to see and understand what the ward sister had meant a few weeks earlier. Elsie seemed a little restless and was behaving in an unpredictable way. She was doing simple things wrongly and getting agitated with herself in the process. She was put under observation at Ribbleton Hospital and it was there that the consultant first told me he feared Elsie was suffering the onset of Alzheimer's. It was a massive shock.

Over the weeks and months and years, her condition has continued to deteriorate and I am now her full-time carer. Although still quite active and able to speak, she is aware of very little and finds communication difficult. If you say something, she has forgotten it within seconds; if we visit somewhere, she is keen to go but wants to leave as soon as we have arrived. Her attention span is very limited. She has stopped watching television, cannot read a book (she used to get through four library books a week) and doesn't recognise members of our family and our closest friends. She has lost interest in the house, too – and to think that her entire life used to revolve around her home and her family.

I put her to bed at night and get her up in a morning, choose her clothes, apply her make-up, do her hair, make her meals, take her for drives in the car and try to entertain her the best I can.

Then there is the security angle, making sure she doesn't leave a cigarette burning (she has smoked since the age of 16) or get out of the house alone. One summer afternoon I was engrossed in the Open golf championship on television when there was a ring on the doorbell. It was the woman from the end of the street – and Elsie.

'Here you are, Tom,' said the neighbour. 'Delivered home, safe and sound.'

It transpired that I had forgotten to put the latch on the front door and Elsie had managed to find her way out. Luckily, our neighbour spotted her just as she was walking towards the main road.

She also once escaped from the car while I nipped in to the local bank. I was gone for no more than five minutes but when I returned she was missing. I panicked like I have never panicked in my life before, driving around all the local streets in a frantic search for about half an hour – it seemed like an eternity. Eventually, I headed home and rang the police. I must have sounded in a right old state because the officer said, 'Now, come on Mr Finney, try to stay calm – we'll have her back with you in no time.'

I was advised to stay at home next to the telephone, not an easy task in those circumstances, and within a matter of minutes the police rang back with the great news.

'We have found Mrs Finney,' the officer said, 'and she is quite safe.'

I cannot tell you my sense of relief. Apparently, Elsie had managed to unlock the passenger door and marched off towards town, crossing several busy roads, before she was finally spotted. The funny thing was that she didn't want anything to do with the police, refusing all requests to get into the patrol car until I arrived.

As anyone who has cared for an Alzheimer's sufferer will testify, you cannot afford to lose concentration. This is, in every respect, a round-the-clock job. I'm not complaining. I look upon it as my duty. Elsie has been a wonderful partner and she would certainly tend to me had the roles been reversed. One of the hardest things for me to accept is the fact that, deep down in her soul, I believe she knows that something is wrong. Most mornings she will have a little weep.

'Now then, what's the matter?' I will ask.

'I don't know,' she says, 'but something is.' Then she will reach out and cling on to me. 'I love you,' she will say. 'I want you here.'

'I know that,' I reply. 'I love you, too, and I'm going nowhere.'

Then it's my turn to cry, an outpouring of my inner grief. It can all be very, very upsetting. It can be frustrating, too. Elsie might repeat the same thing to me a hundred times in the same day, sometimes to the extent that I lose my rag and say something I later regret.

She spends a few hours a week at a local day-care centre where the staff are absolutely first class with her, bless them. She never wants to go but as soon as we pull the car on to the drive they rush out to greet her. 'Come on, Elsie, let's go and have a cup of tea and a fag,' they say and she is immediately won over by their warmth and friendship. The time spent there is good for both of us. Elsie gets a change of scene and some different company and I get the chance to cram in some shopping, washing, ironing and general housework, go into town to pay a few bills or nip in for a haircut.

I try to keep up my weekly commitment to Preston Rotary Club and call in at Deepdale to deal with any correspondence, but apart from that my public life has come to a complete standstill. I still receive hundreds of invitations to attend functions, open shops, be a guest at a dinner or suchlike, but my answer is always the same, a polite no. I even had to write to the local authority to decline the opportunity to meet the Queen when she visited Preston. Those are occasions that both Elsie and I would have loved once upon a time, but not now. She is not able to go and I won't leave her behind.

Although we have some good friends who know and understand our situation, this is the first time I have felt able to talk openly and publicly about Elsie, my sweet Elsie. She has not deserved the hand that life has dealt her in her twilight years. I love her dearly and to see her struggling with all the very things at which she once excelled, and so agitated and restless well, God help me, it breaks my heart.

CHAPTER TWENTY-TWO

It's not the same

I t is not so much the game itself that has changed, more the business that not only surrounds it but threatens to strangle it. An ever-decreasing group of big bidders rule the roost, hungrily gobbling up the best players and leaving the rest to scratch around for the crumbs. These super-rich clubs are forgetting a fundamental of team sport – you always need someone to play against. Where will we be when the best 33 players play for three clubs? Well, roughly where we are now – only two or three clubs are capable of winning the championship and the word 'competition' has been lost.

The spread of top players used to be much more even. In the England team of Swift, Scott, Wright, Franklin, Cockburn, Hardwick, Matthews, Mortensen, Lawton, Mannion and Finney, only Stoke City could boast more than one member. Every club had its star turns, usually more than a couple, and as a consequence you got a better competition, a fairer competition, a healthier competition and a competition that was much more attractive to the spectators. It gets dull when the smiles of triumph feature on the same faces all the time.

Of course, there were teams that dominated for a while in the fifties and sixties – Arsenal and Wolves were two great forces of that time – but they were always aware of dangers from elsewhere. No one could sit down at the start of a season and dismiss the title chances of 90 per cent of the competing clubs. They could now. You only have to look at the way the honour has gone since the dawn of the Premiership – what was it, three winners in the first ten years? Says it all.

I fear for the game and the clubs at the wrong end of the pyramid. How can they hope to compete or hold on to a good player?

Despite the lifestyles of modern footballers, I am just glad I played the game when I did. Forget the finances – I have explained at length my views on that subject – and put to one side my age and the undeniable fact that everything looks better in retrospect. Although, hand on heart, I genuinely believe I could have more than held my own out on the pitch in 2003, I don't think I could have coped with the superstar status; and I know Elsie would have positively hated life in a goldfish bowl. Thankfully, when we went out for a bite to eat or to shop or just for a walk, we were largely left alone. It may sound strange considering that even now, 43 years after I played my final game, people still treat me like royalty, but I am essentially a shy person who treasures his privacy. That isn't to say I don't like attending events or having people round, I do. It is just that I have always cherished home life with my family.

When I read of players throwing celebrity parties, attending film premieres and jetting off to far-flung destinations for an overnight photo opportunity, I wonder just how they do it and whether they actually enjoy it.

The top footballers of today are like the film stars of the fifties – although I always felt that my ex-England colleague George Hardwick, the suave and sophisticated half-back, always so smart and with that dapper moustache, had more than a look of Errol Flynn about him. They cannot move without media intrusion, they need security protection for their children and even a minor injury can make front-page headline news. After the game, they are whisked away to spend the evening in the company of celebrity friends and acquaintances at the sort of glitzy gatherings the Sunday tabloids adore.

Much the same sort of routine Stanley Matthews, Wilf Mannion, Tommy Lawton and I experienced, I don't think! I cannot comment with complete confidence on how Stan, Wilf and Tommy lapped up soccer's social scene, but I can tell you exactly how Tom Finney 'lived it up' after matches. If we had played at home, and even after local away games such as those against Blackburn, Blackpool, Bolton or Burnley, we would meet up with a few friends and head off to a restaurant for a quiet meal. The Dog and Partridge in the sublime Ribble Valley village of Chipping was a particular favourite retreat.

Were we constantly pestered by the paparazzi? No. Did we get inundated with autograph requests? No, although sometimes a nervous adult would spot me across a crowded room and send his child over to ask for my signature.

When we really felt like living dangerously, we would go to the coast to see a show – Blackpool's famous theatres were little more than half an hour away. And there was, of course, the steady stream of personal engagements – no, not the chance to model underwear or sunglasses, more the opportunity to present prizes at the local boys' club.

Forgive me, I do not mean to be frivolous or facetious. I am just trying to paint a picture. Truth is I enjoyed the many talks and appearances I made at local youth clubs, men's fellowships and church groups and considered it a most worthwhile contribution as it clearly brought a lot of pleasure to a lot of people. For proof of that, here's a true story from several years ago.

We had just finished our tea and were about halfway through the washing-up when the telephone rang.

'Terribly sorry to bother you, Mr Finney,' said the most courteous of callers. 'But I'm one of the main organisers of a sports function to be held next month and I've been given the job of asking you to be the chief guest.'

'That's very kind of you,' I replied. 'What date have you got in mind?'

When he told me the date, I feared straightaway that I had something else booked in for that particular night.

'Let me check my diary – oh, I'm so sorry but I've already promised to be somewhere else.' I could sense the disappointment as the caller swallowed hard.

'But Mr Finney, this is a major event, one of the biggest of its kind ever held in the county. We have sold five hundred tickets already and expect it to be a complete sell-out.'

I sympathised with his predicament but explained that I always worked on a first-in-the-diary basis. While appreciating that his event was clearly bigger than the one I was down to attend, I just wasn't prepared to cry off.

'Oh OK then,' he said, sounding a touch flustered. 'If you can't make it, you can't make it.' I thought that was to be the end of the conversation until he piped up, 'My committee will inform the five hundred people that the event is cancelled. So, Mr Finney, what dates do you have free?'

Footballers may not have been celebs back then, but they were still heroes and I for one had known what it was like to look up to the men who wore the white shirt of Preston. Therefore I was never too busy to go along and it was gratifying to have the chance to give something back. The club also expected us to attend a given number of sportsmen's services. These could be held anywhere in the county, usually on a Sunday afternoon, and players from other local clubs would also be invited (I almost said dragged along).

When out-of-hours assignments cropped up, we never thought of asking for a fee, regarding it as part and parcel of the job. But there were other limited commercial opportunities. A footballer's capacity to top up his wages with outside earnings is big business now, but sponsorship is nothing new. In my era, it was not on the financial scale of today, but fairly lucrative all the same. Agents were knocking around although fairly low profile and few and far between, and I was approached more than once. My view was to trust my own judgement and look after my own deals. Why give someone a percentage of your income if you don't have to?

Nowadays agents seem to be almost as important as the players they represent. They can cream off an awful lot of money for what doesn't always appear to be an awful lot of work and they also do the game a disservice in my book by unsettling players in the quest for revenue. Would I recruit an agent if I had my time to do over again? No.

In the early fifties I signed up to the country's first-ever football boot deal when I agreed to put my name to footwear made by the Kettering firm of Raundes Limited. The boot – so lightweight it was actually more like a slipper – was styled around one I had come across in Brazil. Raundes made it especially for me and I negotiated my cut at 25 per cent of the sales. I went for a percentage figure because Stanley Matthews, who was doing some promotional work for the Co-operative Society, told me he felt he had slipped up by settling for a fixed fee. It proved a great decision. In no time at all my boots were selling like hot cakes and I was pocketing between £1,000 and £2,000 a year. At that sort of rate, the boots were earning me more than my football.

I was about 27 at the time and I decided to seek some financial advice on the matter. Tom Finney Boot Limited was formed and I spent much of the summer travelling around to shops across the country making personal appearances and posing for photographs. I recently discovered that one youngster who wore Tom Finney boots was none other than Geoff Hurst. Whether he had a pair on when he scored his World Cup winning hat-trick against West Germany in 1966 I'm not sure!

Later, I endorsed a ball manufactured by Crooks of Huddersfield and some shinguards, again linked to sales and again successful. My biggest single sponsorship arrived in 1954 when I was approached by a Canadian advertising firm who said they wanted a famous sportsman and his family to front up a campaign on behalf of Shredded Wheat. It involved filming a commercial in London and we all went along, Elsie and the two kids particularly excited by the prospect. Considering we had no experience of such things, it all went off well, although a slight mistake by Barbara and Brian meant we couldn't claim to have cracked it in one take. It was a bit embarrassing on the train back to Preston, too, when I realised I had forgotten to wash off the studio make-up – but the £500 fee (for just one day's work, mind) was more than adequate compensation.

It makes me laugh when I hear it said that Stanley Matthews would have struggled had he been around now – what claptrap! Joe Mercer believed you could only be considered a great player when you had performed at the very top for at least ten years. According to that criterion, Stan was certainly a great. While I accept that the drawing of accurate comparisons across different generations is nigh on impossible – you can only be as good as the era you are in – I remain convinced that Matthews would have flourished in today's game, and you can say the same for hundreds of others, too. The great players of my day would have been superstars today.

Winning was important to us, but it was never a life-and-death situation and it was treated accordingly. We went into every single game trying to play our best and win, but it has all got a bit silly now. One bad result and the crowd are calling for the manager's head. That's complete nonsense.

Football may well be faster today, but that isn't to say we were slow and sluggish in the fifties. No one has ever played successfully at the top level without having a high degree of physical fitness. Training was graft. At Deepdale, we had players who could run all day and then through the night as well. My first manager was a fitness instructor and all the games I played for England were for a man who spent years as a physical training instructor in the Royal Air Force.

Speed isn't the be all and end all, anyhow. Trying to play at 100 mph often results in more mistakes being made and I sometimes think the game would benefit from being slowed down a touch. The secret is to harness pace with skill and intelligence. Being able to run faster than the other man is not enough on its own. This is football we are discussing, not sprinting.

As a youngster, I was aware of the need to be fit, but the greatest emphasis was always placed on my ability with a ball at my feet. I believe coaches should always encourage youngsters to perfect their skills with the ball. That isn't old-fashioned philosophy from a man from the distant past; it's sound policy for an era when many of the so-called coaching methods disappoint and sadden me. I see many schoolboy matches and positively cringe when I hear teachers screaming orders from the touchline to 'get rid of it' or 'stop trying to dribble'. I was encouraged to get a hold of the ball, look for the pass and move for the return. I can't recall anyone ripping my head off for trying to beat a full-back by skilful play.

I can honestly claim that no one ever tried to coach me. There were people around to offer advice and point out weaknesses and ways to improve, but that was it. But I did believe in practice making perfect. Right from being a young boy dribbling a tennis ball on my newspaper delivery round through my time as a fully fledged international when I would stay behind for extra sessions, I realised that the harder you tried, the better you got.

Jim Taylor once pulled me aside after a youth team practice match and said, 'Tom, you are making good progress, but I cannot emphasise enough to you the need to be two-footed. You have no chance of taking your career to the very top if your right foot is only there for standing on.' It was great advice and from that moment my main aim in life was to make my right foot as useful as my left. Hour after hour, day after day, week after week, during training and after training, on the pitch and in the street, it was practice, practice, practice.

Will Scott gave me personal tuition and we often used the back of the main stand as part of our training regime. I would kick the ball against the wall with one foot, control it with the other and then reverse the procedure. One day Will told me to wear a slipper on my left foot and a boot on my right and just concentrate on using the 'weaker' side until it felt normal to do so. Eventually, I was able to use both feet equally well and what an advantage that gave me as a professional. Irrespective of which wing I played on, I was able to go on the outside and cross, or cut inside and shoot. One manager was more than two years into his spell at Deepdale before he realised that I wasn't a natural right footer. I never felt that I needed to get the ball on my left side and I did once take a penalty with my right foot in the World Cup finals.

I also believe that skill is a natural gift that cannot be implanted, no matter how long you stay behind at the training ground or how many manuals you care to read. Overcoaching of the kind that we have seen in the last decade produces anonymous, manufactured players. Give a player the ball at his feet and let natural ability shine through. If you have a naturally gifted player, let him play. Everything I did on a football field was born out of instinct and I could never have taught anyone how to do a body swerve.

Ryan Giggs is a player who excites me. He has ability, flair and the sense of entertainment about him and I would have no problem shelling out £25 to go to watch him in action. This is not a case of the wingers' union uniting; I just rate Giggs as a wonderful talent, a player with speed and close control who commits defenders into tackles and then leaves them sat on their backsides as he flies up the line.

Damien Duff is another exponent of the dying art of wing play, a dribbler who can twist and wriggle past challenge after challenge in the tightest of spaces and retain possession even when outnumbered by defenders.

They are a couple of outstanding examples of the sort of ball players every team had in the golden era. Matthews and Carter and Doherty had defenders and spectators guessing what might happen next. Consequently matches were far more exciting back then, there was more action and the emphasis was on simply scoring more goals than the opposition. Nowadays I often feel disillusioned after watching a match, be it live or on television. It seems stop-start with few notable incidents and players far too fearful of making an error to try something inventive.

While pure skill is obviously crucial, skill on its own is not enough. High levels of fitness and a desire for hard work are also necessary; only when you mix ability with workrate can you hope to produce the perfect player.

Technically, the players of 2003 are light years ahead of my gang, but I don't honestly think the spectacle is as good. Our approach was quite basic and there was a distinct lack of attention to detail, certainly in relation to matters like diet and nutrition. No one advised us on eating habits; that was left to the individual player to sort out for himself. We knew that fish and chicken and beans and toast were good as pre-match meals and that alcohol on the night before a game was not a particularly good idea, but, by and large, players ate and drank as they wanted.

I think I was fortunate in that Preston North End tried hard to be modern in outlook, always keen to look at new developments within the game. The appointment of Walter Crook, a former player with Blackburn Rovers, as a coach was considered revolutionary. Walter had spent some time in Holland and he was ahead of his time. He introduced many new ideas on training and fitness, and for the first time we started to question the traditional approach. He encouraged us to warm up properly, to stretch our muscles and have oil massaged into our legs prior to games, particularly on bitterly cold winter afternoons. We certainly cut down the number of man hours lost to pulls and strains.

I know that the whole concept of football is different today but I would dearly like to see some of the current players use the kit we played in. The shirts, for instance, were all the same size whether you were 5ft 4ins or 6ft 5ins. Now everything is streamlined for speed.

They certainly wouldn't be able to do the things they do today with the balls we were given to play with. The ball was so heavy – and on a wet day the weight could increase by 50 per cent – no one considered long-range shooting as a sensible option. Very few goals were scored from distance and free-kick specials, such as the kind David Beckham is known for, were very rare indeed. Without taking anything away from David, who has clearly mastered the art, the ball and his footwear work very much in his favour. It is astonishing to watch the ball, still rising, zip into the top corner as Beckham bends one past another bewildered goalkeeper from well outside the box. Tell you what, if someone had smacked home a shot from 30 yards in my day, it would have been heralded as a flippin' miracle!

Statistics

SIR TOM FINNEY

- Born Preston, Lancashire, 5 April 1922
- League debut v Leeds United on 31 August 1946 at Deepdale
- England debut v Northern Ireland on 28 September 1946 at Windsor Park, Belfast
- Second Division champions 1950–51
- First Division runners-up, 1952–53, on goal average
- FA Cup finalists, 1953–54
- Footballer of the Year, 1954
- Footballer of the Year, 1957 (the first man to win the award twice)
- First Division runners-up, 1957–58
- Last game for England v USSR on 22 October 1958 at Wembley
- Last league game v Luton Town on 30 April 1960 at Deepdale
- Played only game for Distillery, v Benfica in European Cup in September 1963
- Awarded OBE in 1961
- Freeman of Preston in 1979
- Awarded CBE in 1992
- Knighted in 1998

ENGLAND APPEARANCES

Cap	Opponents	Venue	Date	Result	Position/Goals
1.	Northern Ireland	Belfast	28 September 1946	W 7–2	OR – scored once
2.	Republic of Ireland	Dublin	30 September 1946	W 1–0	OR – scored once
3.	Wales	Maine Road	13 November 1946	W 3–0	OR
4.	Holland	Huddersfield	27 November 1946	W 8–2	OR – scored once
5.	France	Highbury	3 May 1947	W 3–0	OR – scored once
6.	Portugal	Lisbon	25 May 1947	W 10–0	OL – scored once
7.	Belgium	Brussels	21 September 1947	W 5–2	OL – scored twice
8.	Wales	Cardiff	18 October 1947	W 3–0	OL – scored once
9.	Northern Ireland	Goodison Park	5 November 1947	D 2–2	OL
10.	Sweden	Highbury	19 November 1947	W 4–2	OR
11.	Scotland	Hampden Park	10 April 1948	W 2–0	OL – scored once
12.	Italy	Turin	16 May 1948	W 4–0	OL – scored twice
13.	Northern Ireland	Belfast	9 October 1948	W 6–2	OL
14.	Wales	Villa Park	10 November 1948	W 1–0	OL – scored once

15.	*Scotland*	*Wembley*	*9 April 1949*	*L 1–3*	*OL*
16.	Sweden	Stockholm	13 May 1949	L 1–3	OR – scored once
17.	Norway	Oslo	18 May 1949	W 4–1	OR – scored once
18.	France	Paris	22 May 1949	W 3–1	OR
19.	Republic of Ireland	Goodison Park	21 September 1949	L 0–2	OL
20.	*Wales**	*Cardiff*	*15 October 1949*	*W 4–1*	*OR*
21.	*Northern Ireland**	*Maine Road*	*16 November 1949*	*W 9–2*	*OR*
22.	Italy	White Hart Lane	30 November 1949	W 2–0	OR
23.	*Scotland**	*Hampden Park*	*15 April 1950*	*W 1–0*	*OR*
24.	Portugal	Lisbon	14 May 1950	W 5–3	OL – scored four
25.	Belgium	Brussels	18 May 1950	W 4–1	OL
26.	**Chile**	**Rio de Janeiro**	**25 June 1950**	**W 2–0**	**OR**
27.	**USA**	**Belo Horizonte**	**29 June 1950**	**L 0–1**	**OR**
28.	**Spain**	**Rio de Janeiro**	**2 July 1950**	**L 0–1**	**OL**
29.	*Wales*	*Roker Park*	*15 November 1950*	*W 4–2*	*OR*
30.	*Scotland*	*Wembley*	*14 April 1951*	*L 2–3*	*OL – scored once*
31.	Argentina	Wembley	9 May 1951	W 2–1	OR
32.	Portugal	Goodison Park	19 May 1951	W 5–2	OR – scored once
33.	France	Highbury	3 October 1951	D 2–2	OR
34.	*Wales*	*Cardiff*	*20 October 1951*	*D 1–1*	*OR*
35.	*Northern Ireland*	*Villa Park*	*14 November 1951*	*W 2–0*	*OR*
36.	*Scotland*	*Hampden Park*	*5 April 1952*	*W 2–1*	*OR*
37.	Italy	Florence	18 May 1952	D 1–1	OR
38.	Austria	Vienna	25 May 1952	W 3–2	OR
39.	Switzerland	Zurich	28 May 1952	W 3–0	OL
40.	*Northern Ireland*	*Belfast*	*4 October 1952*	*D 2–2*	*OR*
41.	*Wales*	*Wembley*	*12 November 1952*	*W 5–2*	*OR – scored once*
42.	Belgium	Wembley	26 November 1952	W 5–0	OR
43.	*Scotland*	*Wembley*	*18 April 1953*	*D 2–2*	*OR*
44.	Argentina	Buenos Aires	17 May 1953	D 0–0	(abandoned) OR
45.	Chile	Santiago	24 May 1953	W 2–1	OR
46.	Uruguay	Montevideo	31 May 1953	L 1–2	OR
47.	USA	New York	8 June 1953	W 6–3	OR – scored twice
48.	*Wales**	*Cardiff*	*10 October 1953*	*W 4–1*	*OR*
49.	*Scotland**	*Hampden Park*	*3 April 1954*	*W 4–2*	*OR*
50.	Yugoslavia	Belgrade	16 May 1954	L 0–1	OR
51.	Hungary	Budapest	23 May 1954	L 1–7	OL
52.	**Belgium**	**Basle**	**17 June 1954**	**D 4–4**	**OL**
53.	**Switzerland**	**Berne**	**20 June 1954**	**W 2–0**	**OR**
54.	**Uruguay**	**Basle**	**26 June 1954**	**L 2–4**	**OL – scored once**
55.	West Germany	Wembley	1 December 1954	W 3–1	OL
56.	Denmark	Copenhagen	2 October 1955	W 5–1	OL
57.	Wales	Cardiff	22 October 1955	L 1–2	OL
58.	Northern Ireland	Wembley	2 November 1955	W 3–0	OR – scored once
59.	Spain	Wembley	30 November 1955	W 4–1	OR – scored once
60.	Scotland	Hampden Park	14 April 1956	D 1–1	OR
61.	Wales	Wembley	14 November 1956	W 3–1	CF – scored once
62.	Yugoslavia	Wembley	28 November 1956	W 3–0	CF
63.	Denmark*	Molineux	5 December 1956	W 5–2	OL

64.	Scotland	Wembley	6 April 1957	W 2–1	CF
65.	Republic of Ireland*	Wembley	8 May 1957	W 5–1	OL
66.	Denmark*	Copenhagen	15 May 1957	W 4–1	OL
67.	Republic of Ireland*	Dublin	19 May 1957	D 1–1	OR
68.	Wales	Cardiff	19 October 1957	W 4–0	OL – scored once
69.	France	Wembley	27 November 1957	W 4–0	OL
70.	Scotland	Hampden Park	19 April 1958	W 4–0	OL
71.	Portugal	Wembley	7 May 1958	W 2–1	OL
72.	Yugoslavia	Belgrade	11 May 1958	L 0–5	OL
73.	USSR	Moscow	18 May 1958	D 1–1	OL
74.	**USSR**	**Gothenburg**	**8 June 1958**	**D 2–2**	**OL – scored once**
75.	Northern Ireland	Belfast	4 October 1958	D 3–3	OL – scored once
76.	USSR	Wembley	22 October 1958	W 5–0	OL

Matches in italics = Home International Championship games
Matches in bold = World Cup finals games
* = World Cup qualifying games

	Played	Won	Drawn	Lost	Abandoned	For	Against
All games	76	51	12	12	1	227	102
Home Ints	29	20	6	3	0	85	36
World Cup	7	2	2	3	0	12	12

TOP TEN LIST OF ENGLAND GOALSCORERS

Player	Goals	Caps	Player	Goals	Caps
1. Bobby Charlton	49	106	4= Alan Shearer	30	63
2. Gary Lineker	48	80	7. Vivian Woodward	29	23
3. Jimmy Greaves	44	57	8. Steve Bloomer	28	23
4= Tom Finney	**30**	**76**	9. David Platt	27	62
4= Nat Lofthouse	30	33	10. Bryan Robson	26	90

MOST APPEARANCES FOR ENGLAND

1. Peter Shilton	125	7. Ray Wilkins	84
2. Bobby Moore	108	8. Gary Lineker	80
3. Bobby Charlton	106	9. John Barnes	79
4. Billy Wright	105	10. Stuart Pearce	78
5. Bryan Robson	90	11. Terry Butcher	77
6. Kenny Sansom	86	12. Tom Finney	76

Details correct to 1 February 2003.

CAREER AT PRESTON NORTH END

Season	Division	Postion	Appearances	Goals	FA Cup Apps	Goals
1946–47	1	7th	32	7	3	2
1947–48	1	7th	33	13	4	1
1948–49	1	21st	24	7	2	2
1949–50	2	6th	37	10	1	1
1950–51	2	1st	34	13	2	0

Season	Division	Postion	Appearances	Goals	FA Cup Apps	Goals
1951–52	1	7th	33	13	0	0
1952–53	1	2nd	34	17	3	2
1953–54	1	11th	23	11	8	3
1954–55	1	14th	30	7	3	2
1955–56	1	19th	32	17	1	1
1956–57	1	3rd	34	22	6	5
1957–58	1	2nd	34	26	1	0
1958–59	1	12th	16	6	0	0
1959–60	1	9th	37	17	6	4
Totals			**433**	**187**	**40**	**23**

Index